A

COLLECTION OF LECTURES

ON

THEOSOPHY AND ARCHAIC RELIGIONS,

DELIVERED IN INDIA AND CEYLON

A COLLECTION OF LECTURES

ON

THEOSOPHY AND ARCHAIC RELIGIONS,

DELIVERED IN INDIA AND CEYLON

COLONEL H. S. OLCOTT

GYAN

Published by

Gyan Publishing House
5, Ansari Road
Daryaganj, New Delhi-110002
Phone: 011-47034999, 9811692060
E-mail: books@gyanbooks.com

Distribution Network
gyanbooks.com
India, USA, Canada, UK, Australia

ISBN: 978-93-6780-120-8 (PB)

First Published, 1883

2nd Impression 2024

Printed at: Gyan Press, Delhi.

A Collection of Lectures on Theosophy and Archaic Religions, Delivered in India and Ceylon
Author: COLONEL H. S. OLCOTT

A COLLECTION OF LECTURES ON THEOSOPHY AND ARCHAIC RELIGIONS,

DELIVERED IN INDIA AND CEYLON

BY

COLONEL H. S. OLCOTT,

PRESIDENT OF THE THEOSOPHICAL SOCIETY.

PUBLISHED BY A. THEYAGA RAJIER, F. T. S.,

Assistant Secretary, Madras Theosophical Society.

Madras:

1883.

CONTENTS.

	PAGE.
The Theosophical Society and its aims	1
The Fourth Anniversary Address	18
Theosophy and Buddhism	26
The Life of Buddha and its lessons	39
The Occult Sciences	47
Spiritualism and Theosophy	56
India, Past, Present and Future	76
Theosophy : its friends and enemies	89
The Civilization that India needs	108
The Sixth Anniversary Address	117
* An Address to lady Theosophists	130
The Spirit of the Zoroastrian religion	138
Theosophy, the scientific basis of religion	161
The common foundation of all religions	186
An Address to Indian graduates	205

* From the pen of an eminent Anglo-Indian Theosophist.

PREFACE.

THE following pages contain a re-publication of the bulk of the numerous Lectures delivered in India and Ceylon by Col. H. S. OLCOTT, the President of the Theosophical Society, since his arrival in this country in 1879. The intense interest evoked by the delivery of these Lectures, and the oft expressed wishes of many friends, students, and members of the Society have induced the publisher to bring out the present collection. It was, however, his original intention to have prefaced the work by a short treatise on Occultism, and to have appended certain explanatory foot notes to certain portions of the Lectures, as well as to have added a catechism of the ancient Brahmanic Faith. Such a publication has, indeed, been advertised for some months past; but, in consequence of certain unforeseen and unavoidable circumstances, it has been impossible to fulfil that programme. As, moreover, subscribers to the Lectures are growing impatient, and the Lectures themselves have been ready for sometime, the publisher begs to present this publication as a sort of first instalment, so to speak, of the work originally advertised; and hopes, before very long, to be able to bring out the treatise on Occultism and the catechism already mentioned—these two forming a complete volume.

It must be added that the present re-print of his Lectures has been submitted to and revised by Col. H. S. OLCOTT, who has been so kind as to permit this work to be published under the auspices of the Theosophical Society.

MADRAS,
February 1883. } A. T.

THE THEOSOPHICAL SOCIETY AND ITS AIMS.

Delivered at the Framji Cowasji Hall, Bombay, on the 23rd March 1879.

WHEN a new Society asks a hearing of the world it is sure to be challenged. The public has that vested right, and none but fools will object to its exercise. Infallibility is out of fashion, notwithstanding the Roman comedy of July 13th, 1870, where, as the Syllabus of the Vatican Council tells us, the Holy Ghost sat with the Bishops and judged with them. Men nowadays take nothing on faith; the era of enquiry and proof has come.

The Theosophical Society expects no exemption from the rule; has asked none; and my presence before this great audience, so soon after the arrival in India of our Committee, shows our readiness to give a reason for its existence. We believe it was a necessary outgrowth of the century: I hope to show you that the hour demanded its coming, and that it was not born before its appointed time. I will not wonder if, when you reflect upon the facts I shall present, you, who trace every earthly event to a supernal cause, will see the indication of Providential purpose in the simultaneous creation of the Theosophical Society at one side of the world, and that of the Arya Samaj of Āryavarta, by Swami Dya Nand Saraswati at the other, without the slightest pre-arrangement or understanding between that pious and learned man and ourselves. And you others, who retain the word "unknowable" in your dictionaries, you, who trace *no* phenomenon to any remote and primitive, but only to a secondary, cause, will not fail to wonder at the "coincidence," as, to avoid trouble, you call whatever is otherwise inexplicable.

Our society points to four years of activity as one proof that there was room for it in the world. And this activity, please observe, was not in the midst of friendly environments, with no one to question or oppose; but in the enemy's country, with foes all about, public sentiment hostile, the press scornful and relentless, traitors working with honest opponents to break up our organization and neutralize our labours. Occupying, as most of us did, positions of influence, we have had to suffer, in ways that will suggest themselves to each of you, for the privilege of free speech. While the press has lampooned us, in writing and pictorial caricatures, by the clergy we have been denounced as the children of Satan, doomed to eternal damnation along with the wretched "Heathen."

We throve on opposition. The more we were abused, the greater interest was created to know what the Theosophical Society really was, how strong, and what were its aims? These questions, which have been put to us, in every possible variation since our arrival here, we answered, without concealment or equivocation, face to face with the enemy, eye to eye. We had nothing to be ashamed of, whether in doctrine, motive, or deed, and so we spoke—and now speak—with the boldness of one who loves the truth and hates a lie.

All this discussion, carried on for months, even years, in journals of world-wide circulation, drew to us large numbers of sympathizers. Scattered throughout America and Europe were men and women of intelligence, influence, courage, who had long been interested in the topics to which we applied ourselves, and who needed only such a rallying point as our society offered, to combine their strength. So they joined us, cheering us by their activity of deed no less than by their friendliness of word. A branch society sprang up in England, under the presidency of a barrister of the highest capabilities, and the conjoint direction of a University professor and medical and other professional men. Other branches were formed in Russia, France, Greece, at Constantinople, and elsewhere. One is now forming in Ceylon under that strong-souled Megittuwatte. Our membership increased to thousands. We received as brothers, with equal cordiality, Hindoos, Jains, Parsis, Buddhists, Jews, and free thinking Christians. At different times the press has described us as specially representing each of those sects; a proof, certainly, of our strict impartiality and the general resemblance all these great religions have to each other at their roots. There was room for all upon our platform, and none need jostle his neighbour. What that platform is, will be made clear before I have done speaking. You will have already inferred from what has preceded, that we were not in favor of Christian theology or any of the sects of which it is the prolific mother.

Believing it good generalship to force the fighting when one feels sure of his supports, we not only struck blow for blow at our antagonists, but contrived more than once to put them on the defensive. Often without obtruding ourselves upon public notice, we aroused an interest in everything related to the East. Oriental science, literature, chronology, tradition, superstitions, magic and spiritualism, afforded themes for our allies to speak and write upon, throughout the two parts of Christendom. Those who have seen the Western journalistic and periodical literature during the past four or five years, must have been struck with the apparently sudden growth of a deep interest in such matters. They will also have noticed the increased number of books published on Oriental subjects. How much of that activity is traceable to the Theosophical Society, *we* only know who have been in the thick of the fighting.

We have been asked, scores of times, why our Society has established no periodical nor issued any volumes of Reports. Our answer is that a wider activity could be achieved by utilizing presses already established. We have thus reached millions of readers, where, through any special organ of our own, we might only have caught the eye and provoked the thought of a few thousands. How many in India, think you, have read about the visit of our Committee and its objects; and how many would have done so if we had depended upon a journal of our own? Papers in English and the several vernacular tongues have been sent us, and letters from the extreme North to Ceylon, have come to us from those who have an interest in our work. It has been remarked at the West that no Society has, within so short a time, been talked about in so many different countries as ours. We gratefully accept the fact as proof that we are welcomed to a standing-room in the arena of the century.

And now what is the Theosophical Society, and what are its aims? How much appears upon the surface, and how much is concealed? What is the plan of work? How is the public to be benefited by the Society, and is mutual co-operation practicable? What attitude do we assume toward religious beliefs, and what ideas, if any, does the Society hold about God and His government? Do we believe in the immortality of the human soul, and, if so, on what grounds? What importance do we attach to the study of the occult sciences, so called? What use has been made by many or few of our Fellows, of any knowledge of those sciences? To what highest good do we aspire, here or hereafter? What are our ideas of the next world? These questions *you* have come here to ask, *I* to answer. I have copied them from written documents, handed to me since this address was announced by the native committee. And here are others propounded by one who wishes to join us:—On one's becoming a member, is any course prescribed for him to follow with a view to his continual progression and the acquisition of mastery over his baser nature? What constitutes the difference between the degrees in the Society? Will instruction be imparted to individual members or groups, on what subjects, and how often? Theosophy has been defined (it is Webster's definition) as "a direct as distinguished from a revealed knowledge of God, supposed to be attained by extraordinary illumination, especially a direct insight into the processes of the Divine mind and the interior relations of Divine nature;" how far does this agree with the doctrines of the Theosophical Society? Is a member of the Arya, Brahmo, or Prarthana Samaj debarred from joining it, and will his joining affect his position in relation to the social rules and duties of his caste? How much time would be required to become proficient in a degree? Will any library be established and accessible to the Fellows? Will there be social gatherings to discuss Oriental philosophy and kindred subjects?

We have here seventeen enquiries, covering ground enough for thirty-four lectures, but I will attempt to cursorily glance at all in the hour that is at my disposal. All, except those of a strictly personal character, have been treated at great length and with signal ability by H. P. Blavatsky, Corresponding Secretary of our Society, in her 'Isis Unveiled', a work which the London *Public Opinion* styled "a stupendous monument of human industry," and the *New York Herald*, "one of the great achievements of our century." Those who care to really sound this question of the relative supremacy of ancient and modern science and religion can easily do so, as the work is to be had of the Bombay booksellers.

But, to begin with our answers I affirm, then, that everything essential as regards principles, recommendations and ideas appears upon the surface of our Society, and nothing is concealed that *should* be made known. We do not say one thing and mean another. We have no mental reservations, nor make any equivocations. What we believe we say—always and everywhere. If we have survived all the battles through which we have passed; if, after a four years' struggle against Christianity, in the very heart and stron hold of Christendom, we are a strong, compact, successful Society, daily increasing in influence, having daily accessions of able coadjutors; if, at this juncture, our outposts are entrenched in the most widely separated countries, and garrisoned by men of the most diverse speech, complexion, and ancestry; if here, upon the threshold of Aryavarta, we find our hands clasped with fraternal warmth by the Hindu, the Parsi, the Jain, and the Buddhist; it is because we have not feared to speak the truth at any cost.

When our Society was organized—at New York in 1875—the very first section of the bye-laws adopted, after fixing upon our corporate title, affirmed that the object of the Society was to obtain knowledge of *all* the laws of nature. This covers the whole range of natural phenomena, and everything that concerns mankind and his environments. The inaugural address of the President was delivered, November 17th, 1875, and in it, after attempting a comparison of our Society with the Neoplatonists and theurgists of ancient Alexandria, the fire-philosophers of the middle ages, and the ancient and modern spiritualists, and finding no exact parallel, I said: "We are neither of these, but simply investigators of earnest purpose and unbiassed mind, who study all things, prove all things, and hold fast to that which is good." "We seek, inquire, reject nothing without cause, accept nothing without proof: we are students, not teachers." Does not this utterance of 1875 answer most of the questions of 1879?

The Society has its secrets, nevertheless, but they harm no one. Composed, as we are, of people who live at the two extremities of the earth, and who speak different tongues, we have the same necessity as Freemasons for some means of mutual identification in special cases.

These are afforded by certain signs and tokens which, of course, are witheld from strangers, and are changed as required. Again, operating, as we do, mainly in Christian countries, in some of which, as in France, Spain, and Russia, for instance, religious intolerance prevails, the corporate perpetuity of our branches would be imperiled by allowing our membership to be known, and our plans for religious and scientific agitation might be baffled by exposing them. Our existence threatens no Government, feeds no political cabal, attacks no pillar of social order. We do not concern ourselves in the least with affairs of State, nor lay impious hands upon the marriage, filial, or parental relation. We would not admit man or woman who was in rebellion against the existing laws or government of his or her country, or engaged in plots and conspiracies against the public peace and safety. In New York we expelled one of our most active charter officers, an Englishman, one of the founders of the Society, in fact—because he allowed himself to be mixed up with a lot of French Communistic refugees in their wicked conspiracies. Judge for yourselves, therefore, how malicious and unfounded are the libels that have been circulated in this country as to our being political spies, and, most ridiculous of all, Russian spies! The only Russian in our party became a citizen of the United States of America last July, for which act, unprecedented among Russian women, she cannot put her foot again on Russian soil without risking transportation to Siberia. Even her book, "Isis Unveiled," is not allowed to cross the frontiers. As to our conspiring against British rule in India, were we such lunatics as to dream of aiding sedition against the most stable, wise, and just Government, it appears to me, this country ever had since the Mogul conquest, it suffices only to remark that two of our party are English and loyal to the very core. Besides which, we have as many, if not more, real Theosophists in the United Kingdom as in America, and the President of our British branch is one of the most loyal of barristers, the son of a Member of Parliament! Nor would we admit into our fellowship any one, who taught irreverence to parents or immorality to husbands or wives. Nor have we any room for the drunkard or the debauchee. If Theosophy did not make men better, purer, wiser, more useful to themselves and to society, then this organization of ours had better never have been born. That it lives, and is respected even by those who cannot sympathize with its ideas, is evidence of its beneficent character. This answers one of the above questions, and I have also shown you that our plan of work is to employ existing agencies to create an interest in Eastern philosophies and religions, and make the Press our helper, even when it fancies it is killing us off with its fine sarcasm or abuse.

And now, we are asked, what attitude do we hold to religious beliefs, and what do we believe as to God and His government? The Society, I have already told you, is no Propaganda, formed to disseminate fixed dogmas; therefore, as a society, it has no creed to offer for the world's acceptance. It recognizes the great philosophical principle that while there is but one Absolute Truth, the differences among men only mark their respective apprehensions of that Truth. It is not for me to say to you what this Absolute Truth is. If I were capable of doing so, then, for the first time since the world began, there would have appeared an infallible, omniscient human mind upon earth. There is no educated sectarian so bigoted that when you calmly discuss with him the bases of his faith, he will not admit that its Founder was not equal to the one Supreme God in omniscience and other attributes. The Parsi will not claim it for Zoroaster, the Buddhist for Sakya-Muni, the Jain for Parasnatha, the Jew for Moses, the Mahommedan for the Prophet of Islam, nor the Hindu for any of the Rishis, who

> "Above all fleshly, wordly feelings soared,
> And sought what worldly comforts Indra poured."

Revere his spiritual intermediator and teacher as either of these may, he will only claim that, in his opinion, more of this Absolute Truth flowed from Heaven to Earth through this particular channel, this minor God, if you will, than through any other. And to settle these disputes, all the spilt blood of religious wars has been shed. Then why should we accord to Christians that which we refuse to other people? Why should we accept Jesus rather than Vasishta, Goutama or Zoroaster? Until the close of the second century no sect believed him to be more than a man, "a good and just man," as James, his alleged brother, is made to call him. Every student of history is aware that when the polite and learned Gnostics of that period were exposing the pious frauds and the chicanery of the early Christian writers, and unriddling their mythical tales of Jesus and the Apostles, Irenæus, that arch plotter and forger, produced the Fourth Gospel according to John, and converted the previously accepted man Jesus, who contained within his form the heaven-descended Logos* of Philo, to the God Jesus, the equivalent of the second person of the Platonic Trinity, and who, being "Very God," was the equal of the Deity in every essential attribute. With such a theology, of course, argument is pointless, and we can find no common ground upon which to invite other religionists to meet Christians. While, therefore, the Theosophical Society can and does co-operate in the dissemination of the philosophical principles of these Eastern, primitive faiths, it neither seeks the favour nor asks the indulgence of a secondary one, which can only live by the destruction of every other, and which finds no room in the love, mercy, or justice of its God for men who never heard of Jesus, nor even read a page of its Bible. And so one thing is made clear, that whatever other God any officer of the Theosophical Society may or may not worship, he

* The Concealed wisdom of Ensoph and the Sacred Tetragram of the Kabalists.—T. S.

or it is not the Irenæan anthropomorphic Logos, nor the Jehovah of Palestine. Yet there is another and better Christian God. Far be it from me to scoff at the simple faith of those thousands of Christians who have pictured to themselves a Deity all love and beneficence, and who exemplify in their lives and conversation all that is beautiful in human nature. The recollection of my nearest and dearest ones, and of those others whom I have known from boyhood up, in different lands and various social conditions, would stop my mouth were I so unjust and cruel. I myself come from a line of ancestors who have left behind them historical records of their unselfish and courageous devotion to Christianity. Just as I have left my home, and business, and friends, to come to India to worship the Parabrahm of primitive religions, so, in 1635, one of my ancestors left his home in England to seek in the savage wilderness of America that freedom to worship the Jewish Jehovah which he could not have at home under the Restoration. But, as the author of "Isis" remarks, these people would have been equally good in any other religious sect, they are better than their creed; goodness, virtue, equity are congenital with them.

But when we have shown in what we do *not* believe, we have to say what is our faith. We *do* believe in the immortality of the human soul* —the "we" meaning all the representative Theosophists whose minds have been opened to me. In truth, there is not much elbow-room in our Society for those who persistently deny this assumption, for what advantage is there in studying all those primitive, sublime utterances of the Vedas, the Zend Avesta, the Tripitika, about the soul and future life, if a man is incapable of realizing the idea of a spiritual self at all? Let such an one take his balances and weigh and count over, and christen the motes of nature's dust-heap; and get ribbons for catching a new bug; and titles for impaling a new beetle. He will die happy in the thought that his name, though Latinized or Hellenized past recognition, will be transmitted to posterity in connection with the solar refrangibility of the cucumber, or some other discovery of equally momentous importance!

The study of occult science has a twofold value. First, that of teaching us that there is a world of Force within this visible world of Phenomena; and, second, in stimulating the student to acquire, by self-discipline and education, a knowledge of his soul-powers and the ability to employ them. How appropriate is the term "occult science," when applied to the careful observation of the phenomena of force, is apparent when we read the confessions of scientific leaders as to the limitation of their positive knowledge. "We have not succeeded," says Professor Balfour Stewart, "in solving the problem as to the nature of life, but have only driven the difficulty into a borderland of thick darkness, into which the light of knowledge (*Western knowledge*, he should say) has not yet been able to

* The seventh principle in man—the Atma of the Hindoos.—T. S.

penetrate."* Says Le Conte, "Creation or destruction of matter, increase or diminution of matter, lies beyond the domain of science."† And even Huxley,‡ the High Pontiff regnant of materialism, confesses ". . . . it is also, in strictness, true that we know nothing about the composition of any body whatever, as it is."

Did time permit, I might cite to you scores of similar utterances from the mouths of the most worshipped biologists and philosophers who happen at the moment to have the stage of notoriety to themselves. You cannot open a book on chemistry, physiology, or hygiene, without stumbling upon admissions that there are fathomless abysses in all modern science. Pére Felix, the great Catholic orator of France, taunted the Academy by saying that they found an abyss even in a grain of sand. Who, then, can tell us of the nature of life, the cause of its phenomena, the qualities of the inner man? Who guards the keys of the secret chamber, and where do they hang? What dragons lie in the path? America cannot tell us, Europe cannot—for we have questioned both. But in the Western libraries we found old books which tell us that in the olden times there was a class of men, who had discovered these secrets, had interrogated nature behind her veil. These men lived in the lands now called Thibet, India, Persia, Chaldea, Egypt, and Greece. We find traces of them even in the sacred literature of Mexico and Peru. And we have been told that this sacred science is not extinct, but still survives, and is practised by men who carefully guard their knowledge from profane hands. Some of us have even had the inestimable good fortune to meet with such wonder-workers and see their experiments. So we have come in quest of the places and opportunity to learn for our own benefit and that of humanity, what occult law of nature can be brought out of Dr. Stewart's "borderland of darkness" into the lighted and odoriferous class-rooms of Western Science.

To what highest good do we aspire? What *is* the highest good, but to know something of man and his powers, to discover the best means to benefit humanity—physically, morally, spiritually? To this we aspire: can our interrogator conceive of a nobler ambition? In common with all thinking people we have, of course, our individual speculations about that infinite and awful something which Anglo-Saxons call God; but, as a Society, we say, with Pope—

"Know, then, thyself; presume not God to scan;
The proper study of mankind is Man."

As to our ideas of the next world the aid of metaphysics would have to be invoked to answer the question. Suffice it that we do not fancy the

* "The Conservation of Energy," by Balfour Stewart, L.L. D., F.R.S., Professor of Natural Philosophy at the Owens College, Manchester. (p. 163).

† "Correlation of Vital with Chemical and Physical Forces," revised for Dr. Stewart's book, *Supra*, (see page 171).

‡ "On the Physical Basis of Life," by Thomas H. Huxley, L.L.D., F.R.S.

other world to be gross like this; lighted by the same solar vibrations, filled with such houses, such Framji Cowasji Halls, as ours! Most men are apt to brutalize the next world in trying to construct a tangible idea for the mind to rest upon. The Heaven of Milton, which, and not at all that of any Biblical authority, is the one believed in by Christians—is a place of shining stairs, golden pavements, and bejewelled thrones, on which without an inch of cushion to mitigate their metallic hardness, the redeemed saints sit for ever and ever singing hymns to the accompaniment of the harp. So the Moslem Paradise teems with physical delights, and even the "Summer Land" of our Western Spiritualists has been sketched, mapped out and described by all the recent authorities, from A. G. Davis downward.

Is it not enough to conceive of a future state of existence corresponding with the new necessities of the soul that has passed through and out of the cycle of matter and become a subjective entity? Can we not realize a life apart from the use of pots and ladles, easy chairs and mosquito curtains? Even the *Jivan-Mukta*, or soul emancipated, while living in this world, loses all sense of relationship to it and its grossness. How much more perfect the contrast, then, between our narrow physical life and the *Mukhtatma*, or soul universalized—the soul having sympathies with the Universal Good, True, Just, and being absorbed in Universal Love.! Let us not drown ourselves in oceans of vague metaphysical speculation, in trying to drag the next sphere down to this, but rather strive to elevate our present plane of matter, so that one end of it may climb to some sort of proximity to the higher realm of spirit.

What an important question is this which heads the second series that I read to you! How can one be helped to acquire mastery over his baser nature? Mighty problem—how change the brute into the angel? Why ask for the obvious answer to so simple a question? Does my friend imagine there is more than one way in which it can be done? Can any other but one's own self effect this purification, this splendid conquest, in comparison with whose glory all the greatest victories of war sink into contemptible insignificance? There must be, first, the belief that this conquest is possible; then, knowledge of the method; then, practice. Men, only passively animal, become brutal from ignorance of the consequences of the first downward step. So, too, they fail to become god-like because of their ignorance of the potentiality of effort. Certainly one can never improve himself who is satisfied with his present circumstances. The reformer is of necessity a discontented man—discontented with what pleases common souls; striving after something better. Self-reform exacts the same temperament. A man who thinks well of his vices, his prejudices, his superstitions, his habits, his physical, mental, moral state, is in no mood to begin to climb the high ladder that reaches from the world of his littleness to a broader one. He had better roll over in his mire, and dismiss Theosophy with a grunt of impatience.

Great results are achieved by achieving little ones in turn; great armies may be beaten in detail by an inferior force; constant dripping of little water-drops wears away the hardest rock. You and I are so many aggregations of good and bad qualities. If we wish to better our characters, increase our capabilities, strengthen our will-power, we must begin with small things and pass to greater ones. Do you want to control the hidden forces of Nature, and rule in her domain as a king-consort? Then begin with the first pettiness, the smallest flaw you can find in yourself, and remove that. It may be a mean vanity, a jealousy of some one's success, a strong predilection, or a strong antipathy for some one thing, person, caste; or a supercilious self-sufficiency that prevents your forming a fair judgment of other men's countries, food, dress, customs, or ideas; or an inordinate fondness for something you eat, drink, or amuse yourself with. It matters not; if it is a blemish, if it stands in the way of your perfect and absolute enfranchisement from the rule of this sensuous world, "pluck it out and cast it from thee" This done, you may pass on.

You understand now, do you not, the meaning of the various sections and degrees of our Theosophical curriculum? We welcome most heartily across our threshold every man or woman of ascertained respectable character and professed sincerity of purpose who wishes to study the ancient philosophies. He is on probation. If he is a true Theosophist at bottom, he will show it, by deeds, not words. If not, he will show it, and go back to his old friends and surroundings, apologizing for having even thought of doing different from themselves. And as one who brings peace-offerings in his hand, he will try to do some meanness to us, who only took him at his word and thought him a better man than he proves to be. I know this is true, for we have had experience—even in India.

I must here clear up one point which some profess to be in doubt about after reading a certain circular issued by our Society. That circular states that for a Fellow to reach the highest degree of our highest section, he must have become "freed from all exacting obligations to country, society, and family"; he must adopt a life of strict chastity. I have been asked whether no one could become a thorough Theosophist without relinquishing the marriage relation. Now our circular makes no such assertion. A man may be a most zealous, useful, and respected Fellow, and yet be a patriot, a public official, and a husband. Our highest section is composed of men who have retired from active life to spend their remaining days in seclusion, study, and spiritual perfection. You have your married priests, and your sanyasis and yogis. So we have our visible, active men, seen in the world, mixed up in its concerns, and a part of it; and we have our unseen, but none the less active, adepts,—proficients in science, physical and occult,—masters of philosophy and metaphysics—who benefit mankind without their hand being ever so much as suspected. Though I am ostensibly President of the whole Theosophical Society, yet I am less than the least of these Emancipated Ones,—and not yet worthy to enter this highest section.

It is evident from the foregoing that there is room in our Society for the Arya, Brahmo, Prarthana, and all the other minor Samajes which represent the progressive mind of Young India. *Divided*, they are comparatively powerless to do much; *united*, they would make a strength to be felt by the reactionists. Remember the Roman *fasces*, my friends, and put that emblem up over the door of every *mundir*. My own country, the Great Republic of the West, has this motto: *E Pluribus Unum*—one out of many, one country out of many smaller States. Just so it might be *one* National Samaj of Aryavarta, out of a shoal of local societies. That is the plan of our Theosophical Society; we have various branches, but one central guiding authority, and surely there are no greater differences between you here, than there are between the red, brown, black, yellow, and white men who call themselves Theosophists, the world over.

The relations of a man to his country and his caste are, as it appears to me, quite distinct from his relations to the study of natural law, of philology, of philosophy, and of esoteric science. Your brown faces and oriental costumes show me, even without the fact that this audience understands the language I speak, the authors I cite, and the thoughts I utter, that education has no caste, colour, creed, or nativity. Why, then, ask if one must adopt a certain dress or put himself in a certain chair, or before a certain dish of food, to study your forefathers' philosophy? Here am I, with a white skin, an European dress, and a life-experience, coloured and shaped after the notions of the section, society, and class in which my parents brought me up. When I began to ponder over this magnificent Eastern philosophy, I was not told that I must dress in this way or that, or do this, that or the other thing, not vitally injurious,—such as the drinking of liquors and indulgence in sensuality. I was simply shown the path, my way was pointed out, and I was left to my own choice. Well, like all men of the world, I had certain bad habits, bad ways of thinking, foolish ways of living. I put an inordinate valuation upon things really worthless, and undervalued things really important. I was looking at things through bad spectacles. After a while, I discovered this myself, and, as I was in dead earnest and determined to succeed or die in the attempt, I began to reform myself. I had been a moderate drinker of wines after the Western fashion, I gave them up. I had been a frequenter of clubs, theatres, social parties, race-courses, and other places wherein men of the world vainly seek contentment and pleasure. I gave them all up; not grudgingly, not looking back at them with regret, but as one flings from him some worthless plaything when its worthlessness becomes known to him. You will, perhaps, pardon the employment of my personal experience as the illustration of the moment, in view of the fact that it is the only one which, without breach of confidence, I can use to answer the interrogatory that has been put to me.

If India is to be regenerated, it must be by Hindoos, who can rise above their castes and every other reactionary influence; and give good example as well as good advice. Useless to gather into Samajes, and talk prettily of reform, and print translations and commentaries if the Samajists are to relapse into customs they abhor in their hearts, and observe ceremonies that to them are but superstitions, and throw all their enlightenment to the dogs. Useless for native gentlemen to sit at the tables of Europeans, in apparent cordial equality, if they have not the moral courage to break bread with them in their own houses. Not of such stuff are the saviors of nations made.

But we will pass on to the next question. No time can be specified for the progress of a Theosophist from one stage to another. Some would take years, others days, to reach a given result. We are asked if any library be established by us? I hope and trust so. A nucleus already exists; who of you will help to build it up? What rich native loves his countrymen more than money? Or is it your notion that the Indians should do nothing, and the strangers all? We are willing to give even our *lives*, if need be, to this cause; what more will any of *you* give?

Yes, there will be social gatherings to discuss our congenial themes. In point of fact, there are such already, for every Wednesday and Sunday evening, since our arrival at Bombay, we have held a sort of *durbar*, or reception, at our bungalow. There we will be happy to see all—even spies—who care to see us, and those who live out of the city can always communicate with us by letter. Being people who try to take a practical view of things, and are disposed to work rather than talk, we have set our minds to accomplish two things. We want to persuade the most learned native scholars—such men, for instance, as the distinguished Sanskrit Professor of Elphinstone College, who occupies the chair of this meeting, and the equally distinguished President of the Pali and Sanskrit College of Ceylon, and the eminent Parsi scholar who also honours us with his presence—to translate into English the most valuable portions of their respective religious and scientific literatures, so that we may help to circulate them in Western countries. At the same time we wish to aid, as best we can, in the extension of non-sectarian education for native girls and married women, which we regard as the corner-stone of national greatness, and in the introduction of cheap and simple machines that can be worked by hand labour and that will increase the comfort and prosperity of our adopted country. We have chosen this land for our home, and feel a desire to help it and its people in any way practicable, however humble, without meddling ourselves with its politics, into which, as American citizens, we have, as I have remarked, neither the right nor inclination to intrude ourselves.

Let me before leaving this part of our subject make one point very clear. The Theosophical Society is no money making body, nor has it anything to do, as such, with financial affairs. Its field is religion, philosophy, and science—not politics or trade. For two years it did not even exact an initiation fee nor dues. I paid its entire expenses out of my own pocket, and we only restored the initiation fee because we had formed a Vedic Section to co-operate with the natives of this country in reviving Vedic philosophy, and certain expenditures were necessary. Even now, while the Freemasons, beside a costly Initiation Fee, are called upon for large annual subscriptions, we take nothing but the small sum which each applicant contributes upon being admitted, towards the expenses of the Society in India, and not a dollar of which is disbursed in Western countries.

And now, having answered, *seriatim*, the questions embraced in the list, I will pass on to some obvious deductions that suggest themselves, and then conclude.

The Indian press have spoken of it as a very strange thing that Western people should have come here to learn instead of to teach—as though there was nothing in India worth the learning. This conveys a sad impression to my mind. It makes me realize how completely modern India ignores the achievements of ancient Aryavarta. It shows how complete is the eclipse of Aryan wisdom when people from the other side of the globe could know more of the essence of Vedic philosophy than the direct descendants of the Rishis themselves. Since we landed on your shores we have met hundreds of educated Hindoos, Parsis, and men of other sects. They have thronged our parlors, filled our compound, and gathered about us day after day. Out of all these we have found few—so few that we might almost reckon them upon the fingers—who really know what Aryan, Zend, Jain, and Buddhistic philosophies teach. There have been scores upon scores able to recite slokas and whole puranas and chapters with accurate accent and rhythm, but they but repeated words without understanding; they had not the key to the mysteries. I have met those who had seen the marvelous phenomena performed by ascetics, and amply corroborated all the stories we had heard and circulated through the Western press. But scarcely one who, having known and seen such things, had set himself to work with determination to learn the science and explore the *adytum* of nature. In this throng of visitors there was no end of students of Mill, of Darwin, of Spencer, of Huxley, Tyndall, Bain, Schlegel, Renan, Burnouf. Their minds were whole arsenals of propositions in logic, metaphysics, mathematics, and sophistry —all the weapons which reason uses against intuition. They could out-wrangle a Cambridge double-first, and

"Make the worse appear the better reason."

They had persuaded themselves into error against their own inner consciousness. We have noted, and I repeat it, that a larger cluster of acute intellects we never encountered than this of Bombay. Part had become thorough materialists. To them, as to Balfour Stewart, the Universe seemed "a vast physical machine . . . . . . composed of atoms with some sort of medium between them as the machine." The apprehension of a God had died out, the feeling of having in them a soul had been smothered. With polite incredulity they have listened to our tales of phenomena witnessed by us, similar to those described in the biography of Sankara Achariya and Sakya Muni, sometimes unable to repress a smile. They seemed to come to us more to observe the lengths and depths to which Western credulity can go, than to gather corroboration of the narratives contained in their own sacred literature. And, I am sorry to say, some few, when out of earshot, have made themselves merry over our testimony to the truth of the primitive philosophies.

Another class we have met, with minds full of misty speculations which prevented their having any clear and defined views of either of the great questions of universal human interest. Drawn hither by the reveries of Swedenborg and Davis, or thither by those of Boëhmen and St. Martin, they had found no sure ground upon which to plant their feet.

To us strangers, this has been a most instructive study, and we have tried to discover the best means to combine all this intellectual vigor, this learning, this mental agitation upon one objective point. We see in this state of things the promise of future good results. Here is material for a new school of Aryan philosophy which only waits the moulding hand of a master. We cannot yet hear his approaching footsteps, but he will come; as the man always does come when the hour of destiny strikes. He will come, not as a disturber of the peace, but as the expounder of principles, the instructor in philosophy. He will encourage study, not inflame passion. He will scatter blessings, not sorrow. So Zoroaster came, so Goutama, so Confucius. O for a Hindoo great enough in soul, wise enough in mind, sublime enough in courage to prepare the way for the coming of this needed Regenerator! O for one Indian of so grand a mould that his appeals to his countrymen would fire every heart with a noble emulation to revive the glories of that by-gone time, when India poured out her people into the empty lap of the West, and gave the arts and sciences, and even language itself, to the outside world! Are her sons all sunken in selfishness and the soft ooze of little things? Has their scramble for meagre patronage deadened the noble pride of race, and replaced it with an obsequious humility tinged with unreasonable hate? Can they not forgive their fellow countrymen for wearing a different style of turban and having a different line of ancestors?

Is the love of caste so passionate and deep as to make an object of righteous hatred every one not in their own social circle? Ah, young men of promise, beloved brothers, and companions, objects of our solicitude and hopes, to see and dwell among whom we have crossed three oceans and threaded two seas, be Indians *first*, and caste-men afterwards if you will. Is there not one of you to send the electric spark through this inert mass and make it quiver with emotion? Here lies a mighty nation like a giant benumbed with sloth and no one to arouse its potential energies. Here lavish nature has provided exhaustless resources, that combined talent and applied knowledge would turn into fabulous national wealth. Here rich mines, a fat soil, navigable waters, forests of valuable timber, a multiplicity of natural products that might be manufactured at home into portable and profitable articles of commerce. All that is lacking is a share of that energy and foresight which, in two centuries and a half have transformed the United States from a howling wilderness into a scene of busy prosperity. In vain the efforts of statesmanship to spread the blessings of education and promote the industrial arts, if they are not seconded by the patriotic endeavours of enlightened Young India. Are these great Colleges and Universities founded for the sole purpose of turning out placemen and dreamers? Have schools been opened only to help to hatch debating societies and metaphysical training clubs, where minds that should be directing great economical enterprises are engaged in splitting hairs, and voting whether love is an essence and man a molecule? I have observed with deep regret that there is among the youth of Bombay an eager desire for the empty honours of University degrees, and no disposition to fit themselves for the management of practical affairs. There are far too many native barristers and doctors, and far too few qualified superintendents of mills and manufactories, geologists, metallurgists and engineers. There are L.L.B.'s in plenty, but of educated carpenters, millers, sugar-makers, and paper manufacturers none—or next to none. The great and crying want of modern India to-day is a scientific school attached to every College, such as we have in America, and, in each great centre of population, a school of Technology with appropriate machinery where the most improved methods of the principal handicrafts could be taught to intelligent lads.

Do not imagine that I have the idle notion that India can be reformed in a day. This once enlightened, monothiestic and active people have descended, step by step, in the course of many centuries, from the level of Aryan activity to that of idolatrous lethargy and fatalism. It will be the work not of years but of generations to re-ascend the steps of national greatness. But there must be a beginning. Those sons of Hindoostan who are disposed to act rather than preach cannot commence a day too soon. *This hour* the country needs your help. Leave your molecules to themselves; put away for a time your speculations upon the descent of species, cease vain endeavours to count the number of times an atom may be split in halves, and go to work in earnest to help yourselves and your Mother land. The atoms in space will evolve new worlds without you; your *country* is growing weaker and poorer every day and wants you.

But you lack capital, you say. Then unite into clubs and committees to find out where capital can be profitably employed, and spread the facts before the Western nations. In London alone there is lying, in bank vaults, idle capital enough to set every possible Indian industry on its feet. Those acute and daring English merchants and capitalists ransack the world in search of opportunities to earn interest on their surplus incomes. Turkish bonds, Peruvian railways, Egyptian consols, Bohemian glassworks, American schemes, are all tried in this hope of profit. What does Europe or America know—really know—of Indian resources, trade, customs, business opportunities? A mere handful of bankers and traders have only such facts as lie upon the surface of this unworked national mine. A few military officers and civil servants may have published the records of their casual observations. But, in comparison with what ought to be known, and might be made known under a proper system of general and sub-committees, this is as a mere drop in the bucket. As to my own country, which would gladly exchange commodities with India as with any other nation, I can speak by the book. For my people, this land is but a geographical abstraction, whose capes, rivers, and chief cities are known by name to the school boy, and straight way forgotten for lack of subsequent reminders. And yet I hear my native brothers complain of poverty. I hear of thousands of stalwart labourers dying of hunger for want of employment at three pice per day. I see Indian gums, fibres, seeds, and grains going abroad in the raw state, and coming back manufactured, to be sold at large profit to natives. I see men, as well educated, as strongminded, as capable to succeed in independent business as any young men in new York, or London, or Berlin, demeaning themselves to throng the ante-rooms of public officials in search of employment, and ready to fall upon each other's faces for the sake of miserable little clerkships. This is what we behold at even a first glance at the country of our adoption.

I will make no apology for my plain speech, for I come from a practical country, where we have learnt that smooth speeches and true friendship do not always go together. There is too much talk here and too little enterprise; too much suavity and not enough available perseverance. There is unmeasured ability to suffer and endure, but not the master spirit which laughs at trouble, and rushes to meet adversity with the joy of the athlete who hails the coming of his adversary as the opportunity, long sought, to show his prowess.

Cast your eye over the Western world and see what an intense activity pervades the whole scene. Let the picture unroll like a great panorama before you. Behold the struggles of all those nations not only to extend commerce, but also to settle the weightier problem of religious truth. See Christianity in America broken up into innumerable sects, and science leading the public far away from the Church into the dry pastures of Materialism and Nihilism. See the clergy being stripped of the last shreds of their influence and the free secular press attaining predominant sway. Look at Great Britain agitating the question of disestablishment, the Catholics emancipated from the incubus of the Irish National Church, and Bradlaugh preaching bold atheism in London, Sunday after Sunday. In France, behold the revolution in politics that has passed the reins of power into Republican hands, and flung out the Jesuits from their cosy nest behind MacMahon's chair. In Germany, open rupture with the Pope, and the abolishment of Ecclesiastical privileges. In Russia, the red spectre of the Nihilist Party menacing both Church and State. Everywhere as it were the boiling and seething of a vast cauldron—the conflict between Theology and Science.

This conflict, so eloquently described by Professor John William Draper, began with the discovery of the printer's art, and its progress has been marked by a thousand victories for science. Born out of the womb of the Reformation, she has proved the benefactress of humanity by facilitating international intercourse, developing national resources, surrounding mankind with a multitude of comforts and refinements, and bringing education within the reach of the humblest labourer. India, as conspicuously, if not more so than any other great Oriental country, has not availed itself of these material advantages. The fault does not lie with the masses, for they know nothing of all that has been going on in the busy world. It lies at the door of the educated class I have heretofore described. And *you* are the very men! *You* have run through the curricula of science and literature, and made no practical application of your acquired knowledge. The sentries of this sleeping nation neglect their duty.

But as the unrestful ocean has its flux and reflux, so all throughout nature the law of periodicity asserts itself. Nations come and go, slumber and re-awaken. Inactivity is of necessity limited. The soul of Aryavarta keeps vigil within the dormant body. Again will her splendour shine! Her prosperity will be restored. Her primitive philosophy will once more be interpreted, and it will teach both religion and science to an eager world. Her ancient literature, though now hidden away from the quest of an unsympathetic West, is not buried beyond revival. The hoof of Time, which has stamped into dust the vestiges of many a nation, has not obliterated those treasures of human thought and human inspiration. The youth of India will shake off their sloth, and be worthy of their sires. From every ruined temple; from every sculptured corridor cut in the heart of the mountains; from every secret *vihar* where the custodians of the Sacred Science keep alive the torch of primitive wisdom, comes a whispering voice saying " Children, your Mother is *not dead* but only *sleepeth*;".

THE FOURTH ANNIVERSARY ADDRESS.

Delivered at the premises of the Society's Head Quarters, Bombay, in November 1879.

On the evening of the 17th day of November 1875, I had the honor of delivering, in the city of New York, my inaugural address as President of the Theosophical Society. That was the first regular meeting of this body, and here, in my hand, I hold the printed notice sent to the members to attend the same. During the four years that have since come and gone, we have experienced those changes which time always brings to societies as well as to individuals. Of the thirteen officers and councillors elected at the meeting above referred to, only three remain; the rest have dropped off for one reason or another and left us to carry on our work with new associates who replaced them. But the work has gone on, day by day, month by month, year by year, without one moment's interruption, and always growing more important. Our field has widened so as to embrace almost the whole world. The little company of one score of men and women has increased to thousands. Instead of my remarks being addressed, as then, to Americans alone, I am now, at this fourth annual celebration confronted by Hindus, Parsis, Mohamedans, Jains and Buddhists, besides many English representatives of Her Gracious Majesty's Imperial Government in India. Committees to represent the Arya Samaj,—whose anniversary this is, as well as ours—and the Poona Gnyana Samaj, honor us with their presence. Here are great merchants and bankers, some titled, some untitled; here the executive officers of native princes. From others at the North, the South, the East and the West, who could not be present, we have letters of affection and encouragement. Instead of occupying the platform of a hall in the Metropolis of the Western Hemisphere, I stand to-night in an Indian bungalow, dedicated to the use of our Library to celebrate the opening of that Library in the commercial Metropolis of Western India and to commemorate the foundation of the Society's new magazine, the THEOSOPHIST which has proved an unprecedented success from the very start and which, within the first two months of its existence, has been called for by subscribers all over India and Ceylon, and in every quarter of Christendom, as well. Friends, one and all, brothers of every race, complexion, creed and tongue, I give you the right hand of fellowship and bid you welcome. Written in letters of fire, on this arch over my head, is that word of friendship, WELCOME; let their flame typify that purer light of Truth, which burns for every man who seeks it. Here, at the door of this Library, it most eloquently speaks in the language of symbols, to bid all enter and search, with the help of books, after that hidden glory of spiritual knowledge which the ancient sages and mystic saw, but which the present sceptical generation falsely supposes to have been long since extinguished. This fact, that we deny that the sun of Aryan Wisdom has set to rise no more, is the one memorable feature of this evening's festivity. Brothers, that glorious sun will again shine over the world through the gloom of this Kali-Yug. Already, the patient watchers see the first golden gleam of its coming. From afar, as though it were a whisper borne on the breeze, the voice of the Past murmurs the promise of a revival of spiritual learning. Our ears have caught the welcome sound, and our souls are refreshed and made strong to continue our efforts. As, at the first streak of dawn, one, standing at some distance from a camp, first hears the confused rustle of arms, of stamping steeds, and the calls of the relieving sentries, before the sleeping army awake us to the day's march and battle, so we may now perceive the premonitions of the active struggle that is cominig between the Old and the New, in the domain of thought. The touch of the magician has been laid upon the lips of the sleeping Aryan Mother, and she is ready to instruct her willing descendants in the knowledge which her immediate sons learned at her knees.

How often since we came to India have I heard it said by Natives, that it was a strange anomaly that white men had to journey from the antipodes—from *Patál*—to tell them about their forefathers' religion! And yet it ought not to surprise you so very much, after all. Have we all not looked from a height upon the plain, and noticed how much more we could see of the movements of people there than could the people themselves? It is so as regards all human affairs—the distant observer can often take a more correct view of a national question than the people most immediately interested. Our late civil war looked very different to you than it did to us, and so we are in a position to get a quicker glimpse of this question of Aryan learning, than you who have long got out of the habit of consulting your ancient literature, and must break through many prejudices and fixed habits of thought before you will be ready to resume the study of the Vedas. And, moreover, is not our coming like the reflux of the wave which casts up upon the beach that which in its flux it bore away at the last turn of the tide? We bring no new doctrine to you, teach no new thing; we only remind you of the facts of *your* own history, expound but the philosophy and science which *your* own wise men taught. In the far distant Past—so far removed from the present that our modern books of history contain no records of it, but which the archæologists and philologists vouch for upon the stength of intrinsic probabilities—the Aryan wisdom was carried from these shores to the other side of the globe. Among the remains of the prehistoric nations of North and South America, the explorer finds vestiges of this trans-mundane outflow of Aryan ideas, in the religious symbolism of their lithic remains, and the lingering traditions of degenerate tribes. If the Zoroastrian Magi fed the sacred fire on their Chaldean towers, so did the priests of the Sun in Mexico and Peru. Nay, so, to-day do the wretched (?) Zuni Indians of Arizona and New Mexico, who go out every morning to greet the rising sun with reverential prayers and prostrations. I cannot enlarge upon this most wonderful theme in the few minutes during which I shall now speak, but it will be treated, as occasion offers, in our journal where you may all read it.

You will see then, in view of the above facts, that—as I remarked before—the coming of our party to India for the purpose of studying the Aryan philosophy is but a natural result of events occurring thousands of years ago—ages before my own people or any other white race of the West existed. I wish I might say that we find you as a body *willing* to help our studies, or even capable. It is a melancholy fact that modern India knows so little of the Vedas that their contents are not even suspected; while the Rishis, and even the founders of the several philosophical schools, were long ago turned into gods, or made incarnations of the Supreme Power, set up as images to worship. Your young men, totally uneducated in Hindu literature, and stuffed with the hot-spiced scraps of guessing Western Scienc, turn away from thee to them superstitious stories of Sankaracharya's miracles, and pronounce Patanjali's "aphorisms of the Yoga philosophy" as the ravings of a credulous mind. And when we tell the modern Parsi the secret meaning of his *Dasátir*, or show the modern Hindu that every so-called supernatural phenomenon, ascribed to the old Yogis, can be explained and proved possible by scientific rules, they reply in one breath "Show us a miracle and we will believe; let one of these adepts, that you say still live, come forth from his hiding-place, and do wonders before us, and we will be willing to admit that you are speaking the truth." We have had a score of messages sent us by rich men to the effect that if we would show them one of these pretended magical feats, they would make us rich presents and join our Society. Poor, ignorant men, they imagine that their money gives them importance in the eyes of a student, and that the divine powers of the soul can be made the subject of barter and traffic! If they have any desire to earn the secrets of nature and of man, let them throw all their vanity and conceit behind them, and humbly, and in the spirit of truth, set to work to study. If they would enjoy the presence and counsel of the Yogis let them wash off the dirt of the world, and *then* seek the feet of those holy men, in the presence of whose purity and learning even kings are unfit to stand with covered feet.

The best friends of India, her most patriotic sons, have deplored to me the moral darkness and degradation of her people. Native Judges, who have sat on the bench for many years to administer justice, have bowed their white heads in shame when they said that the vice of lying and the crime of perjury prevailed to a fearful extent. And the worst part of it was that the moral sense was so far gone, that people confessed their falsehood without a blush, and without an idea that they were to be pitied. Has it indeed come to this, that modern India has lost the power to discriminate between truth and falsehood ? Are the descendants of the Aryas fallen so low ? Forbid it, O Thou Infinite and Inexorable Law of Compensation, the Embodiment of Justice and Law ! For, when a nation plunges to the very bottom of the mire of immorality, its doom is written. When falsehood is set above truth, when man loses his confidence in man, when respectability counts in proportion to success, and villany is not reproved if it only pour wealth into the hungry coffer, then do the pillars of a nation rock and totter, and the building that took so long to rear crumbles to its fall. But, for my part, I do not believe things are come to this pass in this India of my love, this land of my adoption. Falsehood there is, a dulled moral sense, a failing to keep up to promises, lack of patriotic fervor, treachery and mutual over-reaching. These are too painfully evident for us even, to attempt to deny or conceal the fact. But I tell you, and I fling it in to the teeth of all India's slanderers, that these are but the ulcers on a strong body, and that they will pass away. I say that India has touched bottom and, already, is beginning to rise. I see the elements of a great revival of learning, of national health, gathering together. These influences are streaming out from every school, college, and university that a wise and humane Government has established in this land. They are diffused broadcast by every newspaper, whether English or Vernacular, that is circulating. They come from every reforming samaj, society and league. They are pouring in by every mail-steamer that brings Western thought, ideas, and enterprising suggestions. Our Native youth enrolled at English Universities, are fitting themselves to become the apostles of national reform, the heralds of a new dispensation. Ideas of political economy are slowly but surely infusing themselves throughout the nation, through the agency of the Native clerks who drudge in public offices where these grave questions are discussed, and who, insensibly to themselves, are being gradually educated in practical affairs. How can this change, so desirable for *both* governors and governed, so auspicious for the world at large, be hastened ? Let this be the theme of my closing remarks.

First, then, we must all promote education to the utmost of our united powers. That is the key-stone of the arch of a nation, the foundation of true national greatness. And this education must be given to *both* sexes. An educated wife is the real companion and comforter of her husband, the worthy mother of great sons. It is not shallow ornamental education that is needed by the Indian youth, but that kind of education which will fit them for the active pursuits of life, and help them to earn an independent livelihood. The first, most imperative demand of the hour is for technical schools. *Not* great empty palaces that serve only as monuments to a rich man's vanity, but institutions where the industrial and ornamental arts are taught by capable teachers in a thoroughly practical way. Schools which can turn out young carpenters, blacksmiths, carvers, builders jewellers, printers, lithographers and other artisans who can do work so much better and more ingeniously than others that they will never lack employment at the highest price paid to skilled labor. My talented colleague, Mr. Wimbridge, has written upon this theme in our journal, and shown that, in the present low state of Indian art, the apprenticeship system is only perpetuating bad workmanship, and that technological schools are a prime necessity. You will find in the exhibition of products of native industry that will be thrown open to you as soon as the speeches are concluded, some specimens sent for this exhibition by the Pandharpur School of Industry. I hope you will examine them closely, for you will, in them, practically see what Mr. Wimbridge means. Their workmanship is not perfect, yet I venture to say that you will search through the whole of the Bombay bazaar and not find a lock, a key, a steel box, or a hand device, of Native workmanship, to be compared with these Pandharpur samples for quality of finish.Now why cannot such schools be established everywhere? Think of the crores of rupees—now spent every year on paltry shows and foolishness, only to put men's names and sweetmeats into their neighbours' mouths for a day, at the cost of a week's subsequent dyspepsia—as good as flung into the fire, when one-fourth the money would set all these schools in operation! People tell me the nation is starving for want of grain, that their industries are rooted out, their workmen selling their tools for bread! Well, charge it upon Native millionaires who have the money to waste upon the gratification of their own vanity and greediness, but not a pice to give for education. What does the starving agriculturist know of the law of rainfall or of the ultimate poverty and famine that has befallen his district because the faggot-gatherers and lumbermen have stripped the hills and mountain slopes of their forest growths? If any of them have sons in town at school, ten to one they are being taught hard Greek names for alleged scientific discoveries, and not a word that will be of use to them outside the public offices. Charge this upon the rich men who stint themselves to get up showy feasts to unsympathetic strangers, but can spare nothing for Schools. And charge it all the more upon them when they will screw the wages of skilled Native artisans down to the lowest point, and import foreigners to do the very same work, and pay them three times or five times as much again for their services. Why should we import skilled labour except to help and found technological schools? Answer me that, ye capitalists of India. Was there ever turned out of Western looms a fabric *so* fine as the muslin of Dacca? Have

European weavers produced a shawl to rival the shawls of Cashmere? Are there any *better* swords than those blades of the Indian temperers, which would cleave through an iron bar and then slit a veil of lace floating on the air? Are the mosaics of Florence *finer* than those of Surat, Ahmedabad and Bombay, that you will see in our present exhibition; the carvings of the Swiss mountaineers *more* cunning than those that lie in those cases there in all their beauty? Where, in all the Western world, can you point me to *more* titanic engineering feats than the ancient hydraulic works of this country, or the rock-temples of Elephanto, Karli and Ellora? And where is there an edifice to rival the Taj Mahal? Shame, then, upon the Aryan who talks of the ignorance or incapacity of his countrymen. The men are here, and the talent; all that is needed is education and patronage.

My friend and Brother, Lalla Mulraj of the Lahore Arya Samaj, has just sent me a most valuable pamphlet of his upon the science of Sanitation. I wish it might be read and pondered over by every intelligent Native, for the laws of health are universally ignored and violated here, and the welfare of the nation correspondingly suffers. And among other causes of national degeneration is one that has entered upon its fatal work. I refer to the use of intoxicating liquors and stupifying drugs. Those accursed pest-holes, the toddy shops, are multiplying on every side, the maxims of the good old religion are being forgotten, even priests are becoming drinkers. This should be stopped at once. The whole influence of the Brahmins should be at once thrown on the side of Temperance. Total Abstinence Societies should be organized by them everywhere, and *they* should be the first to pledge. I know it will be said that their very religion forbids their touching liquor and so there is no need for them to sign; that, in fact, their signing would be a lowering of their prestige. But this is an argument of no weight. It matters not what any religion forbids, *the real question is whether its commands are obeyed.* Christianity forbids many things—adultery, hypocrisy, lying, murder, false-witness, for instance—yet this does not prevent the whole Christendom from being filled with divorce-suits, perjury, manslaughters and every other mentionable and unmentionable crime. Are the Hindus falling into habits of drunkenness? If so, the Brahmins should be the first to rescue them. Believing this, to be the common-sense view to take, my Brahmin friend who occupies the chair of this meeting, has accepted the Presidency of the Aryan Temperance Society, a body organized this very day under the auspices of the Theosophical Society, and himself was first to sign the pledge. People have asked what practical good we would do for India: let them have a partial answer in this beginning of a crusade against intemperance. As we have made our Theosophical Society a success, despite a thousand obstacles, and just founded a paying journal in the face of difficulties which Indian journalists painted to us in blackest colors, so we mean to help to make a success of this Aryan Temperance Society, until there shall be branches of it working for the regeneration of the people in four quarters of India. Why should we leave to Christians a work that we can do far better ourselves; why leave Temperance to be used by the American Methodist cat, to pull the heathen chestnuts out of the everlasting fire?

Besides our library, our journal, and this Temperance Society, we have begun another practical work for India. In that bungalow across the compound is a work-shop in which we have placed a lathe for metal turning, a lithographic press, a drill, saw and other machines for doing various kinds of work. It is not a school of technology but our private workshop, where we have begun manufacturing certain articles for export. The money realized from their sale in foreign countries will come back here and be spent here in useful ways. You may judge whether it is likely to be of any practical use to the country, when I tell you that a large number of the beautiful invitation cards issued for this occasion, were printed in that shop by a young Parsi who has entirely learned his art from Mr. Wimbridge within the past few weeks. I venture to challenge every lithographer in Bombay, Calcutta, and Madras to produce a specimen of native work to compare with it. And yet, work, equally as good, ought to be turned out of every one of them, and *would be* if the proper kind of technical education had been accessible. You will see at work this evening a number of machines and working models of machines made by Native artisans. Compared with the number which ought to be here they are few, but there was no time for us to make known our intention to hold this exhibition and induce artisans to contribute. But it is at least, you will admit, a fair beginning: when the native workmen discover that we are their friends they will come to us—self-interest will compel them. We have called you here to look at what they have brought; I hope we may often call you again, and that good results will come—as they have in my own country and everywhere else—from the bringing together of capital and skilled labor.

I must give place to other and more able speakers to address you in your own vernacular tongues, and testify to their love of the country and hopes for its resuscitation. I thank you for your presence to-night and I trust that you may go away feeling an interest in us and our work. That work is one in which you have a deep interest. We aim with the help of the various Samajes to revive the study of the Vedas, the formation of Sanskrit classes, and an enquiry into the alleged latent powers of the human soul, stated by the ancient Aryas to exist, and affirmed by thousands of experimentalists since their time and even in our own days. We would call in the aid of modern science to help us to understand that ancient mystical philosophy. For the debased forms of religion that so widely prevail, we would substitute the noble faiths of the olden time. We would teach India the useful arts, and thus assist in reviving Indian prosperity and greatness. We would help to abolish vicious habits, and to form habits of temperance, manliness and self-respect. We call upon every man of you, and every lover of India to rally around us. We do not ask you to be our followers but our allies. Our ambition is not to be considered leaders or teachers; not to make money, or gain power, or fame. Choose any man here, of either of the old races represented, and show us that he is the right man to lead in either branch of this reformatory movement and I will most gladly enlist as a common soldier under him, just as I have under my brother, Gopalrao Hurry Deshmuk, in this Temperance Society. Come, let us labor together like brothers for the welfare of our Motherland.

There is one regret that comes to mar the pleasure of this evening, and somewhat dim the lustre of all these lamps—our Buddhist brothers of Ceylon are absent. And absent too, is that most beloved Teacher of ours, that elder brother, so erudite, so good, so courageous,—Swámiji Dayánund Saraswati. Were he and those others but here, nothing would be left to desire—nothing but that the Theosophists of our branch societies of Europe and America might at least have reflected by some magician's skill upon the sky above them the picture of the joyful scene that we are witnessing. From afar, their longing eyes are turned towards India, and they are waiting to catch the words of instruction and good cheer that our Eastern teachers may utter. This is a novel thing, is it not, that Western men of high position—authors, journalists, university professors, physicians, lawyers, merchants; Russian princes, English lords, German barons and counts—people of high birth and low birth, should be looking to India for instruction in religion and science. Yet this is the very fact, for all these are Fellows of the Theosophical Society, and disposed to listen to Dayánund Swami in his saffron robe and puggaree, and to all *your* other bright minds, rather than to the paid ministers who occupy Western pulpits, and to the guessing scientists who so often pretend to a knowledge of man and nature they do not possess.

THEOSOPHY AND BUDDHISM.

Delivered at Colombo, Ceylon, on the 3rd June 1880.

THE party of Theosophists whom you see here represent two distinct organizations—the THEOSOPHICAL SOCIETY AND UNIVERSAL BROTHERHOOD, and the Bombay Theosophical Society. This lady, Madame Blavatsky, whose name and deep learning are now everywhere known, and myself, were founders, and are officers of the first named body, the parent of all Theosophical Societies now existing throughout the world. The other gentlemen, to wit, Mr. Edward Wimbridge, of London, and Messrs. Panachand, Purshotam, and Damodar, (Hindus), and Padshah and Ferozshah Dhunjibhai (Parsees) are special delegates sent by the Bombay Branch of the parent Theosophical Society to be present at the organization of a Buddhist Branch society or societies in Ceylon. The spectacle of a friendly union of so many different nationalities and such diverse creeds, in the persons of this party, for the carrying out of this mission, is so exceptional a circumstance, that it must be long remembered in the history of this Island. Some may have fancied that we were all Buddhists but this is a great mistake: these Parsee gentlemen worship the sun and fire as the emblems of their deity, Hormazd; one of these Hindus is a staunch Vedantist, another a follower of that great reformer, Pandit Dayanand Saraswati Swami, the third is of the highest Brahmin caste, was religiously inclined from his boyhood, and, since coming to Ceylon with us, has been so impressed with the beauty and simplicity of Buddha's religion and its improving influence upon its votaries that he has renounced his Hinduism and publicly recited the Five Precepts. We three Europeans were reared under the influence of three different sects of the Christian religion. My teacher, Madame Blavatsky, saw the inner character of the Greek Church of which a man—the Russian Czar—is declared to be the Head and God's Vicegerent on earth; Mr. Wimbridge had a like chance to see the inside of the Anglican Established Church, of which a woman—a good and revered Lady, alike a mother to her family and people—is the Head "by the Grace of God," as by statute made and provided. I come from that Puritan stock which went to the American wilderness, two centuries and a half ago, to escape from the hated tyranny of that very Established Church—and in their turn persecuted the Quakers and the Baptists as soon as they were fairly settled in their new home! I need hardly add that neither of us three holds to his or her ancestral sect, nor has any belief in, or connection with, Christianity in any form whatsoever.

This diversity of race and opinion which our present delegation represents, prevails throughout the whole parent Theosophical Society and its branches in America, Europe and Asia. Ours is a republic of conscience in the perfect sense of the word. Every member enjoys absolute freedom in religious matters, and, if sincere in his belief, is respected and protected in its exercise on the sole condition that he will equally respect each one of his fellow members in his religion. How can any one who is not an incurable bigot object to such a reciprocal compact? Is there anything in it revolutionary, anything subversive of public morality, of the well-being of the state or the rights of the individual? What more or less can any reasonable person ask than to be allowed perfect freedom to pursue studies and form and advocate opinions at the bare price of giving every other person the same rights? Let others set themselves up as infallible in religion and science; let them claim monopolies of knowledge or inspiration; let them found faiths or split them up into sects upon minor issues until, like a great tree divided into splinters, all strength and massiveness is gone out of them,—the parent Theosophical Society stands by its principle of mutual tolerance and universal brotherhood, and, as a body, has no creed, sect, or school of its own. You see, therefore, gentlemen that the Theosophical Society is not a Buddhist, any more than it is a Parsee, a Hindu, a Jain, a Jew, or a Christian Propaganda. If it were, then there would be no room in its membership for any but Buddhists, whereas, here before your very eyes, you see that its Hindu and Parsee fellows are throughly devoted to its interests. The salutation of brotherhood has smoothed all the common asperities that keep man and man asunder, and a responsive thrill from every heart attests the tie of common humanity that links us all together beneath our varied complexions, costumes, and creeds.

So careful have we been to prevent our parent Theosophical Society from turning into a sectarian propaganda, that our Rules prohibit any officer from officially favoring any one Branch Society more than another. He may enjoy and, in his private capacity, teach his favourite religion as much as he chooses, but, as an officer speaking for the Parent Society, he cannot give any more of the Society's power or influence in behalf of one branch than another.

How then, it is asked, can the president of this Parent Society, its responsible executive, come to Ceylon as he has now come, and agitate for the formation of a distinctly Buddhistic Theosophical Society; and; in fact, what possible connection can there be between Theosophy and Buddhism? To answer these natural and reasonable questions I am here.

Our Society was formed at new York, in the year 1875, to investigate the laws of nature and disseminate the knowledge of the same, and to study the ancient religions and philosophies from which all modern ones have been derived. We determined to give special attention to such natural laws as were least understood by modern nations but which the ancients appear to have known well. An intimate knowledge of these laws had enabled the priests of ancient Persian, Indian, Egyptian, Hebrew, Chaldean, Christian, Grecian, Roman, Keltic, Scandinavian, Peruvian, Mexican and other religions to produce phenomena which the ignorant viewed as miraculous, and to use them for selfish purposes. By the help of these phenomena, creeds most despotic and corrupt, had, in different ages, been fastened upon mankind, and superstition made a fat soil in which to grow religious fungi. There have always been fools to deny the reality of these weird and occult phenomena, but, until the Englishman Harvey was born, the same class denied the circulation of the blood, and, before Columbus cracked the egg-shell and made the egg to stand upright, the same wiseacres said it could not be done. The fact is that despite all scepticism, all denials, and all anathemas, these occult phenomena seem to have occurred since man first appeared on earth, occur now, and are likely to occur to the end of the world. Our century is one of bold research and enquiry, nothing is permitted to baffle our researches; and the Theosophical Society is the very Offspring of the century. It could not have been formed, except secretly, before now. In the good old days when men were roasted for reasoning, decapitated for logic, and killed for heresy, we would have had a short and troublesome time of it. A secret denunciation to a secret tribunal, the burning of our books by the common hangman, the breaking of our bones with iron bars, and other tortures, would have preceded the last acts of burning us alive and confiscating our estates. This was done in ancient Greece and Rome, and has been done under later religions. Happily those days are gone for ever, and so this branch of occult scientific study was chosen by us as one of the chief objects to which our Society should devote itself.

To study these mysterious laws of nature we were naturally obliged to acquaint ourselves with the philosophies taught in the different ancient schools, where they were best understood. The very basis of all occultism is a broad philosophy, which takes in Man and Nature and their mutual relations. And religions are the formal expression of the devotional feelings inspired in us by the sense of those relations. We may, I think, lay down the proposition that that religion is noblest, most 'divine,' which takes the broadest views of the relationship between the Cosmos and man; which least conflicts with our intuitions and reason, and exacts least from 'faith'—which is but credulity and fetishism in a mild form. This is a severe test no doubt, but still an infallible one. At any rate, it is the test that our century is determined to apply, and you can all see how the base metal is showing itself as the various creeds and dogmas are being rubbed with the touchstone of science. What a day is this for the smashing of idols, the tearing down of pretended revelations, the exposure of priestly craft and dishonesty by which people have been so long deceived and beguiled! This is a day of judgment; let false priests, false scientists, false philosophers, take warning and set their houses in order.

So long as the world was kept in ignorance of the ancient histories, philosophies, religions and sciences, Theology was strongly entrenched. It had a certain remnant of its old power over the masses, and could exercise it; but the opening of the religious books of China, India, Ceylon, and Egypt to Western students inaugurated a new era. It was that we found that philosophies had sprung from the far East, and must recast almost all our pet theories and superstitions. We discovered that we had been standing midway along the course of the river—the stream of knowledge—with our backs turned towards its real sources, and our faces towards its mouth where it empties itself into the dark ocean of the 'Unknowable'; fancying that wisdom began with us, or, at the very worst, the 'ancient' Greeks.

If the progress of comparative philology unsettled the bases of Christian theology, no less did Western scholarship affect the theologies of the Hindus and Parsees. As one who bursts a dam that holds back the waters of a stream, gives them free course to rush into their old bed and sweep everything before them, so it seems as if the power of European scientific research had let loose the stagnant stream of Eastern superstition and a whole pantheon of gods were floating down its tide, never to return. We have personally met some thousands of educated Hindus, and find them as a rule perfect sceptics. They are passing from one phase of belief to another, have abandoned their ancient faith, but not yet received any substitute.

One must travel through India and enjoy with the Natives such affectionate personal relations as subsist between them and ourselves to appreciate the intellectual agitation that is going on. One great agency is at work to stem the materialistic drift among the Indian youth, and it is a very important one. I refer to the revival of Aryan monotheism under the leadership of Pandit Dayȧnand Saraswati Sawmi. This splendid Aryan scholar and orator began the work of founding his Arya Samaj at the very same time that we, without any knowledge of the fact, were establishing our society in America with almost an identical purpose. The coincidence, it must be confessed, is striking, and it has been often noticed by the Swami and his followers. With him and his Samaj a brotherly alliance has been formed. Just as we are now here to make a Branch specially Buddhistic and devoted to the study of Buddha's philosophy and religion, so there is in existence a Branch specially devoted to the Aryan Vedic philosophy and religion, composed of the admirers or followers of the Swami, and entitled the "Theosophical Society of the Arya Samaj."

Speaking for myself, as a founder of the Theosophical Society, I will say that it was not so much of what I had read of Buddhism, Zoroastrianism and other religions, that induced me to take up this work, as what I heard from this lady of her personal observations of religions and sciences in Asia, and other remote quarters of the globe. Her expositions of the various ancient philosophies were so lucid, and they so clearly indicated a common basis for human thinking and aspiration, that such a Society as ours seemed a necessity. If we could only secure the affectionate co-operation of the pious of all creeds and the learned of all schools of philosophy and science in a search after truth, it was inevitable that immense good should result to the world. Such a co-operation could only be brought about by a union upon the basis of mutual toleration and mutual help. Behold the genesis of our new league of Theosophy !

Having decided upon a Society, we were obliged to give it a name. What should it be ? How could we best indicate the general purpose of our organization ? There was long debate of this question, various names were considered, but our choice was finally made, as you see it, for the following reasons :—

I. The general drift of thought in countries under the influence of English, French and German literature is to a hard materialism. The tendency is to cramp all our feelings, observations, aspirations and pleasures within the narrow limits of our five senses. This ignores entirely the far nobler, vaster, more exquisite experiences that a man can have by the awakening within himself of certain latent faculties or powers to which the Buddhists give the name *Irdhi,* and which the Hindus call the *Siddhis* of Krishna. We have the testimony of every devotee, ascetic, mystic, adept, clairvoyant and seer, that what the inner eye of man can see, his inner ear hear, infinitely transcends in beauty, majesty and delightfulness the things of this grosser world of shifting pains and pleasures, through which we are passing. The founders of all the great religions have either exercised those usually latent powers or had their possession ascribed to them. And, as Buddhists treasure, as infinitely precious, the relics of their *arhats* and of the holy founder of the Perfect Doctrine, so are the relics of the founders, or holy proficients, in this occult science, of every other religion, treasured up and endowed by its followers with miracle working powers.

Now we know that the tendency of physical culture of any kind is in the direction of physical excess, and we also know that the tendencies of spiritual culture is towards purity, peace, wisdom, and religious exaltation—that is to say, the lifting up and ennobling of mankind. Reason requires no religion but instinct does. Reason deals with the world of the five senses and builds upon their limited testimony, though nothing can be plainer than that each and every one of them is constantly liable to be deceived. But intuition when fully cultivated takes man into the farthest corridors of the Universe, unlocks the most secret doors, lays bare everything within him and without, making him to know the mysteries of his own being and of the Nature of which he forms so important a part. The rationalist learns only what he and other equally blind persons can discover by looking at the surface of things; he must put his 2 and 2 together, and weigh his grains of truth in scales that are fitted to indicate little weights and measures. But the one who, by contemplation, self-discipline, and trained efforts, succeeds in opening the sealed fountains within the shell of his physicial nature, goes at a bound to the very sources of the One Truth, and knows what he desires to know.

So clearly contrasted is this species of knowledge with that which may be painfully and slowly gained through the five bodily senses that those who first, among comparatively modern people, gave it a name, called it *Theosophia* or the divine wisdom. It was not meant to convey the crude idea of a wisdom similar to that ascribed to any personal god, for the concept of those who coined the term was of an all-pervading eternal Principle in Nature, with which the interior intuitive faculty in man was akin. It has always been attested by those who have acquired this faculty that it gives its possessor the power to understand the philosophies as well as the religions, sciences and languages of men, and this was one reason why we adopted it as the title of our Society.

2. Another reason was that the name had been borne by societies like our own in the sixteenth century. Their philosophy was derived from that of Plato, and Plato's had its source in the ancient schools of India, where Sâkya Muni first studied, thought, and devoted himself to the redemption of mankind from misery. The theosophical faculty had always been known, always cultivated, and, in calling our new organization by that name, we were perpetuating the memories of both the older Alexandrian and the later German schools where that science of sciences had been studied. It was a title to which, when properly understood, no exception could be taken by any one, whatever his religion. It fitted all without conflicting with any, and it possessed the merit of being familiar among Western people.

Thus, then, we had a Society, with a defined policy and a name. Our next step was to put forth a declaration of our principles, and invite the help of all men to discover the truth of which we were in search. What the responses were is now a matter of history. We were opposed, ridiculed, denounced, but we were also encouraged and aided. Our young organization prospered. Hundreds joined us. The press busied itself immensely with all we said and did. Every trifle that could be distorted to use against us was caught up by the enemies of truth. We were preached against from the pulpit, and held up to public execration as infidels, atheists, social agitators. Ever since we came among you these very epithets have been showered upon us. Calumny busied itself in spreading attrocious falsehoods against our private characters. One would have thought we were leagued together to overthrow good morals and strip religion of its most sacred prerogatives. But truth was on our side, and we held our ground. Not only held it, but won many a victory and many a friend among the lovers of justice. Nothing that we ever said nor any action of ours ever shewed that we professed any principle that was against the publc interests, or conduced to the spread of vice, ignorance, misery or crime. Our message was one of universal brotherhood among nations, families and people; a message of kindness, forbearance, mutual help, and the courageous search after and acceptance of truth. Sympathizers in London, in Paris, in Germany, Hungary, Greece Russia, Holland, Denmark, Australia, India and South America, flocked to our assistance, and branch Societies were formed, one after another. Among our friends were men of all ranks and all professions. Though our bitterest, almost our only, foes were the Christian theologians and those whom they could influence, nevertheless a Christian clergyman had the courage to be one of the founders of our Society, and others of his profession re now avowed Fellows. Our message was not to the rich, the noble, the learned, or the powerful alone, but equally to the poor and humble. If we could count in our number princes and other European aristocrats, we had also among our most respected colleagues mechanics in America, England, Ireland and Scotland, who had educated themselves in their snatches of leisure, and felt that our aims were worthy of universal commendation.

At last we two founders came to India from America, with this English gentleman—Mr. Wimbridge—and an English lady, who is now at Bombay. Our coming having been announced in advance, crowds flocked to see and talk with us every day. Hindus of all the principal castes, Parsees, Jains; the Marattas from Poona, the Babus from Bengal, Madrasees from the south, Rajpoots and Punjabis from the north. We held durbars daily, discussed metaphysics with acuter disputants than we had ever met at the West. To one and all we expounded the same doctrine of universal brotherhood. Soon, we began to have applications for membership, and in the commercial metropolis of India a branch Theosophical Society at last sprang into existence. I wish you could attend a full meeting of that Branch to see the perfect kindness with which men of so many opposing castes and religions greet each other, and hear them tell what new light Theosophy has thrown upon their respective religions. You would then understand that the bitterest differences between man and man can be made to melt like wax in the fire before the genial warmth of tolerance and kindness.

We had no easy time of it, however. Our enemies did not mean we should lie on feather beds or beds of roses. The selfish Indian priests would no more accept our scheme of Theosophical study and co-operation than had the priests and clergymen of America and Europe. The reformers of the Brahmo and Prarthana Samajes were no more disposed to join us. But we had a worse antagonist than they to contend against —the Government of India had been made to think us political emissaries, and watched our every movement. When I tell you that every one of these difficulties was conquered in detail, that many enemies were converted into friends, that the Government voluntarily ceased its watch over us, and that H. E. the Viceroy wrote us a letter expressing his satisfaction that we were so zealously studying Indian philosophy, you may judge whether or not we are standing on firm ground. Just before we left Bombay for Ceylon, the *Pioneer* which you know is the organ of the Government, editorially comments upon us in language which I will briefly quote from :—

" The progress of their work in India is well worth attention, quite apart from all questions as to the relative merits of creeds. Hitherto the motives which had brought Europeans to India have been simple and easily defined. They have come to govern, to make money, or to convert the people to Christianity. Curiosity and philological study may have tempted a few stragglers, but these have come and gone and left no trace. The Theosophists, on the other hand, have come because they are filled with a loving enthusiasm for Indian religious philosophy and psychological science. They come neither to rule nor to dogmatise, but to learn. They regard the ancient civilization of India as having attained to higher truths concerning nature and the human soul than have been conquered yet by the science of the West. So far as they seek to teach or influence the native mind, they come to recall the heirs of this ancient knowledge to a sense of the dignity of their own inheritance, and this is the secret, apparently, of their great success with the natives. We need not here consider the absolute merits of the Theosophical theory concerning the philosophical value of ancient Indian literature, but we have no hesitation in recognising the Theosophical Society as a beneficent agency in promoting good feeling between the two races in this country, not merely on account of the ardent response it awakens from the native community, but also because of the way in which it certainly does tend to give Europeans in India a better kind of interest in the country than they had before To find reason even to conjecture that, from the midst of what seems mere primitive superstition, one may be able to extract a knowledge of facts calculated to throw a new light on natural sciences and on the highest mysteries of humanity, is to be put in a new relation with the people of India—in one which conveys a large and interesting promise. So there is ground for watching the progress of the Society with a friendly eye, and we shall look forward with interest to news of its establishment in Ceylon. In India—Anglo-India as well as Native India—they have now many friends, and have lived down the idiotic fancies to which their advent first gave rise. The objects they have in view, have no connection with politics, and their indirect influence on their native friends, so far as this may touch their behaviour as citizens, is wholly in favour of good order and loyalty to the powers that be."

So much for the history of our Society and its principles. Let me now tell you why this delegation has come to Ceylon.

While investigations of other religions had been set afoot, and learned Hindus and Parsees had begun to assist us, we had made no proper alliance with Buddhists. We felt how great an anomaly this was, for to conduct a Theosophical Society without counting in the Buddhists would be the height of absurdity. To say nothing of the fact that Buddhism is the religion of one-third of the human race, the philosophy of Gautama is so profound, so comprehensive, so sounds the depths of human nature, opens up such limitless vistas of progressive unfolding of the spiritual out of the physical—that it deserves the first attention of the student of Theosophy. Our Society had long been in correspondence with the High Priest Sumangala and others, but nothing could be done without organization and system. We felt that to do justice to the subject, a Branch Society must be formed in Ceylon, which should embrace all the scholarship and practical ability among the priests and laity. This society should devote itself to all matters that concerned the interests of Buddhism. As the Christians have their Society for the diffusion of Christian knowledge, so this should be a society for the diffusion of Buddhistic knowledge. The plan which had proved so effective in the one case ought to prove equally so in the other. And so, after taking everything into account and leaving our business in India, we sailed for Ceylon, and here we are.

Our first and most natural desire was to see with our own eyes the effect that Buddha's religion has upon its votaries. For, allowing for the natural imperfections of our common nature, the philosopher judges of the merits of a popular faith by the criminal statistics of a nation. Anything above the average of morality proves the restraining power of a good faith; anything below it proves a bad one. We had all our lives been observing the state of public morals in America and Europe. As a reading American, I had learnt about the decimation of the wild nomadic Indians, the aborigines of our continent, by whiskey sold to them by my countrymen. We had seen that more than 90 per cent. of the crime of Great Britain and the United States was traceable to the influence of intoxicating drinks. We had noticed that the traffic in these accursed poisons was only too gladly protected by Governments, which, though professing the most exalted moral sentiments and a desire to convert the poor Heathen, were not restrained by any consideration of a religious nature from helping to ruin their subjects, physically and morally, for the sake of revenue.

We had read the said history of the Sandwich Islands where, when the missionary landed about fifty years ago, he found a simple, temperate people numbering, if I recollect aright, more than two millions, but where the liquor and loathsome diseases introduced by white men have 'civilized' them down to a wretched remnant of some thirty-thousand. After coming to India we had noticed that wherever European civilization (!) had gained a strong foothold, there were more toddy-shops and dens of harlotry than anywhere else. Out among the thickest masses of the simple, untainted heathen we had seen but few of these social plague-spots. Idolatry and superstition in their most unmistakeable forms appeared to breed less of these foes to human happiness, than the newest pattern of Western progress—so miscalled. And so, after observing the effects of the white man's morality and the white man's liquor upon the white man himself as well as upon the red Indian, the olive-coloured Tahitian and the brown Hindu, we naturally desired to see the criminal statistics of Ceylon, and supplement them by our own observation of the people. At Galee, in my first lecture, I made public the result, but since the figures have not been published I repeat them in the presence of this intelligent audience.

According to the census of 1871 the population of Ceylon numbered 2,406,262, of which 69½ per cent. were Sinhalese, 22½ per cent. Tamils, 7 per cent. Moormen, and the remaining 1 per cent. Malays, other Asiatics, Africans, half castes and Europeans. Of the whole 2½ millions of inhabitants less than one-tenth are set down as Christians: and an overwhelming majority are Buddhists. This, therefore, is an excellent opportunity for us to judge of the restraining efficacy of Buddha's doctrines upon the passions and weaknesses of human nature.

And now I would be glad to have any one of the parties, who have been airing their ignorance in attacking us for advocating the formation of a Buddhistic Society, compare the criminal statistics of the Island with those of any white man's country. Let them show, if they can, a single mass of 2½ millions of white men with as small a percentage of crime as these poor Buddhist "heathen." I am sorry that up to the present moment I have not been able to procure in Ceylon the statistical reports from which to compile the exact figures, but from recollection I do not hesitate to affirm that not even the centres of western civilization—London, Paris, and New York—where moral influences most concentrate and religion is most numerously professed—will bear the comparison for one moment. Out of 2½ millions Ceylonese but 1,807 in all were tried for indictable offences and but 1,106 convictions were obtained. Of the 1,807 tried, one third, or 555, were arraigned for cattle-stealing, and 274 convicted. For offences against the person there were only 375 convictions; of the same with violence 160; without violence 185; malicious injury 8; forgery and offences against the currency 30; and miscellaneous 74.

Fancy what the London detectives and Bow Street magistrates would say to such a beggarly total of crime !* A Colombo audience will naturally plume itself upon representing the most advanced 'civilization' of Ceylon ; and, since we have seen what 'civilization' means, at least in part, we should expect the richest statistics of drunkenness. The Queen's Advocate's Report does not disappoint this reasonable anticipation. And yet, even in this favored capital, only 7 per cent. of the cases brought up in Court were for drunkenness, as against the 90 to $93\frac{1}{2}$ per cent. that in England and America are ascribed to this cause. Verily the compiler of the Ceylon Directory was warranted in calling this "a favourable contrast to the experience of Police Courts in English towns"—where, we must remember, the people, whatever they may think themselves, are decidedly not "degraded and idolatrous Buddhists" as one of my little critics has permitted himself the insolence to call them. The Directory adds one bit of information which bears upon the question in hand and that is that "in proportion to their number, the Sinhalese in Colombo maintain their character for sobriety, only 37 per cent. of the drunkards charged being of this race." On behalf of the Sinhalese I thank the compiler for this fact.

If we now turn to the religion of Buddha, we shall find, I fancy, an explanation of this orderly and sober habit of the Sinhalese.

Whatever the subsequent fate of all the world's religions and their founders, the name of Gautama Buddha, or Sakya Muni, can never be forgotten ; it must always live in the hearts of millions of votaries. His touching history— that of a daily and hourly self-abnegation during a period of nearly eighty years, has found favour with every one who has studied his history. When one searches the world's records for the purest, the highest ideal of a religious reformer, he seeks no further after reading this Buddha's life. In wisdom, zeal, humanity, purity of life and

* Since these pages were sent to the printer, I have had the great pleasure of a long conversation with Mr. Campbell, Inspector General of Police, who takes exception to the conclusions I have reached upon the subject under notice. His opinion is that the Sinhalese are of a cruel nature, in support of which he drew my attention to the inhuman custom of branding cattle in elaborate designs, sometimes covering the entire body of the poor beast, which is universal. Certainly, I never did see anything more cruel in any country ; but I think Mr. Campbell himself gave an explanation which rather strengthens than weakens my position. These brands are in the main intended as charms against evil spirits and the evil-eye ; the custom is, therefore, attributable to ignorant superstitions totally at variance with Buddha's precepts. For the correctness of the statistics here quoted I do not pretend to vouch. I use them as found in the latest edition of the "Ceylon Directory," a voluminous work of reference which professes to have reprinted them from the Government Reports.

thought; in ardour for the good of mankind; in provocation to good deeds, to toleration, charity, and gentleness, Buddha excels other men as the Himalayas excel other peaks in height. Alone among the founders of religions, he had no word of malediction nor even reproach for those who differed with his views. His doctrines are the embodiment of universal love. Not only our philologists— cold anatomists of time honoured creeds who scientifically dissect the victims of their critical analysis—but even those who are prepossessed against his faith, have ever found but words of praise for Gautama. Nothing can be higher or purer than his social and moral code. "That moral code" says Max Muller, ("Buddhism") "taken by itself is one of the most perfect which the world has ever known." In his work "Le Bouddha et sa Religion." (p. 5.) Barthelemy St. Hilaire reaches the climax of reverential praise. He does not "hesitate to say" that among the founders of religions there is no figure more pure or more touching than that of Buddha, His life has not a stain upon it. His constant heroism equals his convictions. He is the perfect model of all the virtues he preaches; his abnegation and charity, his unalterable gentleness, never forsake him for an instant. And, when his end approaches, it is in the arms of his disciples that he dies, "with the serenity of a sage who practised good during his whole life, and who is sure to have found—the truth." So noble was his life, that even the early Roman Catholic saint-makers, with a flippant unconcern for detection by posterity, characteristic of the early periods of Christianity, claimed him as one of their converts, and under the pseudonym of St. Josaphat, registered him in their "Golden Legend" and "Martyrology" as an orthodox, beatified Catholic saint. At this very day, there stands in Palermo a church dedicated to Buddha under the name of Divo Josaphat.

While most other 'saviours' of mankind had stood, as it were, on the eminence of their own virtue, and surveyed humanity from a distance, Sakya Muni went wherever there was suffering, sickness and pain, and shared them that he might know the secret of their existence. The outcast he made his brother, the leper his companion. As the surgeon learns to alleviate physical pain by studying its victim in the hospital and the camp, so he mingled with the dregs of the people to study the moral sicknesses of humanity. In the story of his life we are told that he practised upon himself every one of the austerities and modes of self-torture in vogue among the Indian ascetics, to see if release from the ills of existence could be thus obtained. Nay, he even exceeded them all, undergoing the unprecedented trial of the six-years' total fast; for which he prepared himself gradually and cautiously, by reducing his allowance of food day by day, until he had the body entirely under control of the will, and could pass the time in a state of uninterrupted hybernation, as we may say. But the secret of pain was not thus to be detected, the flitting phantom still mocked his efforts. It was only when he discovered that this whole physical existence was but one of shadows and phantoms, one stage in human experience, one link in an endless chain of births and being—that the full light burst upon his consciousness and the true path to salvation opened out before him.

The supreme merit of Buddha's doctrine is that it is the perfect embodiment of justice. The balanced scales are a far more appropriate emblem for Buddhism than for any court of justice that I ever heard of; it might well be carved or painted on every Buddhist *dágoba.* The "Perfect Law" teaches that human suffering is the result of human ignorance; its cure, to become wise, and to set only the fair value upon the world's joys and sorrows, rewards and ills. It shows that eternal, immutable law punishes the slightest moral sin as certainly as it does every physical sin; and, that as man creates his own destiny, so *he* must be his own Saviour and Redeemer, and can have no other. O, glorious truth! even the heroic sacrifices of a Sakya Muni were not too great a price to pay for such knowledge. Go, ye who call yourselves Buddhists, and preach it throughout a sinburdened world.

THE LIFE OF BUDDHA AND ITS LESSONS.

Delivered at the Kandy Town Hall, Ceylon, on the 11th June 1880.

The thoughtful Student, in scanning the religious history of the human race has one fact continually forced upon his notice, viz., that there is an invariable tendency to deify whomsoever shows himself superior to the weakness of our common humanity. Look where we will, we find the saintlike man exalted into a divine personage and worshipped for a god. Though perhaps misunderstood, reviled and even persecuted while living, the apotheosis is almost sure to come after death; and the victim of yesterday's mob, raised to the state of an Intercessor in Heaven, is besought with prayer and tears, and placatory penances, to mediate with God for the pardon of human sin. This is a mean and vile trial of human nature, the proof of ignorance, selfishness, brutal cowardice, and a superstitious materialism. It shows the base instinct to put down and destroy whatever or whoever makes men feel their own imperfections; with the alternative of ignoring and denying these very imperfections by turning into gods men who have merely spiritualized their natures, so that it may be supposed that they were heavenly incarnations and not mortal like other men.

This process of *enhemerization*, as it is called, or the making of men into gods and gods into men, sometimes, though more rarely, begins during the life of the hero, but usually after death. The true history of his life is gradually amplified and decorated with fanciful incidents, to fit it to the new character which has been posthumously given him. Omens and portents are now made to attend his earthly avatar; his precocity is described as superhuman; as a babe or a lisping child he silences the wisest logicians by his divine knowledge; miracles he produces, as other boys do soap-bubbles; the terrible energies of nature are his playthings; the gods, angels and demons are his habitual attendants; the sun, moon, and all the starry host wheel around his cradle in joyful measures, the earth thrills with joy at having borne such a prodigy; and at his last hour of mortal life the whole universe shakes with conflicting emotions.

Why need I use the few moments at my disposal to marshal before you the various personages of whom these fables have been written? Let it suffice to recall the interesting fact to your notice, and invite you to compare the respective biographies of the Brahminical Krishna, the Persian Zoroaster, the Egyptian Hermes, the Indian Gautama, and the canonical, especially the apocryphal, Jesus. Taking Krishna or Zoroaster, as you please, as the most ancient, and coming down the chronological line of descent, you will find them all made after the same pattern. The real personage is all covered up and concealed under the embroidered veils of the romancer and the enthusiastic historiographer. What is surprising to me is that this tendency to exaggeration and hyperbole is not more commonly allowed for by those who in our days attempt to discuss and compare religions. We are constantly and painfully reminded that the prejudice of inimical critics, on the one hand, and the furious bigotry of devotees, on the other, blind men to fact and probability, and lead to gross injustice. Let me take as an example the mythical biographies of Jesus. At the time when the Council of Nice was convened for settling the quarrels of certain bishops and for the purpose of examining into the canonicity of the 300 more or less apocryphal gospels, that were being read in the Christian churches as inspired writings, the history of the life of Christ had reached the height of absurd myth. We may see some specimens in the extant books of the apocryphal New Testament, but most of them are now lost. What have been retained in the present canon may doubtless be regarded as the least objectionable. And yet, we must not hastily adopt even this conclusion, for, you know that Sabina, Bishop of Heracha, himself speaking of the Council of Nice, affirms that "except Constantine and Sabinus, Bishop of Pamphilus, these Bishops were a set of illiterate, simple creatures that understood nothing;" which is as though he had said they were a pack of fools. And Pappus, in his *Synodicon* to that Council of Nice, lets us into the secret that the canon was not decided by a careful comparison of the several gospels before them, but by a *lottery*. Having, he tells us, "promiscuously put all the books that were referred to the Council for determination, under a Communion table in a church, they (the bishops) besought the Lord that the inspired writings might get up on the table while the spurious writings remained underneath, and *it happened accordingly*." But letting all this pass and looking only to what is contained in the present canon, we see the same tendency to compel all nature to attest the divinity of the writer's hero. At the nativity a star leaves its orbit and leads the Persian astrologers to the divine babe, and angels come and converse with shepherds, and a whole train of like celestial phenomena occurs at various stages of his earthly career; which closes amid earthquakes, a pall of darkness over the whole scene, a supernatural war of the elements, the opening of graves and walking about of their tenants, and other appalling wonders. Now, if the candid Buddhist concedes that the real history of Gautama is embellished by like absurd exaggerations, and if we can find their duplicates in the biographies of Zoroaster, Sankaracharya and other real personages of antiquity, have we not the right to conclude that the true history of the

Founder of Christianity, if at this late day it were possible to write it, would be very different from the narratives that pass current? We must not forget that Jerusalem was at that time a Roman dependency, just as Ceylon is now a British, and that the silence of contemporary Roman historians about any such violent disturbances of the equilibrium of nature is deeply significant.

I have cited this example for the sole and simple purpose of bringing home to the non-Buddhistic portion of my present audience the conviction that, in considering the life of Sakya Muni and the lessons it teaches, they must not make his followers of to-day responsible for any extravagant exuberance of past biographers. The doctrine of Buddha and its effects are to be judged quite apart from the man, just as the doctrine ascribed to Jesus and its effects are to be considered quite irrespectively of his personal history. And—as I hope I have shown—the actual doings and sayings of every founder of a faith or a school of philosophy, must be sought for under a heap of tinsel and rubbish contributed by successive generations of followers.

Approaching the question of the hour in this spirit of precaution, what do we find are the probabilities respecting the life of Sakya Muni? Who was he? When did he live? How did he live? What did he teach? A most careful comparison of authorities and analysis of evidence establishes, I think, the following data:

1. He was the son of a king;
2. He lived between six and seven centuries before Christ;
3. He resigned his royal state and went to live in the jungle, and among the lowest and most unhappy classes, so as to learn the secret of human pain and misery by personal experience; tested every known austerity of the Hindu ascetics and excelled them all in his power of endurance; sounded every depth of woe in search of the means to alleviate it; and at last came out victorious, and showed the world the way to salvation.
4. What he taught may be summed up in a few words; as the perfume of many roses may be distilled into a few drops of *attar*: every thing in the world of matter is unreal: the only reality is the world of spirit. Emancipate yourself from the tyranny of the former; strive to attain the latter. The Rev. Samuel Beal, in his *Catena of Buddhist Scriptures from the Chinese*, puts it differently. "The idea underlying the Buddhist religious system is," he says, "simply this 'all is vanity.' Earth is a show, and Heaven is a vain reward." Primitive Buddhism was engrossed, absorbed by one thought, the vanity

of finite existence the priceless value of the one condition of Eternal Rest.

If I have the temerity to prefer my own definition of the spirit of Buddha's doctrine it is because I think that all the misconceptions of it have arisen from a failure to understand his idea of what is real and what unreal, what worth longing and striving for and what not. From this misconception have come all the unfounded charges that Buddhism is an 'atheistical,' that is to say, a grossly materialistic, a nihilistic, a negative, a vice-breeding religion. Buddhism denies the existence of a personal God—true; denies the immortality of the *soul—true; holds out no promise of a future unbroken existence in Heaven—true; therefore—well, therefore, and notwithstanding all this, its teaching is neither what may be properly called atheistical, nihilistic, negative nor provocative to vice. I will try to make my meaning plain, and the advancement of modern scientific research helps me in this direction. Science divides the universe for us into two elements—Matter and force; accounting for every phenomenon by their combinations, and making both eternal and obedient to eternal immutable law. The speculations of men of science have carried them to the outermost verge of the physical universe. Behind them lie not only a thousand brilliant triumphs by which a part of Nature's secrets have been wrung from her, but also more thousands of failures to fathom her deep mysteries. They have proved thought material, since it is the evolution of the gray tissue of the brain, and a recent German experimentalist, Professor Dr. Jäger, claims to have proved that man's soul is "a volatile odoriferous principle, capable of solution in glycerine." Psychogen is the name he gives to it, and his experiments show that it is present not merely in the body as a whole, but in every individual cell, in the ovum, and even in the ultimate elements of protoplasm. I need hardly say to so intelligent an audience as this that these highly interesting experiments of Dr. Jäger are corroborated by many facts, both physiological and psychological, that have been always noticed among all nations; facts which are woven into popular proverbs, legends, folk-lore, fables, mythologies and theologies, the world over. Now, if thought is matter and soul is matter, then Buddha in recognizing the impermanence of sensual enjoyment or experience of any kind, and the instability of every material form, the human *soul included, uttered a profound and scientific truth. And, since the very idea of gratification or suffering is inseparable from that of material being—absolute SPIRIT alone being regarded by common consent as perfect, changeless and Eternal—therefore, in teaching the doctrine, that conquest of the material self, with all its lusts, desires, loves, hopes, ambitions and hates, frees one from pain, and leads to Nirvana, the state

* The Astral Man:—not the 7th principal in man—T. S.

of Perfect Rest, he preached the rest of an untinged, untainted existence in the Spirit. Though the soul be composed of the finest conceivable substance, yet if substance at all—as Dr. Jäger seems able to prove, and ages of human intercourse with the weird phantoms of the shadow-world imply—it must in time perish. What remains is that changeless part of man, which most philosophers call Spirit, and Nirvana is its necessary condition of existence. The only dispute between Buddhist authorities is whether this Nirvanic existence is attended with individual consciousness, or whether the individual is merged into the whole, 'as the extinguished flame is lost in the ocean of air. But there are those who say that the flame has not been annihilated by the blowing out. It has only passed out of the visible world of matter into the invisible world of spirit, where it still exists and will ever exist, as a bright reality. Such thinkers can understand Buddha's doctrine, and, while agreeing with him that the soul is not immortal, would spurn the charge of materialistic nihilism if brought against either that sublime teacher or themselves.

The history of Sakya Muni's life is the strongest bulwark of his religion. As long as the human heart is capable of being touched by tales of heroic self-sacrifice, accompanied by purity and celestial benevolence of motive, it will cherish his memory. Why should I go into the particulars of that noble life? You all remember that he was the son of the king of Kapilavastu—a mighty Sovereign whose opulence enabled him to give the heir of his house every luxury that a voluptuous imagination could desire—and that the future Buddha was not allowed to even know, much less observe, the miseries of ordinary existence. How beautifully Edwin Arnold has painted for us, in *The Light of Asia*, the luxury and languor of that Indian court,

"Where love was gaoler and delights its bars."

We are told that:

"The king commanded that within those walls
No mention should be made of death or age,
Sorrow or pain, or sickness........................
And every dawn the dying rose was plucked,
The dead leaves hid, all evil sights removed:
For said the king, 'If he shall pass his youth
Far from such things as move to wistfulness
And brooding on the empty eggs of thought,
The shadow of this fate, too vast for man,
May fade, bee like, and I shall see him grow
To that great stâture of fair sovereignty,
When he shall rule all lands—if he *will rule*—
The kings of kings and glory of his time."

You know how vain were all the precautions taken by the father to prevent the fulfilment of the prophecy that his beloved son would be the coming Buddha. Though all suggestions of death were banished from the royal palace, though the city was bedecked in flowers and gay flags, and every painful object removed from sight when the young Prince Siddartha visited the city, yet the decrees of destiny were not to be baffled, the "voices of the spirits," the "wandering winds," and the Devas whispered the truth of human sorrows into his listening ear, and, when the appointed hour arrived, the Suddha Devas threw the spell of slumber over the household, steeped in profound lethargy the sentinels (as, we are told, was done by an angel to the gaolers at Peter's prison,) rolled back the triple gates of bronze, strewed the red mohra flowers thickly beneath his horse's feet to muffle every sound, and he was free, free ? Yes,— to resign every earthly comfort, every sensuous enjoyment, the sweets of royal power, the homage of a court, the delights of domestic life; gems, the glitter of gold; rich stuffs, rich food, soft beds; the songs of trained musicians, and of birds kept prisoners in gay cages, the murmur of perfumed waters plashing in marble basins, the delicious shade of trees in gardens where art had contrived to make nature even lovelier than herself. He leaps from his saddle when at a safe distance from the palace, flings the jewelled rein to his faithful groom, Channa, cuts off his flowing locks, gives his rich costume to a hunter in exchange for his own, plunges into the jungle, and is free !

"To tread its paths with patient, stainless feet,
 Making its dusty bed, its loneliest wastes
My dwelling, and its meanest things my mates:
 Clad in no prouder garb than outcasts wear,
Fed with no meals save what the charitable
 Give of their will, sheltered by no more pomp
Than the dim cave lends or the jungle-bush.
 This will I do because the woful cry
Of life and all flesh living cometh up
 Into my ears, and all my soul is full
Of pity for the sickness of this world;
 Which I will heal, if healing may be found
By uttermost renouncing and strong strife."

Thus masterfully does Mr. Arnold depict the sentiment which provoked this Great Renunciator. The testimony of thousands of millions who, during the last twenty-five centuries, have professed the Buddhistic religion, proves that the secret of human misery was at last solved by this divine self-sacrifice, and the true path to Nirvana opened.

The joy that he brought to the hearts of others, Buddha first tasted himself. He found that the pleasures of the eye, the ear, the taste, touch and smell are fleeting and deceptive; he who gives value to them brings only disappointment and bitter sorrow upon himself. The social difference between men, he found, were equally arbitrary and illusive, caste bred hatred and selfishness, riches strife, envy and malice. So in founding his faith he laid the bottom of its foundation stones upon all this worldly dirt, and its dome in the clear serenity of the world of spirit. He who can mount to a clear conception of Nirvana will find his thought far away above the common joys and sorrows of petty men. As to one who ascends to the top of the Chimborazo or the Himalayan crags, and sees men on the earth's surface crawling to and fro like ants, so equally small do bigots and sectarians appear to him. The mountain climber has under his feet the very clouds from whose sun-painted shapes the poet has figured to himself the golden streets and glittering domes of the materialistic Heaven of a personal God. Below him are all the various objects out of which the world's pantheons have been manufactured; around, above—Immensity. And so also, far down the ascending plane of thought that leads from the earth towards the Infinite, the philosophic Buddhist describes, at different plateaux, the heavens and hells, the gods and demons of the materialistic creed-builders.

What are the lessons to be derived from the life and teachings of this heroic prince of Kapilavastu. Lessons of gratitude and of benevolence. Lessons of tolerance for the clashing opinions of men who live, move and have their being, think and aspire, only in a material world. The lessons of a common tie of brotherhood among all men. Lessons of manly self-reliance, of an equanimous breasting of whatsoever of good or ill may happen. Lessons of the meanness of the rewards, the pettiness of the misfortunes of a shifting world of illusions. Lessons of the necessity for avoiding every species of evil thought, word and deed, and for doing, speaking and thinking everything that is good; and for the bringing of the mind into subjection so that these may be accomplished, without selfish motive or vanity. Lessons of self-purification and communion by which the illusiveness of externals and the value of internals are understood.

Well might St Hilaire burst into the panegyric that Buddha "is the perfect model of all the virtues he preaches.........his life has not a stain upon it." Well might the sober critic Max Müller pronounce his moral code "one of the most perfect which the world has ever known." No wonder that, in contemplating that gentle life, Edwin Arnold should have found his personality "the highest, gentlest, holiest and most beneficent ....in the history of thought," and been moved to write his splendid verses. It is twenty-five hundred years since humanity put forth such a flower; who knows when it did before?

Gautama Buddha Sakya Muni, has ennobled the whole human race. His fame is our common inheritance. His Law is the law of Justice, providing for every good thought, word and deed its fair reward, for every evil one its proper punishment. His Law is in harmony with the voices of nature, and the evident equilibrium of the universe. It yields nothing to importunities or threats, can be neither coaxed nor bribed by offerings to abate or alter one jot or tittle of its inexorable course. Am I told that Buddhist laymen display vanity in their worship and ostentation in their alms-giving; that they are fostering sects as bitterly as Hindus? So much the worse for the laymen: there is the example of Buddha and his Law. Am I told that Buddhist priests are ignorant, idle fosterers of superstitions grafted on their religion by foreign kings? So much the worse for the priests; the life of their Divine Master shames them and shows their unworthiness to wear his yellow robe or carry his beggar-bowl. There is the Law—immutable—menacing; it will find them out and punish.

And what shall we say to those of another cast of character—the humble-minded, charitable, tolerant, religiously aspiring hearts among the laity, and the unselfish, pure and learned of the priests who know the Precepts and keep them? The Law will find them out also; and when the book of each life is written up and the balance struck, every good thought or deed will be found entered in its proper place. Not one blessing that ever followed them from grateful lips throughout their earthly pilgrimage will be found to have been lost: but each will help to ease their way as they move from stage to stage of Being

"Unto NIRVANA where the Silence lives."

THE OCCULT SCIENCES.

Delivered at Colombo, Ceylon, on the 15th of June 1880.

In the tenth chapter of his famous work, entitled *An Enquiry concerning Human Understanding*, David Hume attempts to define the limits of philosophical enquiry. So pleased was the author with his work that he has placed it on record that with the "wise and learned"—a most necessary separation, since a man may be wise without being at all learned, while modern science has introduced to us many of her most famous men who, though bursting like Jack Bunsby with learning, were far, *very* far from wise—his (Hume's) postulate must be "an everlasting check to all kinds of superstitious delusions." For many years this oracular utterance was unquestioned, and Hume's apophthegm was laid like a chloroformed handkerchief, over the mouth of every man who attempted to discuss the phenomena of the invisible world. But a brave Englishman and man of science—who, we are proud to say, accepted the diploma of our Theosophical Society—to-wit, Mr. Alfred Russell Wallace, F.R.S., has of late called Hume's infallibility in question. He finds two grave defects in his proposition that "a miracle is a visitation of the laws of Nature;" since it assumes, firstly, that we know *all* the laws of nature; and secondly, that an unusual phenomenon *is* a miracle. Speaking deferentially, is it not after all a piece of preposterous egotism for any living man to say what is, or rather what is *not*, a law of Nature? I have enjoyed the acquaintance of scientists who could actually repeat the names of the several parts of a bed bug and even of a flea. Upon this rare accomplishment they plumed themselves not a little, and took on the airs of a man of science. I have talked with them about the laws of Nature and found that they thought they knew enough of them to dogmatize to me about the Knowable and the Unknowable.. I know doctors of medicine, even professors, who were read up in physiology and able to dose their patients without exceeding the conventional average of casualties, good-naturedly allowed the profession. They have dogmatized to me about science and the laws of Nature, although not one of them could tell me anything positive about the life of man, in either the states of *ovum*, embryo, infant, adult or corpse. The most candid medical authorities have always frankly confessed that the human being is a puzzle as yet unsolved and medicine "scientific guess-work." Has ever yet a surgeon, as he stood beside a subject on the dissecting table of the amphitheatre, dared to tell his class that he knew what life is, or that his scalpel could cut away any integumental veil so as to lay bare the mystery? Did any modern botanist ever venture to explain what is that tremendous secret law which makes every seed produce the plant or tree of its own kind? Mr. Huxley and his fellow biologists have shown us protoplasm—the gelatinous substance which forms the physical basis of life—and told us that it is substantially identical in composition in plant and animal. But they can go no farther than the microscope and spectroscope will carry them. Do you doubt me? Then hear the mortifying confession of Professor Huxley himself. "In perfect strictness," he says "it is true that we know nothing about the composition of any body whatever, as it is"! And yet what scientist is there who has dogmatized more about the limitations of scientific enquiry? Do you think that, because the chemists can dissolve for you the human body into its elementary gases and ashes until what was once a tall man can be put into an empty cigar-box and a large bottle, they can help you any better to understand what that living man really was? Ask them;—I am willing to let the case rest upon their own unchallenged evidence.

Science? Pshaw! What is there worthy to wear that imperial name so long as its most noisy representatives cannot tell us the least part of the mystery of man or of the nature which environs him. Let science explain to us how the littlest blade of grass grows, or bridge over the "abyss" which Father Felix, the great French Catholic orator, tauntingly told the Academy, existed for it in a grain of sand, and then dogmatize as much as it likes abut the *laws of Nature!* In common with all heretics I hate this presumptuous pretence; and as one who, having studied psychology for nearly thirty years, has some right to be heard, I protest against, and utterly repudiate, the least claim of our modern science to know all the laws of Nature, and to say what is or what is not possible. As for the opinions of non-scientific critics, who never informed themselves practically about even one law of Nature, they are not worth even listening to. And yet what a clamour they make, to be sure; how the public ear has been assailed by the din of ignorant and conceited criticasters. It is like being among a crowd of stock-brokers on the exchange. Every one of the authorities is dogmatizing in his most vociferous and impressive manner. One would think to read and hear what all these priests, editors, authors, deacons, elders, civil and military servants, lawyers, merchants, vestrymen and old women, and their followers, admirers and echoing toadies have to say—that the laws of Nature were as familiar to them as their alphabets, and that every one carried in his pocket the combination key to the Chubb lock of the Universe! If these people only realized how foolish they really are in rushing in

"· · · · · · where Angels fear to tread,"

—they might somewhat abate their pretences. And if common sense were as plentiful as conceit, a lecture upon the Occult Sciences would be listened to with a more humble spirit than, I am afraid, can be counted upon in our days.

I have tried, by simply calling your attention to the confessed ignorance of our modern scientists of the nature of Life, to show you that in fact all visible phenomena are occult, or hidden from the average inquirer. The term *occult* has been given to the sciences relating to the mystical side of nature—the department of Force or Spirit. Open any book on science, or listen to any lecture or address by a modern authority, and you will see that modern science limits its enquiry to the visible material or physical universe. The combinations and correlations of matter, under the impulse of hidden forces, are what it studies. To facilitate this line of enquiry, mechanical ingenuity has lent the most marvelous assistances. The microscope has now been perfected so as to reveal the tiniest object in the tiny world of a drop of dew; the telescope brings into its field and focus glittering constellations that—as Tom Moore poetically says—

> " . . . . stand
> Like winking sentinels upon the void
> Beyond which Chaos dwells ;"

the chemist's balances will weigh matter to the ten-thousandth part of a grain ; by the spectroscope the composition of all things on earth and suns and stars, is claimed to be demonstrable in the lines they make across the spectrum ; substances hitherto supposed to be elements are now proved to be compounds and what we have imagined compounds, are found to be elements. Inch by inch, step by step, Physical Science has marched, from its old prison in the dungeon of the Church, towards its desired goal—the verge of physical nature. It would not be too much to admit that the verge has been almost reached, but that Edison's recent discoveries of the telephone, the phonograph and the electric light, and Crookes's of the existence and properties of Radiant Matter, seem to have pushed farther away the chasm that separates the confessedly Knowable from the fancied Unknowable. The recent advances of physical science tend to mitigate somewhat the pride of our scientists. It is as though whole domains, previously undreamt of, were suddenly exposed to view as each new eminence of knowledge is gained; just as the traveller sees long reaches of country to be traversed upon climbing to the crest of the mountain that had been shutting him in within a narrow horizon. The fact is that whether regarded from her physical or dynamical side, Nature is a book with an endless variety of subjects to be studied and mysteries to be unravelled. And, as regards science, there is a thousand times more that is occult than familiar and easy to understand.

The realization of this fact, both as the result of personal enquiry and of conversation with the learned, was one chief cause of the organization of the Theosophical Society.

Now, it must be agreed, that while the first necessity for the candid student is to discover the depth and immensity of his own ignorance, the next is to find out where and how that ignorance may be dispelled. We must first fit ourselves to become pupils and then look about for a teacher. Where, in what part of the world, can there be found men capable of teaching us a part of the mystery that is hidden behind the mask of the world of matter? Who holds the secret of Life? Who knows what Force is, and what causes it to bring around its countless, eternal correlations with the molecules of matter? What adept can unriddle for us the problem how worlds are built and why? Can any one tell us whence man came, whither he goes, what he is? What is the secret of birth, of sleep, of thought, of memory, of death? What is that Eternal, Self-Existent Principle, that by common consent is believed to be the source of every thing visible and invisible, and with which man claims kinship? We, little modern people, have been going about in search after this teacher, with our toy lanterns in our hands as though it were night instead of bright day. The light of truth shines all the while, but we, being blind, cannot see it. Does a new authority proclaim himself, we run from all sides, but only see a common man with bandaged eyes, holding a pretty banner and blowing his own trumpet. "Come," he cries, "come, good people, and listen to one who knows the laws of Nature. Follow my lead, join my school, enter my church, buy my nostrum, and you will be wise in this world, and happy hereafter"! How many of these pretenders there have been; how they have imposed for a while upon the world; what meannesses and cruelties their devotees have done in their behalf; and how their shams and humbugs have ultimately been exposed, the pages of history show. There is but *one* truth, and that is to be sought for in the mystical world of man's interior nature; theosophically, and by the help of the "Occult Sciences."

If history has preserved for us the record of multitudinous failures of materialists to read the secret laws of Nature, it has also kept for our instruction the stories of many successes gained by Theosophists in this direction. There is no impenetrable mystery in Nature to the student who knows how to interrogate her. If physical facts can be observed by the eye of the body, so can spiritual laws be discovered by that interior perception of ours which we call the eye of the spirit. This perceptive power inheres in the nature of man; it is his godlike quality which makes him superior to brutes. What we call seers and prophets, the Buddhists know as *rahats* and the Aryans as true *sanyasis*, are only men who have emancipated their interior selves from physical bondage by meditation in secluded spots where the foulness of average humanity could not taint them, and where they were nearest to the threshold of Nature's temple; and by the gradual and persistent conquest of brutal desire after desire, taste after taste, weakness after weakness, sense after sense, they have moved forward to the ultimate victory of spirit. Jesus is said to have gone thus apart to be tempted; so did Mahomet who spent one day in every month alone in a mountain cave; so did Zoroaster, who emerged from the seclusion of his mountain retreat only at the age of 40; so did Buddha, whose knowledge of the cause of pain and discovery of the path to *Nirvana*, was obtained by solitary self-struggles in desert places. Turn over the leaves of the book of records and you will find that every man who really did penetrate the mysteries of life and death, got the truth in solitude and in a mighty travail of body and spirit. These were all Theosophists—that is, original searchers after spiritual knowledge. What they did, what they achieved, any other man of equal qualities may attain to. And this is the lesson taught by the Theosophical Society. As they spurned churches, revelations and leaders, and wrested the secrets from the bosom of Nature, so do we. Buddha said that we should believe nothing upon authority, not even his own, but believe because our reason told us the assertion was true. He began by striding over even sacred Vedas because they were used to prevent original theosophical research; castes he brushed aside as selfish monopolies. His desire was to fling wide open every door to the sanctuary of Truth. We organized our Society—as the very first section of our original bye-laws expresses it—"for the discovery of all the laws of Nature, and the dissemination of the knowledge of the same." The known laws of Nature why should we busy ourselves with? The unknown or occult ones were to be our special province of research. No one in America, none in Europe, now living, could help us, except in special branches, such as Magnetism, Crystal reading, Psychometry, and those most striking phenomena of so called mediumship, grouped together under the generic name of modern spiritualism. Though the Vedas, the Puranas, the Zend Avesta, the Koran, and the Bible, teemed with allusions to the sayings and doings of wonder-working theosophists, we were told by every one that the power had long since died out, and the adepts vanished from the sight of men. Did we mention the name Occult Science, the modern biologist curled his lip in fine scorn, and the lay fool gave way to senseless witticisms.

It was a discouraging prospect, no doubt; but in this, as in every other, instance the difficulties were more imaginary than real. We had a clue given us to the right road by one who had spent a long lifetime in travel, who had found the science to be still extant, with its proficients and masters still practising it as in ancient days. The tidings were most encouraging, as are those of help and succour to a party of castaways on an unfriendly shore. We learned to recognize the supreme value of the discoveries of Paracelsus, of Mesmer and of Baron Reichenbach, as the stepping stones to the higher branches of Occultism. We turned again to study them, and the more we studied the clearer insight did we get into the meaning of Asiatic myth and fable, and the real object and methods of the ascetic theosophists of all ages. The words 'body,' 'soul,' 'spirit,' *Moksha* and *Nirvana* acquired each a definite and comprehensible meaning. We could understand what the Yogi wished to express by his uniting himself with Brahma, and becoming Brahma; why the biographer of Jesus made him say 'I and the Father are one'; how Sankaracharya and others could display such phenomenal learning without having studied it in books; whence Zaratusht acquired his profound spiritual illumination; and how the Lord Sakya Muni, though but a man "born in the purple," might nevertheless become All-Wise and All-Powerful. Would my hearer learn this secret? Let him study Mesmerism and master its methods until he can plunge his subject into so deep a sleep that the body is made to seem dead, and the freed soul can be sent, wheresoever he wills, about the earth or among the stars. Then he will see the separate reality of the body and its dweller. Or, let him read Professor Denton's "Soul of Things," and test the boundless resources of Psychometry; a strange yet simple science which enables us to trace back through ages the history of any substance held in the sensitive psychometer's hand. Thus a fragment of stone from Cicero's house, or the Egyptian pyramids; or a bit of cloth from a mummy's shroud; or a faded parchment or letter or painting; or some garment or other article worn by a historic personage; or a fragment of an ærolite—give to the psychometer impressions, sometimes amounting to visions surpassingly vivid, of the building, monument, mummy, writer or painter, or the long dead personage, or the meteoric orbit from which the last-named object fell. This splendid science, for whose discovery, in the year 1840, the world is indebted to Professor Joseph R. Buchanan, now a Fellow of our Society, has but just begun to show its capabilities. But already it has shown us that in the *Akasa*, or Ether of science, are preserved the records of every human experience, deed and word. No matter how long forgotten and gone by, they are still a record, and, according to Buchanan's estimate, about four out of every ten persons have in greater or less degree the psychometrical power which can read those imperishable pages of the book of Life. Taken by itself, either Mesmerism, or Psychometry, or Baron Reichenbach's theory of Odyle, or Odic Force, is sufficiently wonderful. In Mesmerism a sensitive subject is put by magnetism into the magnetic sleep, during which his or her body is insensible to pain, noises or any other disturbing influences. The Psychometer, on the contrary, does not sleep, but only sits or lies passively, holds the letter, fragment of stone or other object in the hand or against the centre of the forehead, and, without knowing at all what it is or whence it came, describes what he or she feels or sees. Of the two methods of looking into the invisible world, Psychometry is preferable, for it is not attended with the risks of the magnetic slumber, arising from inexperience in the operator, or low physical vitality in the somnambule. Baron Dupotet, M. Cahagnet, Professor William Gregory, and other authorities tell us of instances of this latter sort in which the sleeper was with difficulty brought back to earthly consciousness, so transcendently beautiful were the scenes that broke upon his spiritual vision. Reichenbach's discovery—the result of several years' experimental research, with the most expensive apparatus and a great variety of subjects, by one of the most eminent chemists and physicists of modern times—was this. A hitherto unsuspected force exists in Nature, having, like electricity and magnetism, its positive and negative poles. It pervades everything in the mineral, vegetable and the animal kingdoms. Our Earth is charged with it, it is in the stars, and there is a close interchange of polar influences between us and all the heavenly bodies. Here I hold in my hand a specimen of quartz crystal, sent me from the Gastein Mountains in Europe by the Baroness Von Vay. Before Reichenbach's discovery of the Odic Force—as he calls it—this would have had no special interest to the geologist, beyond its being a curious example of imperfect crystallization. But now it has a definite value beyond this. If I pass the apex, or positive pole, over the wrist and palm of a sensitive person—thus—he will feel a sensation of warmth, or cold, or the blowing of a thin, *very* thin pencil of air over the skin. Some feel one thing, some another, according to the Odic condition of their own bodies. Speaking of this latter phenomenon, viz., that the Odic polaric condition of our bodies is peculiar to ourselves, different from the bodies of each other, different in the right and left sides, and different at night and morning in the same body, let me ask you whether a phenomenon long noticed, supposed by the ignorant to be miraculous, and yet constantly denied by those who never saw it, may not be classed as a purely Odic one. I refer to the levitation of ascetics and saints, or the rising into the air of their bodies at moments when they were deeply entranced. Baron Reichenbach found that the Odic sensibility of his best patients greatly changed in health and disease. Professor Perty of Geneva, and Dr. Justinus Körner tell us that the bodies of certain hysterical patients rose into the air without visible cause, and floated as light as a feather. During the Salem Witchcraft horrors, one of the subjects, Margaret Rule, was similarly levitated. Mr. William Crookes recently published a list of no less than forty Catholic ecstatics whose levitation is regarded as proof of their peculiar sanctity. Now I myself, in common with many other modern observers of psychological phenomena, have seen a person in the full enjoyment of consciousness, raised into the air by a mere exercise of the will. This person was an Asiatic by birth and had studied occult sciences in Asia, and explains the remarkable phenomena as a simple example of change of corporeal polarity. You all know the electrical law that oppositely electrified bodies attract, and similarly electrified ones repel each other. We say that we stand upon the earth because of the force of gravitation, without stopping to think how much of the explanation is a mere patter of words conveying no accurate idea to the mind. Suppose we say that we cling to the earth's surface, because the polarity of our body is opposed to the polarity of the spot of earth upon which we stand. That would be scientifically correct. But how, if our polarity is reversed, whether by disease, or the mesmeric passes of a powerful magnetiser, or the constant effort of a trained self-will. To classify :—suppose that we were either a hysteric patient, an ecstatic, a somnambule, or an adept in Asiatic Occult Science. In either case if the polarity of the body should be changed to its opposite polarity, and so our electrical, magnetic or odic state be made identical with that of the ground beneath us, the long-known electropolaric law would assert itself and our body would rise into the air. It would float as long as these mutual polaric differences continued, and rise to a height exactly proportionate to their intensity. So much of light is let into the old domain of Church "miracles" by Mesmerism and the Od discovery.

But our mountain crystal has another and far more striking peculiarity than mere odic polarity. It is nothing apparently but a poor lump of glass, and yet in its heart can be seen strange mysteries. There are doubtless a score of persons in this great audience who, if they would sit in an easy posture and a quiet place, and gaze into my crystal for a few minutes, would see and describe to me pictures of people, scenes and places in different countries as well as their own beautiful Ceylon. I gave the crystal into the hand of a lady who is a natural clairvoyant, just after I had received it from Hungary. "I see," she said, "a large, handsome room in what appears to be a castle. Through an open window can be seen a park with smooth broad walks, trimmed lawns, and trees. A noble looking lady stands at a marble topped table doing up something into a parcel. A servant man in rich livery stands as though waiting for his mistress's orders. It is this crystal that she is doing up, and she puts it into a brown box, something like a small musical box." The clairvoyant knew nothing about the crystal, but she had given an accurate description of the sender, of her residence, and of the box in which the crystal came to me. How? Can any of the self-conceited little people, who say smart little nothings about the absurdity of the Occult Sciences, answer?

Reichenbach's careful investigations prove that minerals have each their own peculiar odic polarity, and this lets us into an understanding of much that the Asiatic people have said about the magical properties of gems. You have all heard of the regard in which the sapphire has ever been held for its supposed magical property to assist somnambulic vision. "The sapphire" according to a Buddhist writer "will open barred doors and dwellings (for the spirit of man); it produces a desire for prayer, and brings with it more peace than any other gem; but he who would wear it must lead a pure and holy life.

Now a series of investigations by Amoretti into the electrical polarity of precious stones (which we find reported in Kieser's *Archia* Vol, IV., p. 62) resulted in proving that the diamond, the garnet, the amethyst, are—E., while the sapphire is+ E. Orpheus tells how by means of a load stone a whole audience may be affected. Pythagoras, whose knowledge was derived from India, pays a particular attention to the colour and nature of precious stones; and Apollonius of Tyana, one of the purest and grandest men who ever lived, accurately taught his disciples the various occult properties of gems.

Thus does scientific inquiry, agreeing with the researches of the greatest philosophers, the experiences of religious ecstatics, continually —though, as a rule, unintentionally—give us a solid basis for studying Occultism. The more of physical phenomena we observe and classify, the more helped is the student of occult sciences and of the ancient Asiatic sciences, philosophies and religions. The fact is, we, modern Europeans, have been so blinded by the fumes of our own conceit that we have not been able to look beyond our noses. We have been boasting of our glorious enlightenment, our scientific discoveries, our civilization, and our superiority to everybody with a dark skin, and to every nation, east of the Volga and the Red Sea, or south of the Mediterranean, until we have come almost to believe that the world was built for the Anglo-Saxon race, and the stars to make our bit of sky pretty. We have even manufactured, out of Asiatic materials, a religion to suit ourselves, and think it better than any religion that was ever heard of before. It is time that this childish vanity were done away with. It is time that we should try to discover the sources of modern ideas; and compare what, we think, we know of the laws of Nature with what the Asiatic people really did know thousands of years before Europe was inhabited by our barbarian ancestors, or a European foot was set upon the American continent. The crucibles of science are heated red hot and we are melting in them everything out of which we think we can get a fact. Suppose that, for a change, we approach the Eastern people in a less presumptuous spirit, and honestly confessing that we know nothing at all of the beginning or end of Natural Law, ask them to help us to find out what their forefathers knew. This has been the policy of the Theosophical Society, and it has yielded valuable results already. Depend upon it, ladies and gentlemen, there are still "wise men in the East," and the Occult Sciences are better worth studying than has hitherto been popularly supposed.

SPIRITUALISM AND THEOSOPHY.

Delivered at the rooms of the United Service Institution of India,

Simla, on the 7th of October 1880.

Thirteen years ago, one of the most eminent of modern American jurists, John W. Edmonds, Chief Justice of the Supreme Court of New York, declared in a London magazine that there were then at least ten millions of Spiritualists in the United States of America. No man was so well qualified at that time as he to express an opinion upon this subject, for not only was he in correspondence with persons in all parts of the country, but the noble virtue of the man as well as his learning, his judicial impartiality and conservatism, made him a most competent and convincing witness. And another authority, a publicist of equally unblemished private and public reputation, the Hon. Robert Dale Owen, while endorsing Judge Edmonds' estimate adds* that there are at least an equal number in the rest of Christendom. To avoid chance of exaggeration he, however, deducts one-fourth from both amounts and (in 1874) writes the sum-total of the so-called Spiritualists at fifteen millions. But whatever the aggregate of believers in the alleged present open intercourse between our worlds of substance and shadow, it is a known fact that the number embraces some of the most acute intellects of our day. It is no question now of the self-deceptions of boors and hysterical chambermaids with which we have to deal. Those who would deny the reality of these contemporaneous phenomena, must confront a multitude of our most capable men of science, who have exhausted the resources of their profession to determine the nature of the force at work, and been baffled in seeking any other explanation than the one of trans-sepulchral agency of the same kind or other. Beginning with Robert Hare, the inventor of the oxy-hydrogen blow-pipe and Nestor of American Chemistry, and ending with Fr. Zollner, Professor of Physical Astronomy in Leipzig University, the list of these converted experimentalists includes a succession of adepts of Physical Science of the highest professional rank. Each of them—except, perhaps, Zollner who wished to verify his theory of a fourth dimension of space—began the task of investigation with the avowed pupose of exposing the alleged fraud, in the interests of public morals; and each was transformed into an avowed believer in the reality of mediumistic phenomena by the irresistible logic of facts.

---

* *The Debatable Land between this world and the next*, p. 174, London Ed. 1874.

The apparatuses devised by these men of science to test the mediumistic power have been in the highest degree ingenious. They have been of four different kinds—(*a*) machines to determine whether electrical or magnetic currents were operating; (*b*) whether the movement of heavy articles, such as tables touched by the medium, was caused by either conscious or unconscious muscular contraction; (*c*) whether intelligent communications may be received by a sitter under circumstances precluding any possible trickery by the medium; and (*d*) what are the conditions for the manifestation of this new form of energy and the extreme limitations of its action. Of course, in an hour's lecture, I could not describe a tenth part of these machines, but I may take two as illustrating two of the above-enumerated branches of research. The first is to be found described in Professor Hare's work. The medium and enquirer sit facing each other, the medium's hands resting upon a bit of board so hung and adjusted that whether he presses on the board or not he merely moves that and nothing else. In front of the visitor is a dial, like a clock-face, around which are arranged the letters of the alphabet, the ten numerals, the words 'Yes', 'No', 'Doubtful', and perhaps others. A pointer, or hand, that is connected with a lever, the other end of which is so placed as to receive any current flowing through the medium's system, but not to be affected by any mechanical pressure he may exert upon the hand-rest, travels around the dial and indicates the letters or words the communicating intelligence wishes noted down. The back of the dial being towards the medium, he, of course, cannot see what the pointer is doing, and if the enquirer conceals from him the paper on which he is noting down the communication, he cannot have even a suspicion of what is being said.

The other contrivance is described and illustrated in the monograph entitled *Researches in the Phenomena of Spiritualism*, by Mr. William Crookes, F.R.S., Editor of the *Quarterly Journal of Science*, and one of the most successful experimental chemists of our day. A mahogany board, 36 inches long by 9½ inches wide, and 1 inch thick, rests at one end upon a table, upon a strip cut to a knife edge; at the other end it is suspended by a spring-balance, fitted with an automatic registering apparatus, and hung from a firm tripod. On the table end of the board, and directly over the fulcrum, is placed a large vessel filled with water. In this water dips, to the depth of 1½ inches from the surface, a copper vessel, with bottom perforated so as to let the water enter it; which copper vessel is supported by a fixed iron ring, attached to an iron stand that rests on the floor. The medium is to dip his hands in the water in the copper vessel, and as this is solidly supported by its own stand and ring, and nowhere touches the glass vessel holding the water, you see that, should there occur any depression of the pointer on the spring-balance at the extreme end of the board, it unmistakably indicates that a current of force weighable in foot pounds is passing through the medium's body. Well, both Dr. Hare with his apparatus, and Mr. Crookes, with his, obtained the desired proof that certain phenomena of mediumship do occur without the interference, either honest or dishonest, of the medium. To the power thus manifested, Mr. Crookes, upon the suggestion of the late Mr. Serjeant Cox, gave the appropriate name of Psychic Force, and as such it will hereafter be designated by me in this lecture.

I mention these two mechanical contrivances merely to show those who, perhaps, have never enquired into the matter, but have nevertheless fallen into the common error of thinking the phenomena to be all deceptions, that the utmost pains have been taken by the cleverest scientists to guard against the possibility of fraud in the course of their experiments. If ever there was a fact of science proved, it is that a new and most mysterious force of *some* kind has been manifesting itself since March 1848, when this mighty modern epiphany was ushered in, with a shower of raps, at an obscure hamlet in New York State. Beginning with these percussive sounds, it has since displayed its energy in a hundred different phenomena, each inexplicable upon any known hypothesis of science, and in almost, if not quite, every country of our globe. To advocate its study, expound its laws, and disseminate its intelligent manifestations, hundreds of journals and books have from time to time been published in different languages; the movement has its schools and churches, or meeting halls, its preachers and teachers; and a body of men and women, numbering thousands at the least, are devoting their whole time and vital strength to the profession of mediumship. These sensitives, or "psychics." are to be found in every walk of life, in the palaces of royalty as well as the labourer's cottage, and their psychical, or mediumistic, gifts are as various as their individualities.

What has caused this world-wide expansion of the new movement, and reconciled the public to such a vast sacrifice of comfort, time, money, and social consequence? What has spurred on so many of the most intelligent people in all lands, of all sects and races, to continue investigating? What has kept the faith alive in so many millions, despite a multitude of sickening exposures of the rascality of mediums, of the demoralizing tendency of ill regulated mediumship, and the average puerility and frequent mendaciousness of the communications received? This, that a hope has sprung up in the human breast that at last man may have experimental proof of his survival after bodily death, and a glimpse, if not a full revelation, of his future destiny. All these millions cling, like the drowning man to his plank, to the one hope that the old, old questions of the What? the Whence? the Whither? will now be solved, once and for all time. Glance through the literature of Spiritualism and you shall see what joy, what consolation, and what perfect rest and courage these weird, often exasperating, phenomena of the seance room have imparted. Tears have ceased to flow from myriad eyes when the dead are laid away out of sight, and broken ties of love and friendship are no longer regarded by these believers as snapped for ever. The tempest no longer affrights as it did, and the terrors of battle and pestilence have lost their greatest power for the modern spiritualist. The supposed intercourse with the dead and their messages have sapped the infallible authority of dogmatic theology. The Spiritualist with the eye of his new faith now sees the dim outlines of a Summer Land where we live and are occupied much as upon Earth. The tomb, instead of seeming the mouth of a void of darkness, has come to look merely like a sombre gateway to a country of sun-light brightness and never-ending progression towards the crowning state of perfectibility. Nay, so definite have become the fancy pictures of this Summer Land, one constantly reads of baby children growing in spirit life to be adults; of colleges and academies for mortal guidance, presided over by the world's departed sages; and even of nuptial unions between living men or women and the denizens of the spirit world! A case in point is that of the Rev. Thomas Lake Harris-founder of the socialistic community on Lake Erie which Laurence Oliphant and his mother have joined—who gives out that he is duly married to a female spirit and that a child has blessed their union! Another case is that of the marriage of two spirits in presence of mortal witnesses, by a living clergyman, which was reported last year in the Spiritualistic papers, A Mr. Pierce, son of an ex-President of the United States and long since dead, is said to have 'Materialized,' that is, made for himself a visible, tangible body, at the house of a certain American medium, and been married by a minister summoned for the occasion, to a lady spirit who died at the very tender age of seven months and who, now grown into a blooming lass, was also materialized for the ceremony! The vows exchanged and the blessings given, the happy couple sat at table with invited friends, and, after drinking a toast or two, vanished—dresscoat, white gloves, satin, lace and all—into thin air! This you will call the tomfoolery of Spiritualism, and you will be right; but, nevertheless, it serves to show how clear and definite, not to say brutally materialistic, are the views of the other world order which have replaced the old, vague dread that weighed us down with gloomy doubts. Up to a certain point this state of mind is a decided gain, but I am sorry to say Spiritualists have passed that, and become dogmatists. Little by little a body of enthusiasts is forming, who would throw a halo of sanctity around the medium, and, by doing away with test conditions, invite to the perpetration of gross frauds. Mediums actually caught red handed in trickery, with their paraphernalia of traps, false panels, wigs and puppets about them, have been able to make their dupes regard them as martyrs to the rage of sceptics, and the damning proofs of their guilt as having been secretly supplied by the unbelievers themselves to strike a blow at their holy cause! The voracious credulity of a large body of Spiritualists has begotten nine-tenths of the dishonest tricks of mediums. As Mr. Crookes truly observed—in his preliminary article in the *Quarterly Journal of Science*.—"In the countless number of recorded observations I have read, there appear to be few instances of meetings held for the express purpose of getting the phenomena under test conditions." Still, though this is true, it is also most certain that within the past thirty-two years enquirers into the phenomena have been vouchsafed thousands upon thousands of proofs that they occur under conditions quite independent of the physical agency of the persons present, and that intelligence, sometimes of a striking character, is displayed in the control of the occult force or forces producing the phenomena. It is this great reserve of test fact upon which rests, like a rock upon its base, the invincible faith of the millions of Spiritualists. This body of individual experiences is the rampart behind which they entrench themselves whenever the outside world of sceptics looks to see the whole 'delusion' crumble under the assault of some new *buna* critic, or the shame of the latest exposure of false mediumship or tricking mediums. It ought by this time to have been discovered that it is worse than useless to try to ridicule away the actual evidence of one's senses; or to make a man who has seen a heavy weight self-lifted and suspended in air, or writing done without contact, or a human form melt before his eyes, believe any theory that all mediumistic phenomena are due to 'muscular contraction,' 'expectant attention,' or 'unconscious cerebration.' It is because of their attempts to do this, that men of science, as a body, are regarded with such compassionate scorn by the experienced psychologist. Mr. Wallace tells us that after making careful inquiry he has never found one man who, after having acquired a good personal knowledge of the chief phases of the phenomena, has afterwards come to disbelieve in their reality. And this is my own experience also. Some have ceased to be "Spiritualists" and turned Catholics, but they have never doubted the phenomena being real. It will be a happy day, one to be hailed with joy by every lover of true science, when our modern professors shall rid themselves of the conceited idea that knowledge was born in our days, question in an humble spirit the records of archaic science.

We have seen that the existence of a force current has been proved by the experiments of Dr. Hare and Mr. Crookes, so we need trouble ourselves no more with the many crude conjectures about table moving, chair lifting, and the raps, being the result of muscular energy of the medium or the visitor, but pass on to notice some of the forms in which this force has displayed its dynamic energies. These may be separated into phenomena indicating intelligence and conveying information, and purely physical manifestations of energy. Of the first class the one demanding first place is the so-called 'spirit rap.' By these simple signals the whole modern movement called Spiritualism was ushered in. These audible concussions vary in degree from the sound of a pin-head ticking to that of blows by a hammer or bludgeon powerful enough to shatter a mahogany table. The current of psychic force producing them seems to depend upon the state of the medium's system, in combination with the electric and hygrometaic condition of the atmosphere. With either unpropitious, the raps, if heard at all, are faint; with both in harmony, they are loudest and most persistent. Of themselves these rapping phenomena are sufficiently wonderful, but they become a hundred-fold more so when we find that through them communications can be obtained from intelligences claiming to be our dead friends: communications which often disclose secrets known only to the enquirer and no other person present; and even, in rare cases, giving out facts which no one then in the room was aware of, and which had to be verified later by consulting old records or distant witnesses. A more beautiful form of the rap is the sound of music, as of a cut-glass vessel stroke, or a silver bell, heard either under the medium's hand or in the air. Such a phenomenon has been often noticed by the Rev. Stainton Moses, of University College, London, in his own house, and Mr. Alfred R. Wallace describes it as occurring in the presence of Miss Nichol, now Mrs. Volckmann, at Mr. Wallace's own house. An empty wine-glass was put upon a table and held by Miss Nichol and a Mr. Humphrey to prevent any vibration. Mr. Wallace tells us that, "after a short interval of silence an exquisitely delicate sound as of tapping a glass was heard, which increased to clear silvery notes like the tinkling of a glass bell. These continued in varying degrees for some minutes, &c," Again, Mr. Wallace says, that when a German lady sang some of her national songs "most delicate music, like a fairy music box, accompanied her throughout . . . This was in the dark, but hands were joined all the time." Several of the persons in this present audience have been permitted by Madame Blavatsky to hear these dulcet fairy-bells tinkle since she came to Simla. But they have heard them in full light, without any joining of hands, and in whatsoever place she chose to order them. The phenomenon is the same as that of Miss Nichol, but the conditions very different; and of that I will have something to say further on.

Mr. Crookes found the force current to be extremely variable in the same medium on different days, and, in the medium from minute to minute, its flow was highly erratic. In his book he gives a number of cuts to illustrate these variations as well as of the ingenious apparatus he employed to detect them.

Among many thousands of communications from the alleged spirits that have been given to the public, and which for the most part contain only trivial messages about family or other personal affairs the details of which were at least known to the enquirers to whom addressed, and which might be attributed to thought-reading, we occasionally come across some that require some other explanation. I refer to those the details mentioned in which are unknown to any one present at the sitting. Mr. Stainton Moses records one such—a case in which a message was given in London, purporting to come from an old man who had been a soldier in America in the war of 1812 and to have died there. No one in London had ever heard of such a person, but upon causing a search to be made in the records of the American War Department, at Washington, the man's name was found and full corroborative proofs of the London message were obtained. Not having access to books here, I am obliged to quote from memory, but I think you will find my facts essentially correct. In another case, for which Mr. J. M. Peebles vouches, that gentleman received, either in America or somewhere else far away from England, a message from an alleged spirit who said he lived and died at York, and that if Mr. Peebles would search the records of that ancient city the spirit's statements would be found strictly true. In process of time he did visit York and search old birth and burial registers, and there, sure enough, he found just the data he had been promised.

Besides communicating by the raps the alleged spirits have employed many other devices to impart intelligence to the living. Such, among others, are the independent writing of messages upon paper laid on the floor under a table or in a closed drawer, between the leaves of a closed book, or on the ceiling or walls, or one's linen; in neither of these cases there being any human hand near by when the writing has been done. All these phenomena I have seen occurred in full light and under circumstances where trickery or deception was impossible. I have also had satisfactory experience of the rare mediumistic powers of Dr. Henry Slade, who, you recollect, was arrested on a trumped-up charge of dishonesty in London, but afterwards gave Zöllner and his brother *savants* of Leipzig, Aksakof, Boutlerof and Wagner, of St. Petersburg, and the Grand Duke Constantine, a series of most complete tests. It was Madame Blavatsky and I who sent Dr. Slade from America to Europe in 1876. A very high personage having ordered a scientific investigation of spiritualism, the professors of the Imperial University of St. Petersburg organized an experimental committee and we two were specially requested by this Committee to select, out of the best American mediums, one whom we could recommend for the test. After much investigation we chose Dr. Slade, and the necessary funds for his expenses having been remitted to me, he was in due time sent abroad. Before I would recommend him I exacted the condition that he should place himself in the hands of a committee of the Theosophical Society for testing. I purposely selected as members of that

Committee men who were either pronounced sceptics or quite unacquainted with spiritualistic phenomena. Slade was tested thoroughly for several weeks, and when the Committee's report was finally made, the following facts were certified to as having occurred. Messages were written inside double slates, sometimes tied and sealed together, while they either lay upon the table in full view of all, or were laid upon the heads of members of the Committee, or held flat against the under surface of the table top, or held in a Committee man's hand without the medium touching it. We also saw detached hands—that is, hands that floated or darted through the air and had no arm or body attached to them. These hands would clutch at our watch chains, grasp our limbs, touch our hands, take the slates or other objects from us under the table, remove our handkerchiefs from our coat pockets, &c. And all this, mind you, in the light, where every movement of the medium could be as plainly seen as any that my present hearers might make now.

Another form of signalling is the compulsory writing of messages by a medium whose arm and hand are controlled against his volition by some invisible power. Not only thousands, but lakhs of pages have been written in this way; some of the subjects-matter being worth keeping, but the greater part trash. Another method is the impression, by the unseen intelligence upon the sensitive brain of a medium, of ideas and words outside his own knowledge, such as foreign languages, names of the deceased persons, the circumstances of their deaths, requests as to the disposal of property, directions for the recovery of lost documents or valuables, information about murders or about distant tragedies of which they were the victims, diagnoses of hidden diseases and suggestions for remedies, &c. You will find many examples of each of these groups of phenomena on record and well attested.

A very interesting anecdote is related in Mr. Dale Owen's *Debatable Land*, about the identification of an old spinet that was purchased at a Paris bric-a-brac shop by the grandson of the famous composer, Bach. The details are very curious and you will do well to read them, lack of time preventing my entering more at length into the subject at this time.

But of all the forms of intelligent communication from the other world to ours, of course, none is to be compared for startling realism with that of the audible voice. I have heard these voices of every volume from the faintest whisper close to the ear, sounding like the sigh of a zephyr through the trees, to the stentorian roar that would almost shake the room and might almost have been heard rods away from the house. I have heard them speak to me through paper tubes, through metal trumpets, and through empty space. And in the case of the world-famous medium, William Eddy, the voices spoke in four languages of which the medium knew not a word. Of the Eddy phenomena, I will speak anon.

One of the prettiest—I would say the most charming of all—but for the recollection of the fairy-like music—of mediumistic phenomena is the bringing of fresh, dewbegemmed flowers, plants and vines, and of living creatures such as birds, gold-fish and butterflies, into closed rooms while the medium was in no state to bring them herself. I have myself, in friends' houses held the hands of a medium, whom I had first put into a bag that was fastened about her neck with a sealed drawing-string, and with no confederate in the house, have had the whole table covered with flowers and plants, and birds come fluttering into my lap from, Goodness knows where. And this with every door and window fastened, and sealed with strips of paper so that no one could enter from the outside. These phenomena happened mostly in the dark, but once I saw a tree-branch brought in the day-light. I was present once at a seance in America when a gentleman asked that the 'spirits' might bring him a heather-plant from the Scottish moors, and suddenly one, pulled up by the roots and with the fresh soil clinging to them, was dropped on the table directly in front of him.

A highly interestisg example of the non-intelligent class of phenomena came under my notice in the course of our search after a medium to send to Russia. A lady medium, named Mrs. Youngs, had a reputation for causing a pianoforte to rise from the floor and sway in time to her playing upon the instrument. Mme. Blavatsky and I went one evening to see her, and what happened was reported in the New York papers of the following day. As she sat at the piano playing, it certainly did tilt on the two outer legs—those farthest from her—and, with the other two, raised six or eight inches from the ground, move in time to the music. Mrs. Youngs then went to one end of the piano and, laying a single finger against the under side of the case, lifted the tremendous weight with the greatest ease. If any of you care to compute the volume of psychic force exerted, try to lift one end of a 7½ octave piano six inches from the floor. To test the reality of this phenomenon I had brought with me a raw egg which I held in the palm of my hand and pressed it lightly against the under side of the piano case at one end. I then caused the medium to lay the palm of one of her hands against the back of mine that held the egg, and told her to command the piano to rise. A moment's pause only ensued when, to my surprise, one end of the piano did rise without so much pressure upon the egg as to break the shell. I think that this, as a test of the actuality of a psychic force, was almost as conclusive an experiment as the water-basin and spring-balance of Mr. Crookes. At least it was to myself, for I can affirm that the medium did not press as much as an ounce weight against the back of my hand and it is quite certain that but very few ounces of pressure would have broken the thin shell of the egg.

One of the most undeniable manifestations of independent force is the raising and moving of a heavy weight without human contact. This I, in common with many other investigators, have witnessed. Sitting at a table in the centre of my own lighted drawing-room, I have seen the piano raised and moved a foot away from the wall, and a heavy leather arm chair run from a distant corner towards, and touch, us when no one was within a dozen feet of either of them. On another occasion my late friend and chemical teacher, Professor Mapes, who was a very corpulent person, and two other men, equally stout, were requested to seat themselves on a mahogany dining table and all were raised from the ground, the medium merely laying one hand on the top of the table. At Mrs. Youngs's house, on the evening before noticed, as many persons as could sit on the top of the piano were raised with the instrument while she was playing a waltz. The records are full of instances where rooms or even whole houses were caused by the occult force to shake and tremble as though a hurricane were blowing, though the air was quite still. And you have the testimony of Lords Lindsay, Adare, Dumaven, and other unimpeachable witnesses to the fact of a medium's body having floated around the room and sailed out of a window, seventy feet from the ground and into another window. This was in an obscure light, but I have seen, in the twilight, a person raised out of her chair until her head was as high as the globes of the chandelier, and then gently lowered down again.

You see I am telling you stories so wonderful that it is impossible for any one to fully credit them without the corroboration of their own personal experience. Believe me, I would not tell them at all—for no man desires to have his word doubted—unless I knew perfectly well that such phenomena have been seen hundreds of times in nearly every land under the sun, and can be seen by any one who will give time to the investigation. Despite my disclaimer, you may think that I am taking it for granted that you are quite as well satisfied as myself of the reality of the mediumistic phenomena, but I assure you I do not. I am always keeping in mind that, no matter what respect an auditor may have for my integrity and cleverness, no matter how plainly he may see that I can have no ulterior motive to deceive him—yet he *cannot* believe without himself having had the same demonstrative evidences I have had. He will—because he must—reflect that such things as these are outside the usual experience of men, and that, as Hume puts it, it is more reasonable to believe any man a liar than that the even course of natural law should be disturbed. True, that assumes the absurd premise that the average man knows what are the limitations of natural law, but we never consider our own opinions absurd, no matter how others may regard them. So, knowing, as I have just remarked, that what I describe has been seen by thousands, and may be seen by thousands more at any time, I proceed with my narrative as one who tells the truth and fears no impeachment. It is a great wonder what we are having shown us in our days, and, apart from the solemn interest which attaches to the problem whether or not the dead are communing with us, the scientific importance of these facts cannot be undervalued. From the first—that is to say, throughout my twenty-eight years of observations—I have pursued my inquiry in this spirit, believing that it was of prime importance to mankind to ascertain all that could be learnt about man's powers and the forces of nature about him.

What I shall now relate about my adventures at the Eddy Homestead in Vermont, America, will tax your indulgence more than all that has preceded. For some years, previous to 1874, I had taken no active interest in the mediumistic phenomena. Nothing surpassingly novel had been reported as occurring, and the intelligence communicated through mediums was not usually instructive enough to induce one to leave his books and the company of their great authors. But in that year it was rumoured that at a remote village, in the valley of the Green Mountains, an illiterate farmer and his equally ignorant brother were being visited daily by the "materialized," souls of the departed, who could be seen, heard and, in cases, touched by any visitor. This tempting novelty I determined to witness, for it certainly transcended in interest and importance everything that had ever been heard of in any age. Accordingly, in August of that year, I went to Chittender, the village in question, and, with a single brief intermission of ten days, remained there until the latter part of October. I hope you will believe that I adopted every possible precaution against being befooled by village trickery. The room of the ghosts was a large chamber occupying the whole upper floor of a two-story wing of the house. It was perhaps twenty feet wide by forty long—I speak from memory. Below were two rooms—a kitchen and a pantry. The kitchen chimney was in the gable end, of course, and passed through the seance room to the roof. It projected into the room two feet, and at the right, between it and the side of the house, was a plastered closet with a door next to the chimney. A window, two feet square, had been cut in the outer wall of the closet to admit air. Running across this end of the large room was a narrow platform, raised about 18 inches from the floor, with a step to mount by at the extreme left, and a hand rail or baluster along the front edge of the platform. Every evening, after the last meal, William Eddy, a stoutbuilt, square shouldered, hard handed farmer, would go upstairs, hang a thick woollen shawl across the doorway, enter the closet and seat himself on a low chair that stood at the extreme end. The visitors, who sometimes numbered forty of an evening, were accommodated on benches placed within a few feet of the platform. Horatio Eddy sat on a chair in front, and discoursed doleful music on a fiddle and led the singing—if such it might be called—without causing Mozart to turn in his grave; a feeble light was given by a kerosine lamp placed on the floor at the end of the room farthest from the platform, in an old drum from which both heads had been removed. Though the light was certainly very dim yet it sufficed to enable us to see if any one left his seat, and to distinguish through the gloom the height and costumes of the visitors from the other world. At a first sitting this was difficult, but practice soon accustomed one's eyes to the conditions.

After an interval of singing and fiddle scraping, sometimes of five, sometimes of twenty or thirty, minutes, we would see the shawl stirred, it would be pushed aside, and out upon the platform would step some figure. It might be a man, woman or child, a decrepit veteran or a babe carried in a woman's arms. The figure would have nothing at all of the supernatural or ghostly about it. A stranger entering at the other end of the room would simply fancy that a living mortal was standing there ready to address an audience. Its dress would be the one it wore in life, its face, hands, feet, gestures, perfectly natural. Sometimes, it would call the name of the living friend it had come to meet. If it were strong the voice would be of the natural tone; if weak, the words came in faint whispers; if still more feeble, there was no voice at all, but the figure would stand leaning against the chimney or hand rail while the audience asked in turn—"Is it for me?", and it either bowed its head or caused raps to sound in the wall when the right one asked the question. Then the anxious visitor would lean forward, and scan the figure's appearance in the dim light, and often we would hear the joyful cry, "Oh! Mother, Father, Sister, Brother, Son, Daughter," or what not, "I know you." Then the weird visitor would be seen to bow, or stretch out its hands, and then seeming to gather the last strength that remained to it in its evanescent frame, glide into the closet again, and drop the shawl before the hungry gaze of the eyes that watched it. But, sometimes, the form would last much longer. Several times I saw come out of the closet an aged lady clad in the Quaker costume, with lawn cap and kerchief pinned across her bosom, grey dress and long housewifely apron, and, calling her son to the platform, seat herself in a chair beside him, and, after kissing him fondly, talk for some minutes with him in low tones about family matters. All the while she would be absently folding the hem of her apron into tucks, and smoothing them out again, and so continuing the thing over and over just as—her son told me—she was in the habit of doing while alive. More than once, just as she was ready to disappear, this gentleman would take her arm in his, come to the baluster, and say that he was requested by his old mother, whom we saw there, although she had been dead many years, to certify that it was, indeed, she herself and no deception, and bid them realize that man lives beyond the grave, and so live here as to ensure their happiness then.

I will not attempt to give you, in these few minutes of our lecture, even the bare outline of my observations during those eventful weeks. Suffice it to say that I saw as many as seventeen of these *revenants* in a single evening, and that, from first to last, I saw about five hundred. There were a certain few figures that seemed especially attached to the medium's sphere or influence, but the rest were the appearances of friends of the strangers who daily flocked to the place from the most distant localities—some as far away as 2,000 miles. There were Americans and Europeans, Africans and Asiatics, Red Indians of our prairies and white people; each wearing his familiar dress and some even carrying their familiar weapons. One evening, the figure of a Kurd, a man whom Madame Blavatsky had known in Kurdistan, stepped from the closet, clad in his tall cap, high boots and picturesque clothes. In the shawl twisted about his waist were thrust a curved sword and other small arms. His hands were empty but, after salaaming my friend in his native fashion, lo! his right hand held a twelve foot spear which bore below the steel head a tuft of feathers. Now, supposing his former medium to have been ever so much a cheat, whence, in that secluded hamlet, did he procure this Kurdish dress, the belt, the arms and the spear at a moment's notice—for Mme. Blavatsky had but just arrived at Chittenden, and neither I nor any one else knew who she was, nor whence she had come. All my experiences there were described by me, first in a series of letters to a New York journal, and afterwards in book form,* and I must refer the curious to that record for details, both as to what was seen and what precautions I took against deception. Two suspicions have doubtless occurred to your minds while I have been speaking—(*a*) that some confederate or confederates got access to the medium through the closet window, or dresses and dolls were passed up to him from below through a trap or sliding panel. Of course, they would occur to any one with the least ingenuity of thought. They occurred to me and this is what I did. I procured a ladder and on the outside of the house tacked a piece of mosquito net over the entire window, sash frame and all, sealing the tack-heads with wax, and stamping each with my signet ring. This effectually prevented any nonsense from that quarter. And then calling to my help an architect and a clever Yankee inventor and mechanician, with those gentlemen I made a minute practical examination of the chimney, the floor, the platform, the rooms below and the lumberloft overhead. We were all perfectly satisfied that if there was any trickery in the case it was done by William Eddy himself without confederacy, and that if he used theatrical dresses or properties, he must carry them in with him. In the little narrow hole of a closet there was neither a candle, mirror, brush

---

* *People from the Other World.*

wig, clothes, water-basin, towel, cosmetic, nor any other of the actor's paraphernalia, nor, to speak the truth, had the poor farmer the money to buy them with. He took no fee for his seances, and visitors were charged only a very small sum for their board and lodging. I have sat smoking with him in his kitchen until it was time for the seance to begin, gone with him to the upper chamber, examined the closet before he entered it, searched his person, and then seen the self same wonderful figures come out as usual in their various dresses. I think I may claim to have proceeded cautiously, for Mr. A. R. Wallace, F. R. S., quoted, and eulogised, my book in his recent controversy with Professor W. B. Carpenter. Carpenter himself went to America to enquire into my character for veracity and publicly admitted it to be unimpeachable. Professor Wagner of St. Petersburg reviewed the work in a special pamphlet, in which he affirms that I fulfilled every requirement of scientific research, and three European psychological societies elected me Honorary Member. It shoud also be noted that four years of very responsible and intricate examinations on behalf of the War Department—during our late American War, the proofs of which service have been shown by me to the Indian authorities—qualified me to conduct this inquiry with at least a tolerable certainty that I would not be imposed upon. Having then seen all that has now been outlined to you, will you wonder that I should have been thoroughly convinced of the reality of a large group of psychic phenomena, that science helplessly tries to offer some explanation for? And can you be surprised that whatever man of science has, since 1848, seriously and patiently investigated modern spiritualism, he has become a convert, no matter what may have been his religious belief or professional bias?

The mention of religion leads me to a certain fact. While the Protestant Church has, in our time, ever resolutely denied the reality of such manifestations of occult agencies, the Church of Rome has always admitted them to be true. In her rubrics there are special forms of exorcism, and one Miss Laura Edmonds, the gifted daughter of the honoured American jurist above mentioned, and one of the most remarkable mediums of this modern movement, united herself with the Catholic Church, her confessor, a Paulist Brother of New York, drove out her obsessing "devils" in due form after—as he told me—a terrific struggle. Mediumship was anathematized by the late Pope himself, as a dangerous device of the Evil One, and the faithful warned against the familiars of the circle as his agents for the ruin of souls. There appeared in France, within the past few years, a series of books by the Chevalier des Mousseaux, highly applauded by the Catholic prelates, especially designed to collate the most striking proof of the demoniac agency in the phenomena. They are all valuable repositories of psychic facts, one especially *Les Moeurs et Pratiques des Demons*, which every student of Occultism should read. The industrious author, of course, convinces no one but Catholics as to his premises, but his facts are most welcome and suggestive. Though there is never a grain of religious orthodoxy in me, and I do not in the least sympathize with the demoniacal theory, yet I find, after learning what I have of Asiatic psychological science, that the Catholics are much nearer right in recognizing and warning against the dangers of mediumship, than the Protestants in blindly denying the reality of the phenomena. Mediumship is a peril indeed, and the last thing I could wish would be to see one whom I was interested in become one. The Hindus—who have known these phenomena from time immemorial—give the most appropriate name of *bhuta dák*, or demons' post to these unfortunates. I do sincerely hope that sooner or later the experience of India in this matter will be studied, and if mediumship is to be encouraged at all, it shall be under such protective restriction as the ancient Sybils enjoyed in the temples, under the watchful care of initiated priests. This is not the language of a Spiritualist nor am I one. In the reality of the phenomena and the existence of the psychic force I do most unreservedly believe, but here my concurrence with the spiritualists ends. For more than twenty years I was of their opinion, and shared, with Mr. Owen and Mr. Wallace, the conviction that the phenomena could not be attributed to any other agency than that of the departed ones. I could not understand how the intelligence behind the manifestations could be otherwise accounted for, especially that shown in such cases as I have mentioned where the facts related were unknown to any one at the seance, and only verified long afterwards in distant countries. But until meeting Mme. Blavatsky at the Eddys' I had not even heard of Asiatic Occultism as a science. The tales of travellers and the stories of the Arabian Nights I set down to fanciful exaggeration, and all that was printed about Indian jugglers and the powers of ascetics seemed but accounts of successful prestidigitations. I can now look back to that meeting as the most fortunate event of my life, for it made light shine in all the dark places and sent me out on a mission to help to revive Aryan occult science, which grows more absorbingly interesting with every day. It is my happiness to not only help to enlarge the boundaries of Western science by showing where the secrets of nature and of man may be experimentally studied, and to give Anglo-Indians a greater respect for the subject nation they rule over, but also to aid in kindling in the bosoms of Indian youths a proper reverence for their glorious ancestry and a desire to imitate them in their noble achievements in science and philosophy. This, ladies and gentlemen, is the sole cause of our coming to India; this explains our affectionate relations with the people, our respect for their real Yogis. Each of you looks forward to the day when you will return to your English homes; our home is here, and here we mean to end our days.

The handbills announce me as the President of the Theosophical

Society, and you gathered here to learn what Theosophy is and what are its relations with Spiritualism.

Let me say then, that in the sense given to it by those who first used it, the word means divine wisdom, or the knowledge of divine things. The lexicographers handicap the idea with the suggestion that it meant the knowledge of God, the Deity before their minds being a personal one; but such was not the intention of the early theosophists. Essentially, a theosophical society is one which favours man's original acquisition of knowledge about the hidden things of the universe by the education and perfecting of his own latent powers. Theosophy differs as widely from philosophy as it does from theology. It has been truly said that, in investigating the divine nature and attributes, philosophy proceeds entirely by the dialectic method, employing as the basis of its investigation the ideas derived from natural reason; theology, still employing the same method, superadds to the principles of natural reason those derived from authority and revelation. Theosophy, on the contrary, professes to exclude all dialectical process, and to derive all its knowledge of God from direct and immediate intuition and contemplation. This theosophy dates from the highest antiquity of which we have preserved any records, and every original founder of a religion was a seeker after divine wisdom by the theosophic process of self-illumination. Where do we find in our day the facilities for pursuing this glorious study? Where are the training schools that are worthy to be called the successors of those of the Neo-Platonists of Alexandria, the Hierophants of Egypt, the Theodidaktoi of Greece, or—and especially—the Rishis of Aryavarta, noblest of all initiates, if we except the stainless, the illuminated Gautama Buddha?

Think for a moment of what this theosophical study exacts of a man who would really penetrate the mysteries and become a true *Illuminatus*. The lusts of the flesh, the pride of life, the prejudices of birth, race, creed (so far as it creates dogmatism)—must all be put aside. The body must be made the convenience, instead, of the despot, of the higher self. The prison bars of sense that incarcerate the man of matter must be unlocked, and while living in and being a factor in, the outer world, the theosophist must be able to look into, enter, act in, and return from, the inner world, fraught with divine truths. Are there,—were there ever—such men, such demigods, rather let us say? There were; there *are*. The legends of the past may seem to us tinged with error, wild and fantastic even; but, nevertheless, such men as these existed and displayed their powers, in many countries, at various epochs. And nowhere more than in India, this blessed land of the Sun—now so poor, so spiritless, so famished and degraded. This was the home of ancient Theosophy; here—upon these very Himalayan mountains that tower so high yonder—lived and taught the men who won the prize of divine knowledge, whose wisdom—a fertilizing stream—flowed through Grecian and Egyptian channels towards the West. Believe me or not, as you will, I am fully persuaded that there still linger among these fastnesses, out of the poisoned moral atmosphere of this nineteenth century, social life, safe from the blight and persecution of bigotry and intolerant modern superstition, safe from the cruel malice of scepticism—those who are true theosophists. Neither pessimist nor optimist, I am not satisfied that our race is doomed to destruction, present or future, nor that the moral sense of society can be kept undiminished without constant refreshment from the parent fount. That fount I conceive to be theosophical study and personal illumination, and I regard him as a benefactor to his kind who points to the sceptical, the despairing, the world-weary, the heart-hungry, that the vanities of the world do not satisfy the soul's aspirations, and true happiness can only be acquired by interior self—development, purification and enlightenment. It is not in accord with the abstract principles of Justice that the world should be left entirely without such exemplars of spiritual wisdom. I do not believe it ever was, or ever will be.

To him who takes up this course of effort the phenomena of mediumship are transcendingly important, for they usher him into the realm of the Unseen, and show him some of the weirdest secrets of our human nature. Along with mediumship he studies vital magnetism, its laws and phenomena, and the Odyle of Baron Reichenbach, which together show us the real nature and polarities of this Force, and the fact that it seems to be akin to the one great force that pervades all nature. Further proof he draws from Buchanan's psychometry, and experiments with those whom he finds to be endowed with the psychometrical faculty. If there are any here to whom this is a new word, I will say that this is a name given by the modern discoverer to a certain power possessed by about one person in four to receive intuitive impressions of the character of the writer of a letter or the painter of a picture by direct contact with the manuscript or the painting. Every one of us is constantly leaving the impress of his character upon everything we touch, as the loadstone imparts some of its properties to every needle it is rubbed against. A subtle something—magnetism, or vital fluid, or psychic force—constantly exudes from us. We leave it on the ground and our dog finds us; on our clothing, and the slaver's blood hounds sniffs the scent and tracks the poor runaway to his hiding place. We saturate with it the walls of our houses, and a sensitive psychometer, upon entering our drawing-room, can unerringly tell, before seeing the family, whether that is a happy home or one of strife. We are surrounded by it as a sensitive vapour, and when we meet each other we silently take in our impression of our mutual congeniality or antipathy. Women have this sense more than men, and many are the instances where a wife's prophetic intuition, unheeded and ridiculed by the husband in the case of some new acquaintance, has afterwards been recalled with regret that it should have been disregarded. Good psychometers can even take from any fragment of inanimate matter, such as a bit of an old building, or a shred of an old garment, a vivid impression of all the scenes of its history. In its highest manifestation psychometry becomes true clairvoyance, and, when that soul sight is indeed opened, the eye within us that never grows lustreless shows us the arcana of the Unseen Universe.

Theosophy shows the student that evolution is a fact, but that it has not been partial and incomplete as Darwin's theory makes it. As there has been an evolution, in physical nature, the crown and flower of which is physical man, so there has been a parallel evolution in the realm of spirit. The outcome of this is the psychic, or inner, man; and, just as in this visible nature about us we see myriads of forms lower than ourselves, so the Theosophist finds in the *terra incognita* of the physicist—the realm of the "Unknowable"—countless minor psychical types, with man at the top of the ascending series. Physicists know of the elements only in their chemical or dynamic relations and properties; but he, who has mastered the Occult Sciences, finds, dwelling in fire, air, earth, and water, sub-human order of being, some inimical, some favourable to man. He not only comes to a knowledge of them, but also to the power of controlling them. The folk lore of the world has embalmed many truths about this power, which is none the less a fact because the modern biologist turns up his nose at it. You who come from Ireland or the Scottish Highlands know that these beings exist. I do not surmise this, I *know* it. I speak thus calmly and boldly about the subject, because I have met these proficients of Asiatic Occultism and seen them exercise their power. This is why I ceased to call myself a Spiritualist in 1874, and why, in 1875, I united with others to found a Theosophical Society to promote the study of these natural phenomena. The most wonderful facts of mediumship I have seen produced at will, and in full daylight, by one who had learnt the secret sciences in India and Egypt. Under such circumstances I have seen showers of roses made to fall in a room; letters from people in far countries to drop from space into my lap; heard sweet music, coming from afar upon the air, grow louder and louder until it was in the room, and then die away again out in the still atmosphere until it was no more. I have seen writing made to appear upon paper and slates laid upon the floor, drawings upon the ceiling beyond any one's reach, pictures upon paper without the employment of pencil or colour, articles duplicated before my very eyes, a living person instantly disappear before my sight, jet black hair cut from a fair haired person's head, had absent friends and distant scenes shown me in a crystal, and, in America more than a hundred times, upon opening letters upon various subjects coming to me by the common post from my correspondents in all parts of the world, have found inside, written in their own familiar hand, messages to me from men in India who possess the theosophical knowledge of natural law. Nay, upon one occasion, I even saw summoned before me as perfectly 'materialized' a figure as any that ever stalked out of William Eddy's cabinet of marvels. If it is not strange that the spritualist, who sees mediumistic phenomena, but knows nothing of occult science, should believe in the intervention of spirits of the dead, is it any stranger that I, after receiving so many proofs of what the trained human will can accomplish, should be a theosophist and no longer a spiritualist ? I have not even half exhausted the catalogue of the proofs that have been vouchsafed to me during the last five years as to the reality of Asiatic psychological science. But I hope I have enumerated enough to show you that there are mysteries in India worth seeking, and men *here* who are far more acquainted with nature's occult forces than either of those much imitated gentlemen who set themselves up for professors and biologists.

It will be asked what evidence I offer that the intelligent phenomena of the mediums are not to be ascribed to our departed friends. In reply, I ask what unimpeachable evidence there is that they are. If it can be shown that the soul of the living medium can, unconsciously to his physical self, ooze out, and, by its elastic and protean nature, take on the appearance of any deceased person whose image it sees in a visitor's memory; if all the phenomena can be produced at will by an educated psychologist; if, in the ether of science—the *Akàsa* of the Hindus, the Anima Mundi of the theosophists, the Astral Light of the cabalists—the images of all persons and events, and the vibrations of every sound, are eternally preserved—as these occultists affirm and experimentally prove—if all this is true, then why is it necessary to call in the spirits of the dead to explain what may be done by the living ? So long as no alternative theory was accessible, the spiritualists held impregnable ground against materialistic science; theirs was the only possible way to account for what they saw. But, given the alternative, and shown the resources of psychology and the nature of the Unseen Universe, you see the spiritualists are at once thrown upon the defensive without the ability to silence their critics. The casual observer would say it is impossible, for instance, for that aged Quaker lady's figure to be anything but her own returning soul—that her son could not have been mistaken, and that, if there were any doubt, otherwise, her familiar knowledge of their family matters, and even her old habit of alternately plaiting and smoothing out her lawn apron, identify her amply. But the figure did nothing and said nothing that was not fixed in the son's memory—indelibly stamped there, however, the long dormant pictures might have been obscured by fresher images. And the medium's body being entranced and his active vitality transferred to his inner self, or 'double', that double could make itself appear under the guise of the dead lady, and catch and comment upon the familiar incidents it found in the son's magnetic atmosphere. This will be hard for you to comprehend, for our Western scientific discoveries have not as yet crossed the threshold of this hidden world of Force. But progress is the law of human thought and we are now so near the verge of the chasm that divides physical from spiritual science, that it will not be long before we will bridge it. Let this stand as a prophecy; if you bide patiently you will see it fulfilled. This then is the present attitude of parties. The promulgation of our views and of many reports by eye witnesses of things done by members of the Theosophical Society has been causing great talk all over the world. A large body of the most intelligent spiritualists have joined us and are giving their countenance to our work. Groups of sympathizers have organized themselves into branches in many different countries. Even here, in Simla, there has sprung up the nucleus of what will be an Anglo-Indian branch. No country in the world affords so wide a field as India for psychological study. What we Europeans call Animal Magnetism has been known here and practised in its highest perfection for countless centuries. The Hindus know equally well the life principle in man, animal and plants. All over India, if search were but made, you would find, in the possession of the natives, many facts that it is most important for Europe and America to know. And you, gentlemen, of the civil and military branches of the public service, are the proper ones to undertake the work with Hindu help. Be just and kind to them and they will tell you a thousand things they now keep profound secrets among themselves. Our policy is one of general conciliation and co-operation for the discovery of truth. Some tale bearer has started the report that our Society is preaching a new religion. This is false: the Society has no more a religion of its own than the Royal Asiatic, the Royal Geographical, or the Royal Astronomical. As those societies have their separate sections, each devoted to some speciality of research, so have we. We take in persons of all religions and every race, and treat all with equal respect and impartiality. We have royal, noble, and plebeian blood among us. Edison is our member, and Wallace, and Camille Flammarion, and Lord Lindsay, and Baron du Potet and the octogenarian Cahagnet, and scores of men of that intellectual quality. We have but one passionate and consuming ambition—that of learning what man is, what nature. Are there any here who sympathize with these aspirations? Any who feel within their hearts the glow of true manhood—one that puts a higher value upon divine wisdom than upon the honours and rewards of the lower life? Come, then, brother dreamers, and let us combine our efforts and our good will. Let us see if we cannot win happiness for ourselves in striving to benefit others. Let us do what we can to rescue from the oblivion of centuries that priceless knowledge of divine things which we call THEOSOPHY.

INDIA, PAST, PRESENT AND FUTURE.

Delivered at Amritsar, on the 29th of October 1880.

THE PAST.

When we look over the accounts that have been written within our own modern historical period about the migrations of peoples, the rise and fall of empires, the characters of great men, the relative progress of science, the arts, literature, philosophy and religion; and when we see how the positive assertions of one writer are denied point blank by another, and then the facts of both proved false by a third who comes after them, is it too much to say that History is, for the most part, a system of bold lying and ignorant mis-statement? I think not. And I am quite sure that out of all the historians who have figured during this epoch that I have mentioned, hardly one can be acquitted, or will be acquitted by posterity, of incompetence or something worse. Of all the untrustworthy historians the worst is he who writes in the interest of some one religion against the religions of others. It would seem as, though no matter what his creed, he considered it a pious duty to lie as much possible for the glory of his particular god. A similar blight is seen resting upon the consciences of political historians, though not so fatally, for if their party interests are but cared for, they can afford to be in a measure fair in other directions. It seems impossible, therefore, to gather any idea of either Egyptian, Greek, Roman, Assyrian, European, or American history without reading all the historians together and extracting the truth out of the clash and conflict of error.

It will not be required that I should give, in the very few minutes for which I shall detain you, either a list of the historians or specimen extracts from their works, upon which the above opinion is based: it being shared by many of the ablest commentators. Suffice it to say that the European historiographers have never had until within a very recent period—say not more than one century—any materials for writing even the most meagre outline of Aryan history. Until the Englishman, Sir William Jones, and his compeers, and the Frenchman, Burnouf, led the way into the splendid garden of Sanskrit literature; until the astonished eyes of the West saw its glorious flowers of poesy, its fruits of philosophy and metaphysics, its crystal like rivulets of science, its magnificent structures of philology; no one dreamed that the world had had any history worth speaking of before the times of the Greek and Roman civilizations. Western ideas of Egyptian, Persian, Babylonian,

Chinese, and Indian achievements—physical, intellectual and moral—were as hazy as a fog. Like the wayfarer who tries, with the help of the street gas lamps and the lanterns of his servants, to pick his way through London streets, when one of those dense fogs of theirs turns noon into dark night, they, the historians, were groping after the facts through the mists of their own ignorance—and religious prejudice. You may look through any great library you please, and you will find there whole shelves of authors who have tried their best to prove that every thing has happened within the last 6,000 years. You will see some not ashamed or afraid to say that Asia derived her religious ideas, her industries, and her very language from the Jews or early Christians, you can find books which try to prove that Sanskrit is a derivative from the Hebrew. You can also read arguments from Christian writers to show that the parental resemblance of Hindu mythology to Biblical stories is due to the fact that St. Thomas, one of the alleged disciples of Jesus, came to India and preached his religion here ! The theory that Aryavarta was the cradle of European civilization, the Aryans the progenitors of Western peoples, and their literature the source and spring of all Western religions and philosophies, is comparatively a thing of yesterday. Professor Max Müller and a few other Sanskritists of our generations have been bringing about this change in Western ideas. Let us hope that before many more years roll by, we may have out the whole truth about Aryan civilization, and that your ancestors (and ours) will be honoured according to their deserts. The pride of modern people may receive a shock, but the ancients will be vindicated and the cause of truth advanced.

The fact will then appear, far more distinctly than even now, that long before the first page of the Bible was written, generations before the Jews had a nationality to boast of, before the foundations of Babylon were laid, or the first stone of the Egyptian pyramids had been hewn—and that, according to Baron Bunsen and Boeckh, must have been more than 5,700 years B. C—the Aryans were enjoying a splendid civilization, and had perfected a grammar and language with which none other can compare. If asked to prove my words, I may do so by propounding a question. To what age of the word's history must the beginnings of the Egyptian State, the monarchy of Mena, the founder of Egypt, be carried back ? Those most interested in the solution of this problem hesitate even as to the duration of Manetho's dynasties—from Mena to the last Pharaoh—the most eminent modern Egyptologers not daring to assign it a more recent period than between 5,000 and 6,000 years B. C. And what do they find on the very threshold of Egyptian history, further back than which Western history cannot penetrate ? Why, a State of the most marvellous civilization, a State already so advanced that in contemplating it one has to repeat with Renan, "one feels giddy at the very idea." *(on est pris de vertige)* and with Brugsch, "there are no ages of stone, bronze and iron in Egypt...........We must openly acknowledge the fact that, up to this time at least, Egypt throws scorn upon these assumed periods." And now, Egyptian history and civilization being the most ancient we have, and this history picturing to us, nearly 8,000 years ago, a people already highly civilized, not in the material sense alone as Brugsch tells us, but in social and political order, morality and religion, the next question would be why we should say that India and not Egypt is the older. My reason may seem at first glance paradoxical, yet nevertheless, I answer—because *nothing is known of India,* 8,000 *years ago.* And when I say nothing is known, I mean known by *us*, the Western nations, for the Brahmins have their own chronology and no one has the means of proving that their calculations are exaggerated. But we Europeans know nothing, or at least have known nothing of it until now, but have a right to more than suspect that India, 8,000 years ago, sent a colony of emigrants who carried their arts and high civilization into what is now known to us as Egypt. This is what Brugsch Bey, the most modern as well as the most trusted Egyptologer and antiquarian, says on the origin of the old Egyptians. Regarding these as a branch of the Caucasian family having close affinity with the Indo-Germanic races, he insists that they "migrated from Asia, long before historic memory, and crossed that bridge of nations, the Isthmus of Suez, to find a new fatherland on the Banks of the Nile........." The Egyptians came according to their own records, from a mysterious land (now shown to lie on the shore of the Indian Ocean) the sacred *Punt*; the original home of their gods—who followed thence after their people who had abandoned them, to the valley of the Nile led by Amon, Hor and Hathor. This region was the Egyptian "Land of the Gods"—PA-NUTER, in old Egptian—or Holy-land, and now proved beyond any doubt to have been quite a different place than the 'Holy Land' of Sinai. By the pictorial and hieroglyphic inscriptions found (and interpreted) on the walls of the temple of the Queen Hashtop, at Der-el-bahri, we see that this *Punt* can be no other than India. For many ages the Egyptians traded with their old homes and the reference here made by them to the names of the Princes, of Punt and its fanna and flora, especially the nomenclature of various precious woods to be found but in India, leave us scarcely room for the smallest doubt that the old civilization of Egypt is the direct outcome of that of the still older India, most probably of the Isle of Ceylon, which was in prehistoric days part and parcel of the great Continent as the geologists tell us.

So then we see that thousands of years before a single spark of civilization had appeared in Europe, before a book had been printed, before the doors of a school had been opened, those great Aryan progenitors of ours were learned, polite, philosophical, and, nationally as well as individually, great. The people were not, as now, irrevocably walled in by castes, but they were free to rise to the highest social dignities, or sink to the lowest positions, according to the inherent qualities they might possess.

If there were great philosophers in those days, so also there were great philologists, physicians, musical composers, sculptors, poets, statesmen, warriors, architects, manufacturers, merchants. In the Chatoosushteekala Nirnaya, of Vatsavana, are mentioned fifty different professions that were followed in the Vedic period, and that shows that not only the actual comforts, but also the luxuries and amusements of a civilized community were common then. We have the enforced testimony of many Christian authors, whom certainly no one will suspect of partiality for India, that neither in what the West calls ancient nor modern times have there been produced such triumphs of the human intellect as by the Aryans. I might fill a separate book with extracts of this kind, but it is unnecessary just now. I will cite only one witness, the Rev. William Ward, a Baptist Missionary of Serampur and author of a well known work on Indian History, Literature, and Mythology. "The grammars," he says, "are very numerous, and reflect the highest credit on the ingenuity of their authors. Indeed, in philology, the Hindoos have perhaps excelled both the ancients (meaning, no doubt, the Greeks and Romans) and the moderns. Their dictionaries, according to him, "also do the highest credit to the Hindoo learned men, and prove how highly the Sanskrit was cultivated in former periods." The Hindoo sages "did not permit even the military art to remain unexamined......... it is very certain that the Hindoo kings led their own armies to the combat, and that they were prepared for this important employment by a military education; nor is it less certain that many of these monarchs were distinguished for the highest valour and military skill." After recounting many important facts, Mr. Ward says, "From the perusal of the preceding pages it will appear evident that the Hindoo philosophers were, unquestionably, men of deep erudition.........and that they attracted universal homage and applause; some of them had more than a thousand disciples or scholars." And, in concluding the fourth volume of his work, he pays your ancestors this merited compliment: "No reasonable person will deny to the Hindoos of former times the praise of very extensive learning. The variety of subjects upon which they wrote prove that almost every science was cultivated among them. The manner also in which they treated these subjects proves that the Hindoo learned men yielded the palm of learning to scarcely any other of the ancients. The more their philosophical works and law books are studied the more will the enquirer be convinced of the depth of wisdom possessed by the authors."

Now I have been often asked by those who affirm the superiority in scientific discovery of modern nations, whether the Aryans or their contemporaries could show anything so splendid as the electric telegraph and the steam engine. My answer is that the properties of steam are said to have been known in those ancient days; that printing was used at a most remote antiquity in China; and that the Aryans had, and certain of their descendants now have, a system of telegraphing that enables conversation to be carried on at any distance, and that requires neither poles, wires, nor pots of chemicals. You wish to know what that is? I will tell you, and tell it to the very beards of those ignorant, half-educated people who make fun of sacred things, and who are not ashamed to revile their forefathers upon the strength of some superficial English education they may have picked up. Your ancient Yogis could, and all who have acquired a certain proficiency in occult science can, thus talk even now, with each other. Some of you may honestly doubt it, but still it is true, as any author who has written on Yoga, and every one who has practised it, from the ancient Rishis down to *some* living Yogis of your day, will tell you.

And then the Aryans—if we may believe that good man, the late Bramachari Bàwà—knew a branch of science about which the West is now speculating much, but has learnt next to nothing. They could navigate the air; and not only navigate it but fight battles in it, like so many war eagles combating for the dominion of the clouds. To be so perfect in aëronautics, as he justly says, they must have known all the arts and sciences related to that science, including the strata and currents of the atmosphere, their relative temperature, humidity, and density, and the specific gravity of the various gases. At the Mayasabha, described in the Bhàrat, he tells us, were microscopes, telescopes, clocks, watches, mechanical singing birds and articulating and speaking animals. The "Ashta Vidya"—a science of which our modern professors have not even an inkling—enabled its proficients to completely destroy an invading army by enveloping it in an atmosphere of poisonous gases, filled with awe striking, shadowy shapes, and with awful sounds.

The modern school of Comparative Philology traces the migration of Aryan civilization into Europe, by a study of modern languages in comparison with the Sanskrit. And we have an equally, if not a still more, striking means of showing the outflow of Aryan thought towards the West, in the philosophies and religions of Babylonia, Egypt, Greece, Rome and Northern Europe. One has only to put side by side the teachings of Pythagoras, Socrates, Plato, Aristotle, Homer, Zeno, Hesiod, Cicero, Scævola, Varro and Virgil, with those of Veda Vyása, Kapila, Goutama, Patànjali, Kánada, Jaimini, Nárada, Pánini, Marichi, and many others we might mention, to be astonished at their indentity of conceptions—an identity that upon any other theory than that of a derivation of the younger philosophical schools of the West from the older ones of the East would be simply miraculous, The human mind is certainly capable of evolving the like ideas in different ages, just as humanity produces for itself in each generation the teachers, rulers, warriors and artisans it needs. But that the views of the Aryan sages should be so identical with those of the later Greek and Roman philosophers as to seem as if the latter were to the former like the reflection of an object in a mirror to the object itself, without an actual, physical transmission of teachers or books from the East to the West, is something opposed to common sense. And this again corroborates our convictions that the old Egyptians were emigrants from India; nearly all the famous ancient philosophers *had been to Egypt to learn her wisdom*, from the Jewish Moses to the Greek Plato.

And now that we have seen—however imperfectly, for the theme is inexhaustible—what India was in the olden times, and what sort of people were her people, let us move the panorama forward and throw a glance at the India of our own days.

THE PRESENT.

If one who loves the memory of this blessed Aryavarta would not have his heart filled with sorrow he ought not to permit himself to dwell too long over the past. For, as the long procession of great men is passing before his inner vision; and he sees them surrounded with the golden light of their majestic epochs, and then turns to view the spectacle that is presented by the India of to-day, it will be hard, though he were the most courageous of souls, to escape a sense of crushing despair. Where are those sages, those warriors, those giant intellects of yore? Where the happiness, the independence of spirit, the self-respecting dignity that made an Aryan feel himself fit to rule the world, and able to meet the very gods on equal terms? Where are the cunning artisans whose taste and skill, as exemplified in the meagre specimens that remain, were unrivalled? Whither are departed the Brahmins in whose custody were all the treasures of Asiatic knowledge? Gone: all gone. Like the visions of the night they have departed into the mist of time. *A new nation is being fabricated out of the old material in combination with much alloy*. The India of old is a figment of the imagination, a faded picture of the memory; the India of to-day a stern reality that confronts and supplicates us. The soil is here, but its fatness is diminished; the people remain, but alas! how hungry and how degenerate. India, stripped of her once limitless forests that gave constant crops and abundant fertility by regulating the rainfall, lies baking in the blistering heat, like a naked valetudinarian too helpless to move. The population has multiplied without a corresponding increase of food supply; until starvation, which was once the exception, has become almost habitual. The difference between so called good and so called bad years, to at least 40 millions of toilers, is now only that in the one they starve a little less than in the other. Crushed in heart, deprived of all hope, denied the chances of much bettering his condition, the poor ryot, clad in one little strip of cloth, lives on from hand to mouth in humble, pious expectation of what to him will be the happiest of all hours—the one that ushers him into the other world. The union of the olden days is replaced by disunion, province is arrayed against province, race against race, sect against sect, brother against brother. Once the names Arya and Aryavarta were talismans that moved the heart of an Indian youth to its depths, sent the flush of blood into the cheek, and caused the eye to glitter. Now, the demon of Selfishness sits athwart all noble impulse; the struggle for life has made men sycophants, cowards, traitors. The brow of a once proud nation is laid in the dust, and shame causes those who revere her memory to avert their gaze from the sickening spectacle of her fallen greatness. Mighty cities, once the homes of hives of population, the centres of luxury, the hallowed repositories of religion and science, have crumbled into dust; and either the filthy beast and carrion bird inhabit their desolate ruins, or the very recollection of their sites is lost. Now and then the delving archæologist exhumes some fragment which serves to verify the ancient Aryan records, but, ten to one, he tries to twist their evidence into a corroboration of some pet theory that denies a greater antiquity than a handful of centuries to Indian civilization.

It is not my province to deal with the political interests involved in the full consideration of our subject. If I were in the least competent to handle it—which I certainly am not, after such a mere glimpse as I have had of the situation, and with the tastes and habits of a life opposed to my dabbling in politics at all—I would nevertheless abstain. For my interest in India is in her literature, her philosophy, her religion, and her science; it was to study them I came. And it is upon glancing at those that I am constrained to express my sorrow that things are as they are. The Brahmins I find engaged as clerks to Government and to merchants, and even occupied in menial capacities. Here and there a learned man is to be found, but the majority, receiving no encouragement to devote their lives to abstract science or philosophy, have given up the custom of their forefathers, and their glory is departed. Some still linger about the temples, and repeat their slokas and sastras in a parrot-like way; and take what gifts the stingy and impoverished public may fling at them; and waylay the European visitor with outstretched palm and the droning cry of *baksheesh*! But in their temples there are no longer any sacred mysteries, for there are few priests who have become initiated, and few who even believe that there are secrets of Nature that the ascetic can discover. The very successors of Patanjali, Sànkara, and Kànada doubt if man has a soul, or any latent psychic powers that can be developed. And this fashionable scepticism taints the minds of all Young India. The flower of Aryan youth are turning materialists under the influence of European education. Hope—that bright angel that gives joy, and courage to the human intellect—is dying out; they have no longer hope in a life of the hereafter, nor in the splendid possibilities of the life of the present. And without hope, how can there be the cheerful resignation under evils that begets perseverance and pluck? We have the authority of Sir Richard Temple, late Governor of Bombay, for saying that "modern education is shaking the Hindoo faith to its very foundation." These are the very words he uttered not long ago, in a speech at the University of Oxford, the pamphlet-report of which I have here in my hand. And he mentions as chief, among the effects of that change, the formation of the three great "religious sects" of the Brahmo Samaj, the Prarthana Samaj and—most absurdly—the Theosophical Society, which never was, nor ever pretended to be, a sect! The Arya Samaj he does not so much as mention, though the President of the Bombay Branch—Rao Bahadur Gopalrao Hurree Deshmukh—is a member of the Bombay Governor's Council, and the forty or fifty branch Samajes, already founded by Dayanand Swami, include perhaps as many registered or affiliated members as the other three societies together. Sir Richard tells the English people that now is the time for them to send out more missionaries, as Young India is ready to turn Christian as it were in a mass! Now I believe this is a perfectly erroneous supposition. As I see it, the young Hindoos, outside the reformatory Samajes, are losing their old religious belief without gaining or being ready to embrace any other. They are becoming exactly like the great mass of educated youth in Europe and America. Influenced by the same causes, they require the same treatment. It is Science which undermined the foundations of Religion; it is Science which should be compelled to erect the new edifice. As an incomplete study of Nature has led to Atheism, so a complete one will lead the eager student back to faith in his inner and nobler self, and in his spiritual destiny. For, there is a circle of Science as of all other things, and the whole truth can only be learnt by going all the way round. This, I think, is the strongest corner of the edifice of Theosophy that we are trying to raise. Other agitators come to the young generation claiming authority for some book, some religious observances, or some man as a religious guide and teacher. We say "We interfere with no man's creed or caste, preach no dogma, offer no article of faith. We point to Nature as the most infallible of all divine revelations, and to Science as the most competent teacher of its mysteries." But the science we have in mind is a far wider, higher, nobler science than that of the modern sciolists. Our view extends over the visible and invisible, the familiar and unfamiliar, the patent and the occult, sides of Nature. In short, ours is the Aryan conception of what science can be and should be, and we point to the

Aryas of antiquity as its masters and proficients. Young India is a blind creature whose eyes are not yet open; and the nursing mother of its thought is a bedizened goddess, herself blind of one eye, whose name is Modern Science. There is an old proverb that "in a company of blind men, the one-eyed man is a king," and here we see it practically exemplified. Our Western educators know just enough to spoil our spirituality, but not enough to prove to us what man really is. They can draw Young India away from their old religion, but only to plunge them into the swamp of doubt. They can show us the ingenious mechanism of our vital machinery, the composition of our digesting fluids, the proportion of fluids and solids in our frame. But *Atma* is an unscientific postulate, and Psychology a species of poetry, in their eyes. Shall we then say that modern education is an unmixed blessing to India? Look at our Indian youth and answer. Sir Richard Temple is right in saying that the foundations of their faith are shaken; they are indeed, but he does not seem to perceive the proper remedy. It is not Christianity, which itself is tottering before the merciless assaults of the liberal minds within its own household. It is pre-eminently uncongenial to the Hindu mind. No imported faith will afford the panacea for this spiritual disease that is spreading on all sides. What is needed is that the Vedas shall be once more restored to their ancient hold upon the Indian mind. Not that they should be accepted as a mere dead letter. Not that they should have a merely tacit reverence; but an intelligent appreciation of thir intrinsic merits. It must be proven, not simply asserted, that the Vedas are the fountain source of all religions, and contain the indications of a science that embraces and explain all sciences. To whom shall we look for this vindication of their majesty? To whom but to those who unite in themselves at once the advantages of modern critical culture and familiarity with the Sanskrit literature; and—most important of all—the knowledge of the hidden meaning of the Vedic allegory and symbolism? For the inspired Vedas are often hidden under the visible writing and nestle between the lines; at least this I have been told by those who profess to know the truth. And ignorance of this fact, and the taking of the Vedas in their dead letter sense, is what has driven thousands of the brightest intellects into infidelity. Comparative Philology will not do our interpretation for us, it can only show the dead letter meaning of the dead letter text. An esteemed Fellow of our Society —Mr. Shankar Pandurang Pandit—is doing this literal translation work at Bombay, while many others are busily tracing the several streams of Western ideas back to the parent spring in the Vedas. But Modern India needs to be instructed in the *meaning* of the Vedic authors; so that the age may have for itself the perfect certitude that in those far distant ages science was so well understood as to leave no necessity for us to cast aside as rubbish that Book of Books at the behest of modern self-styled "authorities" in Science. An Indian civilization resting upon the Vedas and other old national works, is like a strong castle built upon rocks: an Indian civilization resting upon Western religious ideas, and patched with imported ideas that are fitted only to the local traditions and environments of their respective birth places, is a but a rickety house of cards that the first blast of stern experience may topple over. We certainly cannot expect to see, under the totally different conditions of modern times, an exact reproduction of Aryan development; but we can count upon the new development having a strictly national character. Whoever is a true friend of India will make himself recognized by his desire to nationalize her modern progress; her enemy, he who advocates the denationalisation of her arts, industries, lines of thought, and aspirations. There are men of both sorts among the class who have received the priceless blessing of education—and, I am sorry to say, hundreds, if not thousands, who are setting the pernicious example of aping Western ways, that are good only for Western people, and of imitating Western vices that are good for no people, among them the excessive use of spirituous liquors. I see also everywhere a lot of rich sycophants who humbly bow the knee to every European they meet in the hope of recognition and reward. These poor fools do not realize that a people intensely manly, independent and self-respectful like the English, can only feel contempt for those who cast aside their own dignity and self-respect. Nor are they so dull as not to detect, under all this mask of servile politeness, the concealed scowl of hatred, and, under this fawning and cringing, the mean lust after titles and decorations. An Englishman honours a brave foe, and scorns a sneaking hypocrite. Before India can hope to make the first recuperative step up the long slope down which she has been for many centuries descending, her youth must learn the lesson that true manhood is based upon self-respect. And they must learn once more to speak the truth. There was a time when a Hindoo's word pledged to another man, no matter whether Hindoo or stranger, was sacredly kept. English gentlemen have told me, more than once, that, thirty years ago, one might have left a lakh of rupees, even uncounted, with a Native banker without taking a receipt, and be sure of not being wronged out of a single pie. Can it be done now? Friends of mine—native gentlemen connected with the judicial establishment—have told me, some with moistening eyes, that lying and perjury had of late grown so common that magistrates could scarcely believe a word of the testimony offered by either side unless corroborated. The moral tone of the legal profession has been perceptibly raised, but the mendacity of the general public has reached a low level. Do you think a national resuscitation can be even dreamt of with such a bottomless depth of moral rottenness to lay its foundations upon? Many of the best friends of Aryavarta have confessed all these things to me, and in accents of despair foretold the speedy ruin of every thing. Some, the other day, went so far as to say that in all the North-West and

Punjab—to say nothing of other Provinces—six men of the true patriot-hero mould could not be found. This is *not* my opinion. Some of you may recall that in all my addresses to the Indian public I have taken the hopeful view of the situation. I do not wish to deceive myself, let alone others, for I hope to live and die in this land and among this people. I rest my judgment of Indian evolution upon the whole course of Aryan evolution, not upon a fragmentary bit of the same. The new environment is evolving a new India which, in three chief respects, is the complete antithesis of the older one. Old India—and, in fact, even modern India, the one of, let us say, the eighteenth century–was (1) Asiatic to the core; (2) it had more land than cultivators; and (3) its soil was unexhausted. But the brand-new India of to-day, suckling of Manchester, Birmingham and Sheffield, and hunting ground of the shikarri and the missionary, is putting on European clothes, and thinking along European lines; its land is overcrowded; its soil going at a galloping pace towards actual sterility. No prophet is required to forecast what this involves. If 'fertile France,' as Dr. Hunter calls it,* is crowded, with 180 people to the square mile; and green, fair Ireland is so over-populated, with 169 persons to the square mile, that she pours her emigrants into America by millions; and England's people, when they exceed 200 to the square mile, gain their food only by taking to manufactures, mines and city industries—what must we think of hapless India's lot? Throughout British India the average population is 243 persons to the square mile; and there are portions—as, for instance, in thirteen districts of Northern India, equal in size to Ireland—where the land has to support an average of 680 persons to the square mile, or more than one person to each acre! The Famine Commissioners report that in Bengal 24 millions of human being are trying to live upon the produce of 15 million acres, or about half an acre apiece. "The Indian soil" as Dr. Hunter says, "cannot support that struggle." And what then—is it asked? Well, death to crores: that is the grinning skull behind the gold cloth and glitter of these pageants; the terrible words traced in the invisible ink of Fate between the lines of these college diplomas. This state of things is the result of definite causes, and in their turn these effects become causes of fresh results far ahead. From the experience of the past may we always prognosticate what is likely to come. And this brings us to the third, and last, branch of the subject of the evening.

THE FUTURE.

Who shall raise the curtain that now hangs in black, heavy folds before the IS TO BE? Only the eye of the perfect seer can penetrate the secrets of the coming ages. The true Yogi of old could foretell events because he had

---

* *England's Work in India.* By W. W. Hunter, C.I.E., L.L.D London, 1881, Smith Elder & Co.

acquired the power to pass at will into the spiritual universe, and in that condition the Past and the Future are all merged into one conscious Present; as to an observer who stands at the centre of a circle, every point in the circumference is equally distant. But the true Yogis are now few, and if any are to be met among us, they are hiding themselves, more and more carefully every day, from the sight of men. We must then proceed by the deductive, since we may not by the intuitive, process. And, as we are helped by Comparative Philology to theorize upon the origin and destiny of language, so, by the study of Comparative History, we may at least get some idea of the probable outcome of the social forces we see at work in the India of to-day. Through this glass, then, I see the country, after having reached the predestined lowest level of adversity—predestined, I mean by the universal cyclic law which controls the destinies of nations, as the law of gravitation does the orbits of the planets—rising again. Action and reaction—the sway of the pendulum of human events— follow each other. Nations, though ever so splendid and powerful, are stamped out, under the iron heel of reactive destiny, if their inherent vitality be weak. But when it is strong, then, indeed, may we behold the majestic spectacle of a nation reviving from its very ashes, and starting afresh on the road to greatness. To which category shall we assign India ? I know not what others may say, but for my part I do most firmly believe in her future. If she had been weak of vitality she would have been obliterated by various causes; nay, if she had not had an inherent giant strength, her own vices would have destroyed her before now. She has survived every thing, and she will live to renew her strength. Her best sons are being afforded not only opportunities for education, but also of training, in hundreds of offices, practical statesmanship, under the greatest nation of administrators of modern times—my own country of America not excepted. *European education is creating a new caste which is to guide the nation up the hill.* And, as the Aryan of former times was the very prince of philosophers, so it is in the order of nature that his descendant should become in time among the ablest of statesmen. Already broader and higher spheres of usefulness are opening before him, partly as the result of his own importunities, partly because of the greater economy of administration that his admission to the higher preferments seems likely to offer. We are perhaps at the threshold of a new era of Indian civilization, an era of enormous development. The bad crisis may be postponed, perhaps almost averted, by the aid of liberal science. If the present peaceful and stable order of things should continue—and surely such would be the sincere prayer of every one who wishes well to India, for change would mean a plunge back into chaos—we shall see the barriers gradually melt away that have kept the peoples apart. Gradually they are realizing that, however distant the Punjab may be from Travancore, or Cutch from

Bengal, the people are yet brothers, and the children of the same mother. When this conviction shall once possess the whole body of these 24 crores, then there will, indeed, be the re-birth of this nation. And then, with all the modern improvements in arts, sciences and manufactures superadded to abundant labor; with schools thronged with eager students; with the knowledge of the Aryans unearthed from the dust of the ages; with the Vedas reverenced and appreciated by the whole educated class, who are now coquetting with Infidelity, with Atheism, with sciolistic Science—with everything that is calculated to despiritualize and denationalize them; with Sanskrit teachers well supported and honoured as in former days; with the most distant districts bound together by a network of railways and other public works; with the mineral and agricultural resources of the country fully developed; with the pressure of population adjusted to the capacities of the several districts; and with the last chains of superstition broken, and the eyes unbandaged that have been so long withheld from seeing the truth—the day of Aryan regeneration will have fully dawned. Then once more shall Aryavarta give birth to sons so good as to provoke the admiring homage of the world. When shall we see this glorious day? When shall India take the proud place she might have in the family of nations? Ah, when! The oracle is silent, the book of destiny none have read. It may be only after a century or centuries; it cannot be soon, for the pendulum swings slowly, and on the dial of Fate the hours are marked by cycles and epochs, not by hours or single generations. Enough for us the present hour; for out of the present comes the future, and the things we do and those we leave undone weave the warp and woof of our destinies. We are masters of causes, but slaves of their results. Take this truth to heart, you who hear me, and remember that whatever your faith—if you have any faith at all in man's survival after death—whether, as, Hindus, you believe in Karma, or, as Buddhists, you believe in Skandha, you cannot escape the responsibility of your acts. What you do that is good or bad, and what you might do but leave undone will equally be placed to your account by the Law of Compensation. The lesson of the hour is that every Indian mother should recall to the child at her knee the glories of the past, that every son of the soil should keep green the memory of his ancestors and that each should do what he can, in every way and always, to be worthy of the name of an Aryan.

THEOSOPHY: ITS FRIENDS AND ENEMIES.

Delivered at the Framji Cowasji Institute, Bombay, on the 27th of February 1881.

Complying with the good custom of all societies that are really working for the general good, though the latter merit is denied us by some, we now, a third time, come before the Bombay public to give an official account of ourselves. Our anniversary meeting should have been held in the month of November, and would, but that we were then far away in the Punjab, and did not return to Bombay until the last day of the old year. And, having thus unavoidably missed the usual time, we thought it best to wait until we could celebrate the anniversary of the arrival of our party in India. That event, so important to us—I wish I could add, possibly to the country, as regards its future results—occurred on Sunday, February 16, 1879, and I am here to tell you how it has fared with us during the two years that have since passed. I will do my best to.......

"nothing extenuate, nor aught set down in malice."

We only ask that those who love and those who hate us, will alike be governed by the same feeling of moderation. For, to tell you the plain truth, we have suffered quite as much, if not more, by the extravagant expectations and ideas of our friends, as from the malice and falsehoods of our enemies. The one have rushed to as great extremes in one direction, as the other have in another. We have been kept quite as busy in recovering ground we ought never to have lost, and would never have lost if our sympathisers had been reasonable, as in defending ourselves and our cause from the plots and assaults of those who wished for our defeat. I have tried, in many public addresses, to define our exact responsibility to the Indian nation. I have done my best to show exactly what it had a right to demand of us, and what it had not. I have explained, over and over again, what the Hindus had themselves to do, if they really cared to snatch their nationality from the gulf of perdition into which it has been plunging, headlong, these many centuries. I have tried to make Young India see that there can be no real moral reform that does not come from their *own united* effort; and that no foreigner, though he love the country ever so much and be ready to sacrifice ever so much for it, can relieve her own sons of the smallest portion of that duty. Many whom I see around me in this audience heard my first address to the country, from this same platform, on the 23rd of March 1879. I ask these to remember how earnestly I tried on that occasion to impress this solemn conviction upon the native mind. Among other things I said:—"If India is to be regenerated, it must be by Hindus, who can rise above their castes and every other reactionary influence; and give good example as well as good advice. Useless to gather into Samajes, and talk prettily of reform. Not of such stuff are the saviours of nations made." Did you hear me putting ourselves up as the would-be leaders of Hindu regeneration, or as exemplars of virtue or of wisdom to pattern after? No, a thousand times no: I said our chief and sole desire was to help India and her people "in any way practicable, however humble," without meddling with politics, into which as foreigners we "had neither the right nor inclination to intrude ourselves." With the cry of one who sees danger hovering over those he sympathizes with and would have them make an effort to save themselves, I said:—"Here is material for a new school of Aryan philosophy which only waits the moulding hand of a master. We cannot yet hear his approaching footsteps, but he will come; as the man always does come when the hour of destiny strikes. He will come, not as a disturber of the peace, but as the expounder of principles, the instructor in philosophy. He will encourage study, not inflame passion. He will scatter blessings, not sorrow. So Zoroaster came, so Gautama, so Confucius. O, for a Hindu, great enough in soul, wise enough in mind, sublime enough in courage, to prepare the way for the coming of this needed Regenerator! O, for one Indian of so grand a mould that his appeals to his countrymen would fire every heart with a noble emulation to revive the glories of that by-gone time, when India poured out her people into the empty lap of the West, and gave the arts and sciences, and even language itself, to the outside world!" And that I foresaw that the work, even if begun at once, must take long to yield the desired results, is shown in these further remarks:—"Do not imagine that I have the idle notion that India can be reformed in a day. This once enlightened, monotheistic and active people have descended, step by step, in the course of many centuries, from the level of Aryan activity to that of idolatrous lethargy and fatalism. It will be the work not of years but of generations to re-ascend the steps of national greatness. But there must be a beginning. Those sons of Hindustan who are disposed to act rather than preach, cannot commence a day too soon. *This hour* the country needs your help."

So, too, I may refer you to the address I delivered, Nov. 29, at the celebration of our fourth anniversary, when I again recurred to the subject. "We do not ask you to be our followers," I said, "but our allies. Our ambition is not to be considered leaders, or teachers; not to make money, or power, or fame. Choose any man here, of either of the old races represented, and show us that he is the right man to lead in either branch of this reformatory movement, and I will most gladly enlist as a common soldier under him." But this idea of the necessity for personal effort does not seem to have as yet impressed itself upon the public mind. Some would force us to accept without remonstrance the imputation that we want to push ourselves into the attitude of leaders; to ape the state of Alexander, who—Dryden tells us, (*St. Cecilia's Day*)—

> "Assumes the God,
> Affects to nod,
> And seems to shake the spheres."

—and that if we do not at least attempt to lead, or to exhibit all the qualities, intellectual and moral, of the ideal leader, we must confess that we have not made good our claims. But again, for the twentieth time, I protest, and, in the presence of this multitude, declare that the moral Regenerator of Aryavarta will be no European, but must be a son of the soil, and no one else! It is only too evident I say, too sadly so, that a vague notion has gained wide currency that we, Theosophists, must straightway bind up all the gaping wounds in the body of this hapless India, while the Hindus look passively on, or consent to be taken as derelict in duty. "What efforts," asks a correspondent of the editor of a Bombay native paper "have until now been made by this Society to alleviate the sufferings of the Aryans, and how have they succeeded?" Does our questioner know the meaning of words? Did he, before penning those lines, ponder well what relief of the sufferings of the Aryans involves, and what our poor efforts could reasonably be expected to accomplish in that direction? No, but like every other man who has sat down to hale us before the public, he dashed off the first smart phrase that came into his mind, as one shuts his eyes and fires his musket point-blank into a crowd. I can say one thing in reply to this gentleman which can be proved even upon European testimony, let alone the abundant evidence natives can furnish. And that is that we have made every effort in the power of mortal men to interest the paramount race in behalf of the Hindus, and make them respect Aryan philosophy and science. To effect this result, we have spared neither time, trouble, nor the inconveniences and costs of travel. We have also excited respect for Indian achievements, and sympathy with Indian thought in the most distant countries. In ample proof of this, I point you to the articles which have appeared in those countries, many of which are preserved by us in our scrap books at our Head Quarters.

But all this is nothing in the eyes of these drowsing patriots! "Here we are," substantially say they who, perhaps, never sacrificed one *pan-supari* for India, "and here are the Aryans, twenty-four crores strong: here is Aryavarta, stripped to the last rag, and in the last extremes of starvation. Here are one-fifth of the people lying down hungry every night, and rising hungry every morning. Here are fifty millions of wretched human beings fighting famine on a half acre of land each. Here is ignorance holding a nation in chains, and superstition gnawing out the last remnants of hope in their hearts. Here are hungry fathers breeding children by lakhs only to starve; farmers eating the best of their seed grain and saving the worst; giving their land no fallow time for recuperation; burning their manure, because the wood is all cut away; here are taxes multiplying, poverty increasing, and an educated class thinking of Government alone as their employer; here are 500 struggling applicants for ten vacant places, at from Rs. 40 to 60 per month, advertised by the Bombay Telegraph Department; and here are liquor shops springing up like mushrooms in every large town. Come, Theosophists, banish our sufferings and we will not call you impostors or adventurers any more." This is no exaggeration, but the exact tone of nine-tenths of the criticisms upon us with which the native press has teemed, and of the public expectation. Do we not know it? Who should but we who get almost every day letters to this very effect from the four corners of India? And yet how can we utter one angry word in protest, when we know that the cause of all this is in the wretchedness of a people, enwrapped in such a blackness of despair that they clutch at even the faintest promise of relief. In their awful dejection they have tried to cheat their hearts into belief that perhaps the hoped-for Regenerator had come or was just coming from across the ocean. Aye, and just after my first address was made, a native paper said as much. But it is *not* so, it is *not* so, I tell you. We can only sorrow at our helplessness to give the succour so much needed, and try to spur to a sense of their duty those who alone could do something if they only would. And by parenthesis let me remark that it would be a good beginning if those who have said the sharpest things about what the Theosophists have not done, would, when next writing to the papers, prove that they had themselves set us that pattern of unselfish patriotism they would have us imitate! Talk is cheap, gentlemen, and the commodity is not scarce in India. If words could be coined into rupees, our young reformers would long ago have restored the splendour of the Aryan epoch, and lodged every ryot in a marble bungalow. Yet words are useful too, and very necessary to India at this particular juncture. Words of warning, of appeal, of encouragement; burning words that shall sink through the thick crust of selfishness and reach the very core of every patriot's heart. Have you read the history of the world and not learnt the mighty power of the right word spoken at the right moment? Speak then every man of you, but also act; speak and tell your countrymen that the time for dreaming is past, the hour for action has come. Let a great shout go up like the voice of thunder until the Himalayas echo to the cry from Cape Comorin, that if the nation is to be saved every one who can give the slightest help must *now* give it. Even the British themselves with all their might and power, will be unable to save the Indian people from starvation, perhaps annihilation, unless India herself awakens to activity and reform, and helps them to save. You have gained knowledge, scatter it everywhere; for it is Ignorance that has cursed Aryavarta, and this is the demon that has buried his fangs in her fair throat. You remove your shoes and reverently worship when you enter your temples, and, I tell you, you ought to do the same at every school house door. For, if India may be rescued, it is only by the spread of education in the Temples of Knowledge. When one shall see in your country what you can see in America and England, —a school open wherever there are children to be taught—then, aye, then indeed, will the sufferings of the Aryans be "alleviated," and India be prosperous and happy once more. Do not trouble yourselves about the Theosophists; don't waste your time in complaining that they have not accomplished the miracles you expected of them: they will do what little they can—you may count upon that; and they will never do any thing dishonorable or that has to be covered up. Set your own houses in order; live in private up to your public professions,—that is all we, or any one, could ask; be what you pretend to be. If you are idol haters in public meetings, be so when your own family and caste fellows are also by; if you are orthodox at heart, be manly enough to say so to the face of the whole world. If you think Christianity the best religion and your reason is convinced, boldly proclaim it and take the consequences; and if you think it the worst, say that like men. If you expect your neighbour to give in charity, or work for the country's good, set him the example. We have had enough of masks and hypocrisies, and a moral coward every honest soul loathes. Cannot every man in this assemblage put his hand upon one of these two-faced talkers? Are they not in the orthodox sects, in the Arya Samaj, the Prarthana Samaj, and the Theosophical Society—yes, even in that, and not only hypocrites but traitors? Do you not, even while I speak, recall to mind how the man with two faces pretends to be a reformer, but is not; to favor child widows' remarriage, and yet casts the first stone at the one who puts into practice his very sentiments, nay, will himself, if a widower, marry a wife young enough to be his grand-daughter's daughter? Have you not heard him abhor child marriage, and yet know that he had had no sound sleep until his own baby daughter was pledged and bound to a boy husband; or worse yet, to a man older than himself; seen him frown upon the costly ceremonials of investiture with the thread marriage, first pregnancy, &c., and yet beggar himself and his relatives in trying to vie with his acquaintance in empty display? These are the men of mere words, whose counsel no one respects, and no one wants, because they are hypocrites and poltroons. But he who preaches self-denial and practises it; virtue, and keeps no mistresses in secret; he who proves by his acts that he means all he says, ah! *he* is a man to listen to, let his advice be ever so fanciful and impracticable. For we feel that he at least is a conscientious man and is acting up to his best light, even though strength often fail him and he occasionally may fall out of the straight path. These are the kind of men we try to draw into our Theosophical Society. We never ask them what their creed is, we do not care: they may worship the God they see in fire or the sun; or the divinity that for them infuses the substance of a Sivaic Lingam and animates its ultimate atoms; they may search for his glory at Mecca or Jerusalem; in the kábah or fire-temple; at Benares or L'hassa; or in the ocean depths or the morning dawn. Though they wash their sins away in the Ganges or the Jordan; though they pray standing or kneeling, with forms of words or the soundless aspirations of the inmost heart—we care not. They are sincere, and we hail them as our Brothers. They are searchers after the truth, and, in the degree of their spiritual mindedness, Theosophists. What then is Theosophy? you will ask. I reply that *Theosophia*—"God-like wisdom" for us means "search after divine knowledge," the term *divine* applying, as we see it, to the divine nature of the abstract principle, not to the quality of a Personal God. Many may even be rejecting God as a being, be *pucka* atheists in fact, and yet if they accept the existence of *divine* or absolute wisdom and truth, and are honestly and sincerely trying to find it out and live up to that standard, they are *philo-theosophs*, lovers of God-like or divine Wisdom and Truth; the two words being synonymous, for there can be no aboslute Truth without Wisdom, and absolute Wisdom is absolute Truth. Our Society might have added to the name "Theosophical" that of "Philadelphian," (from the two words *philos*-loving and *adelphos*-brother) as it was always meant to be a society of universal brotherhood and for promoting brotherly love among all races—but there were several religious societies of that name already, as the Christadelphians and the Philadelphians. Knowing but of one really divine manifestation on earth—*Humanity* as taken collectively, Humanity with its god-like intellect, its latent promises and spiritual hopes, hidden away under a thick crust of materialism and selfishness—we know of no better form of worship, no higher cultus to the divine principle than that whose oblations are laid on the altar of Humanity. With our hands upon that altar we must all strive to call out these divine, deep hidden intuitions of mutual Help, Tolerance and Love. By "divine" then I mean that which the common intuition of mankind conceives to be the opposite of all that is animal, material, brutish. The knowledge one gains by the help of his physical senses is physical science. It is the orderly classification of the objective phenomena of the visible world. Theosophy, on the contrary, is the discovery of the law and order of the inner world of force or spirit, by the aid of another set of faculties that lie within the human being. What creed the spiritual searcher may outwardly hold to, matters as little as the colour or shape of his turban or scarf; provided only, that he does not let the acid of his creed eat out the precious substance of his nobler nature. There have been true theosophists in every creed; true seers who have lifted the secret veils of nature and penetrated the mysteries. It may astonish you to hear me say that the most materialistic scientists are theosophists;— aye Messrs. Huxley and Tyndall, for instance, who have devoted their whole lives to the search of truth in *hidden* principles in physical nature, and served humanity faithfully and sincerely. This alone would make good my proposition, even did we not know that mankind are substantially the same the world over. Have you ever read the *Dabistan*—that most instructive report by Mohsan Fani, the learned Persian of the seventeenth century, of his observations of the various holy men who were his contemporaries? If not, do so, and you will find quoted the exultant language of Jeallal-Eddin Rumi, in which he describes the extinction of all human prejudices and passions that occurs when the mystic has attained *emancipation*. "O Moslems! what is to be done? I do not know myself; I am neither Jew, nor Christian, nor Gueber, nor Moslem; I am not from the East nor from the West; nor from land nor sea; neither from the region of nature nor from that of heaven; not from Hind nor China; not from Bulgaria nor Irak; nor from the towns of Khorassan...I know but him, Yahu!...... What is the intent of this speech? Say it, O Shams Tabrizi! The intended meaning is; *I am the soul of the world*." The Mobed Peshkär of Patna, we are told, "attained the knowledge of God and himself, and he became eminently divested of prejudice and exempted from human infirmities: being totally unfettered by the bonds or chains of any sect whatever, and studiously shunning the polemic domains of prejudice: in short, the eulogium of one creed and the abhorrence of another, entered not into this system." The Shaikh Bahu-ud-din Muhammed Amali, enchanted by the noble sentiments of Kaivän, a Zoroastrian sage, became his follower, and nobly exclaims:—"As the splendour of the Almighty is in every place, knock thou either at the door of the kabah or the portals of the fire-temple."

The editors of the *Dabistan* say:—"There is scarcely a tenet to be found in any other creed which does not, at least in its germ, exist in the Hindu religion." And yet while thus showing an appreciation of a profound truth, they also say that the common state of a Yogi "is that of complete impassiveness or torpor"; thereby indicating that the Hindu search, through Yoga, after the very spiritual light and powers exemplified in the joyous cry of the Sufi Jellal-Eddin, they did not appreciate. And yet they affirm this great truth that "in all times and places, the religion of the 'Enlightened' was distinguished from that of the 'Vulgar'; the first as interior, being product of universal reason, was everywhere nearly uniform; the second, as exterior, being composed of particular and arbitrary rites and ceremonies, varied according to the influence of the climate, and the character, history, and civilization of a people. But, in the course of time, no religion remained entirely the same, either in principle or form." The core and heart of all was a like aspiration after spiritual truth. This spiritual aspiration for absolute knowledge is true Theosophy, and the word that our Society brought to the Western world was that the acquirement of this knowledge was possible by self-discipline and purification and development. We first proclaim then, the universal brotherhood of man and the duty of all to join in what will promote the welfare of the human race, especially those who are weakest and need most help. We do not claim this as any new doctrine; it has been often enunciated by other societies. But we are trying to make those who accept it in theory, show it in practice. Our plan has been to interest groups of men of different races and religions to co-operate with each other in this direction. We have succeeded to a certain extent—an extent which might surprise some who have imagined that we were doing nothing. I hear we are accused of greatly exaggerating our numbers. We are alleged to have said in India, that we have 40,000 members in America, and to have written to our Americans that we had that number in India. I say this is all a wicked lie, a falsification of facts by our enemies. We never said so. I defy any one to come forward and tell me to my face that Madame Blavatsky ever did so, or I. What we did say we maintain, and that is that we have about 45,000 theosophists scattered all over the world, and I reiterate the assertion here. We have members in the two Americas, in Australia and the West Indies, in Siam and Burmah, in Java, Holland, Austria, Russia, France, England, Scotland, Ireland, Germany, Hungary, Belgium, Italy, Cyprus, Ceylon, Spain, Turkey, Egypt, Syria, Greece, Mexico, Japan, and, here, in India. I am only sorry that by our *Rules*, and the long settled policy of the Society, I am restricted from giving you the details, as I easily might, of the exact locality and strength of our several branches, except of those whose names are already known to the public. And yet, even as regards this last category you are not possessed of all the facts; for we have here in India, in the Punjáb, a branch of active Fellows, formed within the last three months, whose name is known and has been published in the newspapers, and yet whose membership, including the officers, is a *secret*. Our Rule No. XIV. says:—

"Any one who, for reasons that may appear satisfactory to the President admitting him to fellowship, may prefer to keep his connection with the Society a secret, shall be permitted to do so, and no one except the President in question has the right to know the names of all the Fellows under his jurisdiction. The President shall, in such exceptional cases, himself report the names and remit the initiation fees to the President Founder."

I think not more than one per cent. of these 40,000 have ever paid our Parent Society one rupee. We have whole societies formally allied with us in exchange membership—as, for example, the Psychological Society of Paris—of which only individual members are initiated Fellows of the Theosophical Society. Thus are easily answered the cavils of critics who have been figuring up our receipts at Rs. 4,00,000 on the strength of the fact that *if* each of 40,000 members *had* paid Rs. 10 each, therefore we must have collected four lakhs. As to the statement recently copied into the Indian papers, from a New York journal, that there were only two Theosophists in that city, it is simply an absurd falsehood, and no such person as the Mr. N. R. Monachesi, upon whose authority it purports to be given, ever belonged to our Society, nor do I know such a person, though it is pretended that he is a Theosophist. There are various persons of that name, as of most other names, in New York—a city of about 13,00,000 of people. A Mr. *Herbert* Monachesi *is* a Theosophist, and some months ago wrote me he was about to leave America with the intention of ultimately joining us here. Whether he has actually started or not I do not know, but I do know that he is incapable of circulating so transparent a falsehood as this, and the whole thing is evidently a concoction of our enemies. We have not asked the great majority of our sympathisers to pay initiation fees into our treasury; in fact, when in New York, for over two years we took none. Nor in many cases have we even asked them to announce themselves as forming branches of our Society. All we wanted was to see the work going on, and as long as we two could earn enough, by our literary labors, to support the Society of our own creation, we have, as far as possible, excluded the question of money from mixing with that of Theosophy. Thus, the Treasurer's total receipts from all Indian sources—including two donations of the aggregate of Rs. 220, and initiation fees —from February 1878 to date, are Rs. 1,560, while we have actually disbursed, since we sailed from New York and until the 31st of December last, the sum of Rs. 24,951, for public and private objects—the Society's affairs and our own. This reckoning has been made carefully, and it is correct. It is repugnant to the feelings of all right minded persons to thus put forward matters of an entirely private nature. But the opponents of our cause have resorted to the low and mean expedient of trying to make us seem to the public eye as adventurers who have come here to extort money. We have now been living in Bombay as householders more than two years, and I call upon our worst enemy to come forward, either before this audience or in any other way, and show that we owe any man one anna, either for money borrowed or things bought, or ever took, or tried to take a pecuniary advantage of any one, Native or European. They may not like us, or our ideas, they may call us infidels or visionaries, but they dare not insinuate the smallest thing against our private character. There have been public and avowed affiliations of Indian societies with our Society; as, for example, those recently reported of the

Sanskrit Sabha of Benares, headed by Pundits, Bapu Deva Sastri and Bala Sastri; and the Brahmâmrita Varshini Sabha, of which Pundit Rama Misra Sastri is manager; and we have many regularly organized branches—in Ceylon alone eight. But the formally allied outside organizations that are visibly working in concert with us, which number about seventy, and whose members aggregate at least three lakhs, are only a part of the groups who are now imbued with this principle of the brotherhood of man. By the very last mail from America, intelligence has been received that a movement has been started among the spiritualists by an editor of great influence for an organization of the more intelligent among them into a fraternity upon strictly cosmopolitan theosophical lines. Theosophy he calls a "supplementary faith, which Madame Blavatsky and Colonel Olcott seem to have been commissioned to engraft on Spiritualism, pure and simple." The importance of such a step as he proposes will be appreciated when we remember that there are claimed to be over ten millions (100 lakhs) of Spiritualists in that country. Another sign of the drift of public opinion there is—a great call for lectures and books upon the Asiatic religions and philosophies. One venerable member of our Society has his whole time occupied in travelling through the Western States of America to give discourses upon the religions of India and Egypt. And this brave old man—old, since he is about 60—was formerly a Methodist clergyman, having charge of churches! The same mail brought me an application from the Danish West Indies for authority to form a branch society there; the mail before that, one of similar import from a gentleman of high connections at the Hague. On the 23rd of January came one of the same tenor from the Island of Java. Australia made the same application in January also. Thus, in ever widening circles, like the wavelets caused by a stone that drops in water, runs on the impulse given to contemporaneous thought by the Theosophical Society. That impulse is now so marked, and has gone so far beyond any blunders in judgment we may make; so far beyond the reach of anything we, Founders of the Society, could do to check it, were we even to wish to do that thing, that the established and inexorable law of the diffusion of human thought would carry it down the century were we to die tomorrow. See; I have here the photograph of a group of some 300 boys who are regularly attending the school recently opened by our branch Society at Galle, Ceylon—one of the five that have sprung up in that island as the result of our recent visit. Every boy is the son of Buddhist parents, and nearly all were until now being educated in missionary schools, where their minds were being turned away from the religion of their forefathers. The teachers you see here are Buddhist members of our Society, and our noble colleagues pay the school's entire expenses out of their private means. That no such schools have been founded by Theosophists in India, may be accounted for, partly because Government is doing so much for non-sectarian eduation, but mainly because we have not yet received into our Society men with the liberality of Jamsetji Jeejibhoy, Jaggernath Sunkerseth, Gokuldas Tejpal, or Cowasji Jehangir, though we have one member worth fifteen lakhs. And so long as the schools are but founded, it matters little that *we* should have the mere credit of their establishment. Our highest hope is to arouse others to noble deeds, and that the seeds of a great and permanent reform shall be scattered. From the first we have been fortunate in attracting into our membership, many authors, journalists and others who address the public or have a hand in the work of education. This will explain to you why our theosophical ideas should have so rapidly gained a world wide circulation. Theosophy, properly understood, has not one feature calculated to excite the hostility of reasonable men of any school of science or religion. I will lay down two cardinal propositions: (1.) That all men are brothers, all equally entitled to know divine truth, and, without distinction of nationality or faith, should join for the general good of humanity; bound by a common tie and common sympathies. For *united* effort not only mitigates the hardness of the task, but produces tenfold greater results in the same time. One ant can carry but a grain of dust at once, but a colony of ants labouring together can remove the largest house] in time. So one man, unless endowed with extraordinary advantages, can accomplish comparatively little, but with co-operation evey thing is possible. This help we ask, this we have the right to expect and, as I have shown you, we have had it from thousands of well-wishers whose faces we have never seen and never may see. (2.) My second proposition is that every human being has within his own nature, in a greater or less degree, certain sublime faculties which, when fully developed, will give him divine knowledge. The theory upon which almost all formalized religions rest, is that only a certain favoured class of men have these spiritual capacities, and alone can be permitted to exercise them. But, as I said before, there have been "emancipated" or "illuminated" ones under all the various religions, and the testimony they have brought back to us from their soulflights into the inner world has essentially agreed. We have seen that when a certain point of this interior development is reached, the seer loses all sense of his nationality, his theology, even of his personality. His pettiness becomes infinitely expanded, and, from the consciousness of being a microscopic point as compared to the whole, he feels that he is in all, bounds all, is all. The body he so cherished and lavished so much care and thought upon, is now felt to be a clog and impediment; if, indeed, he can cramp himself down to a realisation that it exists. How beautiful, how suggestive the verse of the poet Hafiz, where, in a charming allegory, he describes the ease with which the absolute truth may be attained when the barriers of flesh are once surmounted:—

"The perfect beauty of my beloved is not concealed by an interposing veil;
O Hafiz, *thou art the curtain of the road*: remove away."

There are no secrets of nature impenetrable, he would say: the only obstacle to our gaining full knowledge is SELF. This is the coward, the traitor, the despot, the bigot, the swinish sensualist, the lump of egotism. This Self is the serpent coiled beneath the flowers of life. This is that which stifles all good and noble aspirations, and which makes the Rights of Man as a whole ruthlessly sacrificed to the base greed of the individual man. Ah! the dream of Universal Brotherhood of Man, when nations will cease to enslave nations, and the only strife will be who can best live up to the ideal of human perfectibility! The bright vision mocks us even as we gaze upon its splendour, yet happy he who has even been so blessed as to see it in his dreams. Theosophy is the enchantress that alone can conjure it up; and though hard be the task and disheartening the delay in gaining the divine wisdom, when once gained, the sacrifices of a life seem no adequate price to pay for its acquisition.

Who are the friends of this Theosophy; who its enemies? I utter no paradox in saying that in the case of Theosophy, as of every other cause, those esteemed its friends are sometimes its worst enemies, and its would-be enemies often its best friends. For the zeal of the former is often inordinate, and the poisoned darts of the latter often recoil from the polished shield of truth and wound the one who hurled them. If I frankly include myself in the former category, I should be acquitted of egotism, and so I do. My Cause is far greater than my ability to serve it effectively, and none knows so well as I, how much and often this sacred cause may have been injured by the errors I have myself committed. It is not a question to be considered whether my motives have been good; for results are the current coin in the exchequer of moral justice. The Christian hell, the proverb says, is paved with good intentions; a Christian sect has adopted the motto *Finis coronat opus*—the end justifies the means—and made it the pretext for nameless and numberless crimes against humanity. As regards the moral accountability of the individual, the question is whether he has done all he could with the means at his disposal to realize a worthy ideal. If Theosophy has suffered from my blunders, who profess to be, among its most earnest advocates, its mouth-piece, so has the progress of our Society suffered through the inexcusable heedlessness of our associated fellows and members in holding such extravagant views of the Founders, and expecting them to be above the weaknesses of mortality. This I have touched upon already, but I revert to it from a desire to press home the thought that a would-be friend may convert himself into a dangerous enemy by setting up the illusions of his own fancy, and then growing indifferent, if not hostile, when the clamour passes away. "Are these

Theosophists," asks a certain Mr. Ganpatrao of the editor of the *Indu Prakash*, "in conduct like ordinary people of the world, or like Tukaram, and other *Sadhus* of ancient times?" Now if the false report had not spread that we *were* like Sadhus, our friend would never have thought of asking such a question. If the gentleman is within the sound of my voice, let me answer that we are nothing but ordinary people, and never pretended to be anything else. We never asked people to look upon us as *gurus* or follow our personal example; though we have tried as far as our natural infirmities have permitted to make that example a good one. What we have said to the Hindus is, "Follow the example of your Tukarams and your Harischandras, of your Rishis and your Yogis; follow them as models, and not any foreigner, even though he may think your ancestors fools, and not know he is one himself in saying, or even thinking, so. And we have tried to make the dignity, the virtue and the learning of those ancestors of yours appreciated by you, and respected by the whole world."

"Have they conquered the six passions of Lust, Anger, Greediness, Vanity, Avarice, and Envy?" he asks. Now it is for those who are best acquainted with our daily lives and conversation to answer this question. I leave it to them to answer; not altogether now, but after we are dead and gone, when the truth shall shine out through the clouds of partiality, on the one side, and of prejudice, on the other. Some of these vices we may, I think, justly claim to be exonerated from having even now. For no one in India, even our worst enemy, would dare accuse us of either lust, greediness, avarice or envy. If I were to tell you we are perfectly free of *vanity* it would perhaps be taken as the best proof that we are not, or remain for ever an open question; as nothing is so difficult as to prove whether it is personal Vanity in man or a justifiable Pride which is his secret *motor*. From anger we certainly are not exempt; we have not yet reached the stage where one can suffer in silence and with smiles the cruel stripes of slander, the base return of treachery and ingratitude, the wilful perversion of our motives, the cowardly assaults on character by masked assassins. No, not perfect yet—alas! not yet. But even supposing that we are not to be ranked among the "emancipated ones," does our questioner therefore give us to understand that he is not bound to listen to our advice to put aside his own vices and pattern after the virtues of Tukaram? That is the gist of the whole question; and this interrogatory reflects the now universally prevalent tone of public thought —*viz.*, that to find some holy or supposed holy person, and nominally enrol oneself as his admirer, follower or pupil, will confer merit and secure *moksha* without self-sacrifice or the conquest over evil passions. Not only by word of mouth in private conversations, but I, from many public platforms, and both of us through our journal, the THEOSOPHIST, have tried to compel the public to think of the great problem of Theosophy, and pointed all who would learn, to the ancient Aryan sources of information.

Mr. Gunpatrao's next question is "How far do the Theosophists keep up to the standard of Brotherhood?" I will tell him that he may search the whole history of our Society, and he will find that we have always been on the side of the weak against the strong. We have, as you have seen in what has been shown you respecting the spread of our fellowship to the five quarters of the world, linked many, of many nations and creeds, together with the tie of mutual reciprocity and tolerance. "This new Gospel," says a writer in a London journal, "appears to be now in the ascendancy among spiritualists. Its immense value in behalf of the well-being of mankind cannot be over-estimated. We rejoice to see the Theosophists in Hindustan. . . really labouring towards this goal." "That great project of human fraternity" writes M. Fauvety, President of the Paris Psychological Society, "which you propose to realise by means peculiar to yourselves. . . constitutes the grandest and noblest tentative that has been essayed on the road to universal conciliation." "Such a society as yours" says the venerable French metaphysician Cahagnet, in accepting our diploma of Fellow, "has been the dream of my whole life." Says the *Pioneer* of Allahabad—a paper which before we came to India and promulgated our views, was certainly never charged with any specially weak tolerance of Hinduism—"we have no hesitation in recognising the Theosophical Society as a beneficent agency in promoting good feeling between the two races in this country, not merely on account of the ardent response it awakens from the Native community, but also because of the way in which it certainly does tend to give Europeans in India a better kind of interest in the country than they had before." "No man" remarks the Colombo (Ceylon) *Examiner* "who has a firm faith in what he believes is the truth, and the excellence of his own system of faith, can quarrel with the Theosophists. . . . They tell us they have a conscientious mission to perform, and we see them labouring earnestly in the discharge of their self imposed duties. . . . the spirit of research they are striving to infuse into the torpid minds of our countrymen cannot fail to lead to good results." "Let us" said the noble President of the Ionian Theosophical Society, of Corfu (Greece) in his Inaugural Address "let us place the brotherhood of nations as the first of our wishes, and let us hasten the coming of that blessed moment when the whole of mankind will be gathered in one fold and will have but one shepherd." The *Amrita Bazar Patrika*, that fearless champion of Indian interests, speaking of our journal, says "Since the THEOSOPHIST carefully abstains from politics, and its plan is one of Universal Brotherhood, it should be welcomed by every sect and people throughout the world. And as it recognises the Aryans as the fathers of all religions and sciences, Hindus owe it their enthusiastic support."

But I need not multiply, as I almost indefinitely might, these proofs from all parts of the world and from people of all races and creeds, that the plan upon which we are at work, is doing good in softening prejudices, breaking down barriers that keep men apart, and creating an interest in Aryan philosophy. I will consider Mr. Ganpatrao's question answered and pass on. His remaining queries pertain to our relations with the Arya Samaj, to the subject of phenomena, and to certain recent unpleasant differences that arose in this city between the Founders and some of their fellow members. As to the former the facts are very simple, and they have been already explained minutely, both by Swamiji Dayanand Saraswati to his Samajes, and by myself in a special lecture recently delivered before a number of the Samajes throughout the N.-W.P. and Punjab. Briefly they are as follows :—While in America, we corresponded with two Bombay Samajists and with Swamiji himself upon the subject of a union between our respective Societies for the promotion of Vedic literature and the interests of the Indian people. We had the impression that the Samaj and our Society were organized on an identical basis, and that if we should accept the proposals for an amalgamation made to us by them, it would greatly promote our own objects, as a Society. But upon further correspondence it was found that the Rules of the Samaj conflicted more or less with the theory of our own organization. It was thereupon agreed between the Swamiji and myself that instead of amalgamating we should organize a third society to be regarded as a branch of both of ours, and to be known as the "Theosophical Society of the Arya Samaj of Aryavarta;" the two parent bodies being left free to pursue each its own settled plans and policy. Three personal interviews with him in India have resulted in confirming this step, and we are each doing in our own way and according to our own ideas, what we can for the good of the nation. Our own Society has been so fortunate as to awaken the sympathies of the orthodox Hindu community by alliances with the two Sabhas of Pandits at Benares previously alluded to; and a similar declaration of affiliation with a respectable Hindu Society in the Madras Presidency will shortly be made public.

As regards the purely personal matters respecting which information is asked by Mr. Ganpatrao, good taste dictates that as little as possible be said. The affair has been absurdly magnified into a disruption of the Society. The fact is that in the past year only nine persons in all have resigned from our Society, including all its branches throughout the world, and of these only six left us at Bombay. To say that a great fraternity like the Theosophical Society could be broken up, or even sensibly feel a shock by the retirement of six members of whom only one was a person of importance to us (and whom we still respect and value as a friend) would be almost as foolish as to consider the three little tailors of the Tooley Street as the people of Great Britain. So let the thing pass like an unsavoury breeze from the 'Worli outfall,' with all its sewage of anonymous letters and spiteful newspaper malice. We do feel, with all our desire for self-improvement and final emancipation, as if we could hardly abstain from answering all such attacks by saying that *their* malice and hatred for us can never equal *our* contempt for *them*.

What remains is to dispose of the question of occult phenomena. The *Indu Prakash's* correspondent wishes to know whether Madame Blavatsky has produced real phenomena; whether she will do so again; and whether the correspondent himself may have a special chance to see them. Now, as far as human evidence will go, the proof is apparently overwhelming that at Simla, Benares, and elsewhere strange things of this nature did occur, and that they were real and not mere deceptions. Tricks, gentlemen, are played only by tricksters—persons who have no character to lose, and who have an interested motive in making their dupes believe their lies. You will get no Court in any civilized country in the world to withhold from an accused of previous good character the benefit of the doubt. And now tell me, if you please, what was Madame Blavatsky's interested motive in this case? She is not here, and I may speak freely what I have to say about her. What was the motive? Money? She never asked or received one anna's value for any phenomenon she ever produced either in India or elsewhere. And, mind you, these phenomena have attended her for many years, all over the world, as she has journeyed to occult science. If it were at all worth the trouble I could occupy hours in reading to you reports of the strange feats of this kind she did in America alone, in the presence of all manner of people. I might give you the names and addresses of enough credible witnesses—sceptics—to prove her possession of these powers to the satisfaction of any fair-minded man. And her vindication might be made with the greatest ease by collecting the testimony of eye-witnesses in India, who would certify to facts more remarkable than any that have been reported in the papers. Well, then, if money was not her object, was it fame? A sorry reward, indeed, this sort of fame, which makes her the subject of the scurvy jests and pusillanimous jeers of the ignorant and prejudiced! Her fame is already secured in the author ship of *Isis Unveiled*, one of the most masterly reviews of ancient and modern Science and Theology ever written: a book which one of the best of our contemporaneous critics pronounces "one of the remarkable productions of the century." Only here in India has the book had the honour of being abused by certain petty editors. I say "honor," for it is one to be abused and a disgrace to be praised by such weathercocks. Well, if neither money nor fame forced her to invite such criticisms, what then? Come, you who rake the gutters of human nature for bits of garbage to fling in decent people's faces, what is left for you to insinuate? She is a woman; strike her in the good woman's most sensitive moral part—her motive. Ah, shame on slanderers! See this great, generous hearted soul, filled with love for humanity; longing to throw light into the darkened minds of those who still believe in miracles, and still clank the chains of superstition; devoting her life, sacrificing the sweets of home, and family and ease, and a high social position to go about the world in search of truth, and spreading it so that all may partake. Those who know her best appreciate her abnegation and perfect disinterestedness; and though some who do not understand her motives may think—nay even take upon themselves to proclaim her according to their worldly understanding a hallucinated lunatic—no one had better venture to call her an impostor, unless, indeed, he is prepared to be himself called by dozens of the most renowned men in Europe,—her friends —a vile slanderer! Here, stand I her witness and friend, I whom she took out of the ditch of worldly selfishness and put on the path to divine truth and happiness. I am here to tell you that I should deserve to have my tongue cleave to the roof of my mouth were I to keep silence when her motives are thus called in question.

She has shown her phenomena from what I conceive to be the mistaken idea that when there was no reasonable ground for suspicion of their genuineness that would be acknowledged, and the public would try to learn as she learned, and then whether materialists or religious bigots become wiser and happier. Noticing the impending visit to India of Professor Solavief, the "Herbert Spencer of Russia," the *Pioneer* of Friday, the 25th instant, editorially remarks:—

"He (Prof. Solavief) has been impressed with a sense of the importance of Hindu thought in connection with pure speculation, by the light thrown on this subject by the Theosophical Society and its stupidly maligned, and so far ill-appreciated, founder Madame Blavatsky. The fact is that while we (Englishmen) in India have been in contact with the remains of old native culture for a hundred years without having detected its significance, it has been reserved for the indomitable old lady just mentioned to put an entirely new face on oriental philosophy. It will probably surprise some heedless jokers in the press to hear that already some of the foremost European metaphysicians in India have acknowledged this.

Bitter experience has taught her the truth that human nature is too base to be honest. If I were her, I would never again—at least in India —thus fling myself as a victim to be mangled by the hounds. There are many who would regard the Theosophical Society as a miracle club, by joining which, whether deserving or not, they ought to get their fill of *tamasha*. Some, devoid of patriotism and the instinct of race pride, caring nothing for the vindication in modern eyes of their ancestral fame and glories, but only eager for their senses to be astonished by phenomena, have felt themselves aggrieved because they have seen none. She has been reviled by them and through them, because of their disappointment The published testimony of those who *have* witnessed the most wonderful things, has caused her to be pounced upon by a host of newspaper critics, as though she were not a private individual who never showed anything but to a limited circle of friends, but a sort of professional juggler who had cheated them out of their money. But even though they saw ten thousand phenomena, yet neither studied nor put forth individual efforts, they would never reap the slightest benefit. They would never learn the great truth, that while occult phenomena are possible, a miracle is an impossibility in nature. Spiritualism has for the past thirty-two years been surfeiting the public with phenomena of the most startling description: the known laws of force have been upset, matter has displayed qualities never suspected before, and even the figures, or rather portrait statues of the dead have stalked in our presence and revealed the secrets of the shadow world. Has religion or philosophy been the gainer by all this? No. Have the mass of investigators been stimulated to nobler lives? No. Those that were moral before are for the most part moral still, and the bad continue bad. We are gorged with phenomena, we need philosophy and a sure path to release us from our pain and suffering. Where is this knowledge to be sought for? *Here, in India*; and if you will question either one of the hundreds of European visitors with whom Madame Blavatsky has talked in different countries, you will find that her constant vehement assertion has ever been that what she knows she learned in India and Tibet, and that for what they taught her she gives her love and her life, if necessary, to promote the happiness of their people.

"But is not your Society established for the sole purpose of giving these experimental proofs of psychic power?" some will ask. I say, no; more phenomena have been shown to outsiders than to members, because every man who joins us to study occultism, tacitly pledges himself to try to develop his own latent psychic powers. If he does this he is helped, if not he is left to wait until he can decide to rouse himself to exertion. Adeptship implies the highest success in self-evolution, and the lavish display of phenomena to beginners is as demoralising as overdoses of opium or brandy. It either kills effort, or excites a frenzy of superstitious adulation. Do you know what we might have done in India by this time as easily as I can lift this paper? We might have formed a new sect that would now really count its 40,000 devotees and more. If we had been vain and unprincipled enough to have given ourselves out as two Sadhus bearing a divine commission and preaching under inspiration; and if Madame Blavatsky had publicly done one-fourth the phenomena I have seen her do in America, or even in India, in private, and the occurrence of which is perfectly attested, you would have seen thousands prostrating themselves before the flag of the Theosophical Society, and trampling one another to come and embrace our feet. Do you doubt it? You would not if you stopped to read our correspondence and note the extravagant lengths to which the imagination of our friends has carried them. I can show any of you, if you choose, a bundle of requests for the miraculous cure of physical and mental ailments, the recovery of lost property, and other favours. And, lest my English auditors might be disposed to laugh in their sleeves at Hindu credulity, let me warn them that some of the most preposterous of these requests have come from their own community; some from persons so highly placed that they have asked that their names may be withheld at all hazards. All this is a saddening proof of the unspirituality and rankling superstition of the present age. Adepts do not show themselves or their phenomena because there is no public to appreciate them. It is known that we have affirmed that some of these *mahatmas* are in relations with our Society, and take an interest in its welfare. I reaffirm the statement, and at the same time protest against the daring supposition that for that reason they are responsible for all or any of the mistakes in its management. Those faults are all my own and count against me. I have realised, too late, that a public that could so basely treat a woman who was but their disciple, could not understand anything that might be said about them. So henceforth I shall try to abstain from even speaking of them except to such as are prepared and anxious for the truth. An age that is satisfied with church miracles, mediumistic phenomena, or the most rank materialism, without seeking further for the hidden causes, may as well be left to play with its toys. The thoughtful man need ask no more wondrous phenomenon than his own existence, no greater miracle than the display of his own splendid powers. He is surrounded by a world of phenomena scarcely one of which he has traced to its ultimate source. The steps of science are near the threshold of the sanctuary; her hand held out to feel the lintels of the door which with her bandaged eyes she cannot see. Mystery on mystery of the outer world has been unearthed, until it almost seems as though there were but little left to learn. This blinded goddess of Materialistic Science that has but just begun to dream a universe of vast extent, may lie behind the curtain at the door. She stands without, uncertain, groping; and across thethreshold waits Theosophy—sweetest of all the *devis* into which poetic fancy ever made a thought personified—and holding out her own strong hand says, "Sister science, come! The field is boundless, let us search together."

THE CIVILIZATION THAT INDIA NEEDS.

Delivered at Tuticorin on the 22nd of October, 1881.

In reflecting upon a choice of subjects upon which to address you, it seemed to me that our time would be most profitably spent in examining the modern dogma that "the true test of the civilization of a nation must be measured by its progress in science." I shall consider it in its relation to Asiatic, especially Indian, needs and standards. My discourse will not be exhaustive, not even approximately so. I am not going to attempt an oration or an exegesis. I shall only say a few words upon a subject so profound and exhaustless that one would scarcely be able to consider its lengths and breadths without writing a volume, or even a score of volumes. For, to know what progress really is, and what are the absolute canons of civilization, one must trace back the intellectual achievements of mankind to the remotest past; and that, too, with a clue that only the Asiatic people can place in our possession. If Europe really wishes to estimate the rush of civilization, she must not take her datum line from the mental, spiritual and moral degradation of her own Middle Ages, but from the epochs of Indian and Mongolian greatness. The advancement Europe has experienced in popular intelligence, in religious enfranchisement, and in the multiplication of aids to physical comfort; and the phenomenal leap made by my own country of America within one century to the topmost rank of national power—these are well calculated to make her accept the above-stated scientific dogma without a thought of protest. The quoted words are those of Sir John Lubbock, and I take them from the report (in *Nature*, No. 618, vol. 24) of his presidential address to the members of the British Association for the Advancement of Science, on the 31st of August last—an address that will figure in history. The occasion was the fiftieth anniversary meeting of the Association, and the President properly and most ably and lucidly reviewed the progress of science during this wonderful half-century. How vast has been the increase of knowledge about physical nature, and what vistas it opens out, I need not particularize before so intelligent a Hindu audience as the present. You, who have had the benefit of a modern education, know that most branches of physical science have been revolutionized, and many of them positively created within the past half-century. Biology, the science of living organizations; Surgery; Archæology; Comparative Philology; Anthropology; Geology; Palæontology; Geography; Astronomy; Optics; Physics, including the Kinetic theory of gases; the properties of matter and the conservation of energy, Photography; Electricity and Magnetism, and their correlations; Mathematics, as applied to scientific problems; Chemistry; Mechanical Science, including the processes for utilising metals; Economic Science and Statistics;—the development of these is the splendid triumph of the intellectual activity of the Western world since the year 1830. Sir John Lubbock counts it all up in the following words:—"Summing up the principal results which have been attained in the last half-century, we may mention (over and above the accumulation of facts) the theory of evolution, the antiquity of man, and the far greater antiquity of the world itself; the correlation of physical forces, and the conservation of energy; spectrum analysis and its application to celestial physics; the higher algebra and the modern geometry; lastly, the innumerable applications of science to practical life—as, for instance, in photography, the locomotive engine, the electric telegraph, the spectroscope, and most recently the electric light and the telephone." Truly, if we compare the Europe and America of to-day with what they were five centuries ago, or even one century, we see a reason for the shout of exultation with which the progress of the Western nations is celebrated. And we can quite understand why the learned and most respected President of the British Association should have laid down the dogma already noted in my opening remarks. An educated Hindu would be the last to dissent from his position that there are no probable limits to the power of the human mind to solve all the ultimate problems of natural law. When, by the help of the spectroscope we have been enabled to discover the very composition of the stars of heaven, who shall dare to fix a limit to the capacity of man to unravel the mysteries of the universe around him?

But you must remember that we have been speaking of the progress of *physical* science; and that after that has done its best, after its proficients have pushed their researches to the very verge of objective nature, though not one secret of the phenomenal world is left uncovered, there is still to explore another and a far more important domain of knowledge. At that outermost verge yawns an abyss that separates it from the Unknown, and, as scientific men call it, the Unknowable. Why do they not enter this boundless department of Nature? Why, in all this hurry-skurry of the biologists after knowledge, have they not solved the old problem of the Why, the Whence, the Whither, of Man? Is it not because their methods are faulty, and their canons of science too narrow? Firstly, they have been overshadowed throughout their investigations by the dark and menacing influence of Christian Theology; and secondly been hampered by their ignorant disdain for the claims of Asiatic Occultism, whose adepts alone can tell them how they may learn the secret laws of nature and of man. Read the summary of scientific progress made by Prof. Draper, in his most splendid work, *The Conflict between Religion and Science*, if you want to see how the Christian Church has fought that progress inch by inch. O, the black and bloody record! Bow your heads in reverence, ye friends of human progress, to the martyrs of science who have battled for the truth. And when you go through so-called Christian countries, as I have, and see how that once haughty and all powerful church is crumbling, let your hearts throb with gratitude for the long array of daring scientists who have dissected her pretensions, unmasked her false doctrines, shivered the bloody sword of her authority, and left her what she now is, a dying superstition, the last vestiges of whose authority are passing away. Do you think I am speaking in prejudice or passion? Alas! no, my friends and brothers; I am but giving voice to the facts of history, and every unprejudiced man among you may verify them if he chooses. Prof. Huxley, who, without the least apparent sympathy for Asiatic thought or knowledge of its ancient occult science, is yet unconsciously one of the greatest allies of both, in doing what he is to advance science in spite of Christian Theology, says:—"The myths of Paganism are dead as Osiris or Zeus, and the man who should revive them, *in opposition to the knowledge of our time*, would be justly laughed to scorn; but the coëval imaginations current among the rude inhabitants of Palestine, recorded by writers whose very name and age are admitted by every scholar to be unknown, have unfortunately not yet shared their fate, but, even at this day, are regarded by nine-tenths of the civilized world as the authoritative standard of fact and the criterion of the justice of scientific conclusions, in all that relates to the origin of things, and among them, of species. In this nineteenth century, as at the dawn of modern physical science, the cosmogony of the semi-barbarous Hebrew *is the incubus of the philosopher and the opprobrium of the orthodox.* Who shall number the patient and earnest seekers after truth, from the days of Galileo until now, whose lives have been embittered and their good name blasted by the mistaken zeal of Bibliolaters? Who shall count the host of weaker men whose sense of truth has been destroyed in the effort to harmonize impossibilities—whose life has been wasted in the attempt to force the generous new wine of science into the old bottles of Judaism, compelled by the outcry of the stronger party?" Hail! Huxley, man of the Iron Age!

And how well Prof. Huxley says this :—"It is true that if philosophers have suffered, their cause has been amply avenged. Extinguished theologians lie about the cradle of every science ...... (Christian) orthodoxy is the Bourbon of the world of thought. It learns not, neither can it forget; and, though, at present, bewildered and afraid to move, it is as willing as ever to insist that the first chapter of Genesis contains the beginning and the end of sound science; and to visit, with such petty thunderbolts as its half-paralyzed hands can hurl, those who refuse to degrade nature to the level of primitive Judaism." These are the brave utterances of one of the most respected men among European scientists, and he expresses the opinion of an overwhelming majority of his colleagues. None knows better than we, humble Founders of the Theosophical Society, to what depths of meanness and extremes of malice Christian bigotry can go, to impede the progress of Free-thought. For the last six years we have been pursued with their calumnies against our good names. All the papers in India and Ceylon that could be controlled or influenced by those enemies of truth, have been trying their best to embitter *our* lives. Where falsehood has failed and slander recoiled upon them, they have employed the stinging whips of ridicule, and what has been our offence? Simply that we preached universal religious tolerance, have stood up for the dignity and majesty of ancient Asiatic science and philosophy, and implored the degenerate sons of a glorious ancestry to be worthy of the great names they bear. It is this insatiate enemy that has set police spies to track our footsteps throughout India; they have charged us with being adventurers,—"unscrupulous adventurers" according to the *Saturday Review*—they who have circulated numberless lies about us, and forged letters that we never wrote. Clergymen, from their pulpits; editors, from their desks; catechists, at the street corners; even bishops and other high dignitaries of the church, have tried to weaken our influence and stop our mouths. But as we have stood for truth, so the truth has stood by us; and day by day our vindication has been growing more perfect. An honest life is its own best shield. It has served us in India and Ceylon; and not only have the Government of India called off their detectives, but at Simla, the summer capital of India, we have just organized a Branch—the Simla Eclectic Theosophical Society—that is almost entirely composed of Anglo-Indians.

As for Ceylon, the Colonial Secretary has refused all applications for the Government to molest us, and has opened the prison doors for me to lecture to the Buddhist convicts. So, as you see, my first proposition —that scientific inquiry has been impeded by the bigots of Christian Theology—is made out, and we will now consider the second. The disdain felt for the ancient occultists is well expressed by Prof. Huxley in the passage above quoted. He who would dare to revive the old pagan myths must expect to be "laughed to scorn." Physical science has dissected them, found no "Kinetic energy" in that "gas," could not test them by the spectroscope, and so they must have been sheer nonsense! But we say they were not; and, having not only studied those myths under teachers who could interpret them, but also learned from those who could experimentally demonstrate the truth of their assertions, what the ancient myth-makers of India knew of science, we "laugh to scorn" the whole school of modern scientists, who know so much in one direction and so little in another. Sir John Lubbock quotes approvingly in his address the opinion of Bagehot that the ancients "had no conception of progress; they did not so much as reject the idea! they did not even entertain it." This is the very key to my present discourse. I wish you to realize what should be called real "progress," and why the ancients—your forefathers—"did not even entertain" the idea of what the modern scientists regard as progress. And to comprehend this question, we must first understand what is man, and what is the highest point of progress or improvement to which he may attain.

If you will run your eye over the list of sciences noted by the President of the British Association, you will see that nearly all of them bear upon the material comfort, the educational development of the physical man, and his understanding of the physical facts of the world in which he lives. Thousands of the most startling of modern inventions are to aid Western people against the rigours of climate and the infertility of soil, to facilitate the transport of passengers and merchandize and the transmission of intelligence, and to gratify the appetites and passions of our baser nature. It has been one mad struggle of physical man with natural obstacles; the chief objects, the multiplication of wealth, of power, of means of physical gratification. Some people call this "progress," but what sort of progress is it that arms the lower against the higher part of man's Self? The Christian Bible puts it thus:—"What shall it profit a man if he shall gain the whole world, and lose his own soul?" [Mark VIII. 36.] The words are not like mine, but the idea is the same. There is a kind of "progress" that leads to moral debasement and spiritual death. I put it to you, Hindus, whether you have not become familiar with it since you went in for European shoes, and for that strong stuff that comes in corked bottles and is drunk with soda water, out of a big tumbler.

What has become of Religion in this half-century of turmoil? How fares it with man's better nature; is it purer, nobler than it was when your ancestors were satisfied with their myths, and not troubling themselves about progress? The moderns have grown wise indeed, if the acme of wisdom be to know why birds, and bugs, and animals are striped, or spotted, or of this colour or shape, or the other; why the sky is blue, water will not run up hill, stars wheel around their centres of attraction, and electricity leaps from cloud to cloud. But if, as the ancients held, the highest wisdom be to know the secret causes for all objective phenomena, and the extent to which all our human faculties can be developed, then are these scientists but busy ants, living within a microscopic hillock of great nature. Their boasted progress is, from this ancient point of view, but the beginning of true knowledge, at the wrong end, and all their troublesome activity but vanity and vexation of spirit. Is Civilization measured by the progress of Science? What *is* Civilization? Is it the perfecting of deadly weapons for the better killing of man by man? Is it the wholesale debasement of people by encouraging the consumption of opium and strong drinks? Is it the falsification of commodities for wear, and of articles for food, so as to cheat the unsophisticated? Is it the lowering of the standard of truthfulness to the point where perjury is at a premium, and man has almost lost all confidence in his fellow-man? Is it the extinguishment of the intuitive faculties, and the stifling of religious sentiment? Are *these* the marks of Civilization? Then, indeed, do they abound, and the world has progressed, within the last half-century. But the true moralist, I ween, would call these the proofs of retrogression. If he were a fair man, and could be brought to read what the ancient Hindus had really discovered, and what was their lofty standard of enlightenment, he would have to confess that we, modern people, make but a sorry show in comparison with them. They may not have had railways and spectroscopes, but they had grand notions of what constitutes an ideal man, and the vestiges of their civil polity that remain to us, show that society was well organized, private rights were protected, and domestic virtues cultivated. I am not speaking of the epochs intermediate between them and our own time, but about the real ancients, the progenitors alike of the modern Hindus and the modern Europeans. The biologist of our day is using his lenses and scalpel for what purpose? To discover the secret laws of life, is he not? Well, the ancient philosopher knew these, thousands of years ago; so where is the progress for us to boast of? The modern engineer builds bridges, and railways, and great ships to carry us from country to country. But the ancient mystic could, as quick as thought, project his inner self—to any place he chose, however distant, and see and be seen there. Which is the greater proof of "progress"—to make one's body to be carried in a wooden carriage, over iron rails, at the rate of sixty miles an hour, or by the force of an iron will, aided by a most profound knowledge of the forces of nature, to go in one's *double* around the earth, through the pathless *akasa*, in the twinkling of an eye? Or, take chemistry as an example. We will say nothing about this science having been entirely recreated since 1830 when the radical theory of Berzelius was in vogue; let that pass. We will take the science as it stands now; and what is its characteristic? Uncertainty. most assuredly. Great discoveries have been made, but the lacunæ, or gaps, between the chemist and a full knowledge of the laws of nature are still confessedly as great as ever; for each new discovery is but another eminence from which the experimentalist sees the horizon ever receding. Chemistry can expel life and disintegrate atoms; it can by synthesis rebuild inert matter. But it cannot recall the parted life when it is once gone. It can separate the rose leaf into atoms, but it cannot mould them again into a rose leaf nor restore its vanished perfume. And yet by the creative power of their trained will the ancient occultists could make roses fall in showers, from out of the empty air, upon the heads of sceptics, or fill the room with wafts of any perfume one might ask for. Nay, those who have studied their science have done it in our days, and before our own eyes. Can any member of the British Association with his imperfect methods, show us either one of the phenomena of the *Siddhis* described in the *Shrimat Bhagavata*:—*Animá*, *Mahimá*, *Laghimá Prapti*, *Prákáshyama*, *Ishita*, *Vashitá*, and the eighth which enables one to attain his every wish? Can he display any knowledge of the Buddhist *Iddhiwiddhinána* science, by producing the wonders of either the *Laukika* or *Lokothra*? When he can do any of these, and vie with either the Indian *Rishi* or the Buddhist *Arhát*, then let him dogmatize to us about "progress," and indulge in his witticisms against the "ancients." Until then, we will return him laughter for laughter, scorn for scorn.

Progress, you see, is a relative term. What may be wonderful advancement to one people, may be quite the opposite to another. And as for civilization, I think that we are only justified in applying the name to that state of society in which intellectual enlightenment is attended by the highest moral development, and where the rights of the individual and the welfare of the people as a whole are equally and fully realized. I cannot call any country civilized which, like England and America, spends five times as much for spirituous drink as for religious and secular education. I call that a barbarous, not a civilized, power which derives a large share of its income from the encouragement of opium smoking and arrack and whiskey drinking. I give the same name to a nation which, in spite of the teachings of Economic Science and the dictates of religion and morality, plunges into wars of conquest, that it may make new markets among weaker peoples for its wares and merchandize. That a different theory of civilization prevails, goes but to show the utter perversion of the moral sense which "modern progress" has brought about.

But may we not even ask Sir John Lubbock and his colleagues how they have discovered what the ancients did or did not know of even physical science? In another lecture (*India; Past, Present and Future*), I noted the fact that there were exhibited at the Mayasabha, described in *Bharata*, certain most wonderful specimens of mechanical ingenuity and technical skill. The fourteenth chapter of the first volume of Madame Blavatsky's *Isis Unveiled*, is crammed with illustrations of the profound knowledge possessed by ancient Egypt, Phœnicia, Cambodia, India, and other countries, of arts and sciences. If occasion required, I might show you by chapter and verse that some of the very latest discoveries of modern science are but rediscoveries of things known to the ancients, but long lost to mankind. The more I study the more is the truth of the ancient doctrine of cycles made clear to my mind. As the stars of heaven move in their orbits around their central suns, so does humanity seem ever circling about the Sun of Truth; now illuminated, now in eclipse; in one epoch resplendent with light and civilization, in another under the shadow of ignorance and in the night of moral and spiritual degradation. Four times have the islands now forming the Kingdom of Great Britain and Ireland dipped beneath the ocean and, after intervals to be calculated only by the arithmetic of geological time, been raised again and repeopled. (Huxley: *Lay Sermons*, p. 215.) There was also a time when the Himalayas, as well as the Pyrenees, the Alps and the Andes, were under water, and the ocean rolled where they now rear their towering crests. How vain is it not, then, for people to pretend to say what the ancients did not know, and what is "new under the sun!" You do not find the Hindus or the Chinese making such a mistake; their records, on the contrary, show that the ancestors possessed far more wisdom than their descendants, and the Chinese reverence for them is so strong as to take the form of religious worship. I would not need to go, as I am doing, all over India and Ceylon, and implore you, Asiatic men of to-day, not to dishonour yourselves by sneering at your "ignorant ancestors," if you had ever studied the literature they left behind them. It is your blind ignorance that makes you guilty of this sacrilege. Your education has been prescribed by the men of "progress." They have taught you a little Latin, less Greek, some patches of what they call History, such Logic and Philosophy as they have scraped out of the dry bones of the ancient philosophers, and a terrible lot of misleading physical science. And, with your heads crammed with such poor stuff, you assume airs and "laugh to scorn" the belighted beings who founded the six schools of Indian Philosophy, and the Rishis and Yogis who were able to range unfetterd through all the Cosmos! Aye, and to divest yourselves of the least tinge of suspicion that such progressed minds as yours could sympathize with the "degrading superstitions" of your nation, you vie with each other in efforts to lay your race-pride, your intellectual manhood, and your self-respect in the dirt, for the hob-nailed shoes of "progress" to stamp upon. Shame on such Asiatics!

What the best friends of India and Ceylon most desire is to see their young men cling to what is good of the olden times, while grasping all that is useful of the modern epoch. That is the civilization which India needs. There are certain abstract moral doctrines that are never new nor ever old, for they are the property of our race. The best maxims that Jesus taught were taught by others, ages before his time—if he had ever a time, which is certainly a doubtful question. So we must not measure civilization by the evolution of moral codes but by the national living up to them. Christendom has as fine a moral code as one could wish, but she shows her real principles in her Armstrong guns and whiskey distilleries, her opium ships, sophisticated merchandize, prurient amusements, licentious and political dishonesty. Christendom, we may almost say, is morally rotten and spiritually paralyzed. If interested missionaries tell you otherwise, don't believe them upon assertion: go through Christian countries and see for yourselves. Or, if you will not or cannot go, then get the proper books and read. And when you have seen, or read, and the horrid truth bursts upon you; when you have lifted the pretty mask of this smiling goddess of Progress, and seen the spiritual rottenness there, then, O, young men of sacred India, heirs of great renown, turn to the history of your own land. Read, and be satisfied that it is better to be good than learned; to be pure-minded and spiritual than rich; to be ignorant as a ryot, with his virtue, than intelligent as a Parisian debauchee, with his vices; to be a heathen Hindu practising the moralities of the Rishis than a progressed and civilized European trampling under foot all the rules that conduce to human happiness and true progress.

THE SIXTH ANNIVERSARY ADDRESS.

Delivered at the Framji Cowasje Institute, Bombay, on the 12th of January, 1882.

—:o:—

We meet to-day to publicly celebrate the Sixth Anniversary of the Theosophical Society. On its behalf I bid you welcome. I have here brought with me the original postal-card circular notice which convened the Founders, in the City of New York, on the 16th of October, 1875, to vote upon the Bye-Laws that had been drafted by the committee appointed at the preliminary meeting, on the 17th of September *ante*. Already, our Society has reached a development which gives historic value to this modest document. As the seed contains the germ of the full grown tree, so that little card had in it the potentiality of the great movement that Theosophy has become.

This is the third time we have addressed the Bombay public, in this Hall, on our anniversaries. You now know us, and have had time to watch our movements and gauge our sincerity. We do not address you as strangers, therefore. We have got beyond the preliminary stage of polite phrases on both sides. You know just how we keep our promises, and we know what yours are worth. The scented garlands Bombay brought us in February 1879 withered long ago, its complimentary speeches of welcome long since died away on the air. It seems far away—our first meeting. The three years that have slipped by have been, for us, so crowded with incidents that, though my feet stand on the same spot upon which I then stood, my memory hardly can realise that it is only three years. Such changes, too, as have befallen us! Dreams of hope blasted what other dreams fulfilled; some who then pretended friendship, turned into foes; and hundreds more whose existence then we did not suspect, became our staunchest, most unselfish and self-sacrificing friends. Some who stood beside me then have gone into the dark valley of Death, and some—thanks to the innate nobleness of human nature—have been true as steel to our cause from first to last. But, amid all these vicissitudes, what has been the net outcome as regards our Society; has it expanded or contracted; is it stronger or weaker; will it live and still grow, or die out, as visions fade? I come, obedient to the public voice, to answer these questions. I am here to give an account of my stewardship. To meet you I left my work in the heart of Ceylon, whither I shall shortly return, after a round journey of 3,000 miles. I shall tell you honestly what the Theosophical Society has accomplished within these years; withholding nothing that is not of a confidential nature. And then I shall ask you some questions in return. I want you to tell me how *you* have done *your* duty—not to us, but to your conscience, your race, and your religion. For, understand, I have made my last appearance to you as a suppliant for your kind alliance. The time for me to apologize for candour is past. I come to force the question home upon you whether you have as much right to your own self-respect, as you had at the beginning of 1879, when first I appealed to you to recollect the glories of your forefathers and be worthy of the name of Aryan or Persian. The promises I made in my first address from this place have been, or are being fulfilled. We can now point you to work done, schemes carried out, plans realised. Theosophy was then a new question, scarcely any one in India had heard of us; but now you may go where you like throughout India, and you will find that we are known, have friends and champions, and are exercising a positive and appreciable influence upon the thought of the educated classes. I do not ask you to believe this upon my simple statement, but upon the joint testimony of the public press and our enemies of all shades and degrees. The very abuse that has been showered upon us, when we take note of its authors, is a certificate of our usefulness. Bishops and archdeacons, sectarian or venal writers, bigots and pretended saints or reformers, do not waste their strength in attacking the insignificant. And where will you find a society that has been better abused than ours! No; our credentials are the work we have done, and the attacks upon us, by the enemies of Hindu, Buddhist and Zoroastrian philosophies and sciences, for doing it. Because they hate your religion and would have you despise your ancestors, they have tried to put us down and stop our mouths. But they have failed. *If we could survive your neglect, whose loyal help we had the clear right to count upon, we were not to be put down by their violence.* We have preached nothing but truth, and it is against that eternal rock that these slanderers have been dashing their fists. Let them go on, and stand you by idle, as most of you have done hitherto, if you will: the Theosophical Society is a living fact, and it is fast becoming a power. I read you last May an extract from the letter of a well-known Bengali patriot, in which he says that we are now universally known and respected, and have also performed a miracle. "Only the other day" he wrote "in a company of friends, the question was raised how it was that the educated Babus in general, now showed an inclination towards Hinduism. I said it was owing to the Theosophists, and *it was admitted by all to be so.*" So much for Bengal; now for North India. Says the London organ of the Church Missionary Society (the *Church Missionary Intelligencer and Record)* in its issue of last July:—"In a recently published article we gave some hint of the mischief which is being caused in North India by what is termed Theosophism. If we did not believe that this mischief was real, and a fresh hindrance to the progress of Christianity, it would not be worth while reverting to it.... From what we learn it is spreading, and if it extends much further, it is likely to be quite as noxious as the Brahmo Samaj, about which so much learned nonsense is talked." Well, it is something at least to be abused in good company; but it seems a little queer to yoke the Founders of the Theosophical Society, who do not pray, with the Brahmo Samajists, who do—very much. Now the Church Missionaries ought to know whether we are doing anything in North India to strengthen the love of the Natives for their own religion; and for my part I think their London organ has told the truth about it. But here comes the Very Reverend Archdeacon Baly, and says at the recent Church of England Missionary meeting that Theosophy is only a sort of new religion based on juggler's tricks. "We have two religions growing up among us," he gravely remarks. "The first is Theosophy, of which you must have heard something. At present its principal developments seem to me to savor of a conjuring cleverness on one side, and an easy credulity on the other...........I fear it will never be able to convey any spiritual power to man, or endow him with any spiritual good, until it borrows and adopts, directly or indirectly, some of the beneficent principles of Christianity." For a layman this would be stupid, and show pretty clearly that he did not read the papers— at least not the THEOSOPHIST, and the Native papers; we might almost suspect him of being a subscriber to the *Civil and Military Gazette*, or the *Lucknow Witness*, or the *Calcutta Statesman*, or some other journalistic jewel box of the sort. But for a learned and esteemed gentleman, an archdeacon, and a Very *Very* Reverend to boot, to utter such nonsense is really lamentable. *Imprimis*, we preach no new religion, never did; always vehemently protested against being thought to do so. In fact, as I have reiterated in every speech I ever made in India, our Society as a body has no religion. What we do is to preach the majesty and glory of all the ancient religions, and to warn the Hindu, the Sinhalese, and the Parsi, to beware how they depart from the teachings of the *Veda*, the *Tripitikas*, and the *Avesta*, for any newer faith, before learning well what the older religions contain, and what the newer ones do *not* contain. Theosophy has grown to what it is just, because it teaches that this "spiritual power," and "spiritual good" can be obtained in only one way, and that the religious ascetics of the schools of Sakya Muni, of Zoroaster of Patanjali, of Mahomed, as well as the mystics of Egypt, Greece and Rome, of China, Tibet and Japan, of the Aztecs and Toltecs, of Siam and Cambodia, all, *all*, I say—had the key to the mysteries of Nature and access to the only source of "spiritual power" —the boundless, eternal cosmic ocean of the AKAS. There, in that infinitude of space, that cradle from which new-born worlds and new-born men equally come, that final cemetery of planets and their inhabitants—is the eternal LIGHT. And he who would derive power or good, must raise himself far up to the psychological state of the "divine" ecstacy, in which the gods, and narrow creeds, and bibles of blind men are looked down upon, as the soaring eagle looks down upon the tiny speck of something black in the plain below, that calls itself a man, and may even be an Archdeacon out for a walk. The strength of our movement is that it is built upon the strong foundation of Universal Brotherhood. This is no empty rhetorical phrase with us, but an accomplished fact. The missionaries, after a century of labour in India, and the expenditure of millions of money, have converted so few high caste Brahmins that they can almost count them upon their fingers. But in three short years the Theosophical Society has taken into its brotherhood not only lay Brahmans of the very highest caste, and the most renowned among the Pandits, but it has taught them to work in fraternal unity with Hindus of the lower castes, and even with Parsis, Buddhists and Mussalmans for the spreading throughout the world of the ancient philosophies, for the world's spiritual good. Let Archdeacon Baly be more sure of his facts before he lectures again upon Theosophy.

But we have other and even better credentials to show of our success in North India. Mr. Baly spends his hot-weather at Simla; what does he say to our new Anglo-Indian branch, the Simla Eclectic Theosophical Society? Are such noted men as compose it noted for their "easy credulity?" If so, no one ever discovered it before: and if men of that calibre among the Anglo-Indian community have joined us, and publicly announced the fact, you may be sure of two things, (*a*) that the original theory of the Government of India, that we were Russian spies, and the later one of the *Saturday Review* and the Palamcottah Missions, that we are "unprincipled adventurers," are equally stupid and malicious fabrications. Our good private characters have now been effectually vindicated, and, whether they will or not, the missionaries, who are driven to their last ditch, must seriously go to work and *prove* that their religion is divine, and every other one diabolical.

In India, we have, since I last addressed you—in the month of May, 1881—organised no less than ten branches of our Society, *viz.*, at Simla, Lahore, Rawalpindi, Bareilly (Rohilkund), Lucknow, Muddehpoorah (Bengal), Berhampore (Bengal), Allahabad, Bhaunagar, Tinnevelly. Other branches have been formed at Paris, the Hague, Jamaica (Danish W. I.), in Java, and Australia. Does this not look as though Theosophy had something more and better than "conjuring cleverness" to rest upon? I ask all fair men among the Christians if they do not think they have, perhaps, been a little mistaken about us, our motives and plans.

And now, have any of you read or heard about the circumstances attending upon the formal organisation of our branch at Tinnevelly, Madras Presidency, on the 25th of October last? Do you know that it was marked by one feature of which the like has not been seen in India for two thousand years, an incident which proves more clearly and eloquently than words that our Society is, in fact, as in name, a Universal Brotherhood? I allude to the planting of a king cocoanut in the inner compound of the ancient temple of the Hindu gods by a committee of our Buddhist members of our Buddhist Branch at Colombo, Ceylon, amid the deafening plaudits of 5,000 high caste Hindu idolators. Let the Christians match that if they can. Our Hindu Tinnevelly Brothers received their Buddhist Brothers with a procession and music, the temple elephant, gaily caparisoned, led the van, every native official came to pay his respects, and, as I said before, we planted the cocoanut—ancient emblem of peace and respect—within the temple enclosure where no profane foot had trod before.

I will say a few words about our work in Ceylon, and then give place to the other speakers who will address you. During our visit of 1880, the Sinhalese people *en masse* gave us a princely reception. We moved through the Island, from Galle to Kandy and back again, in almost a "royal progress." They exhausted their ingenuity to do us honour, as in the ancient days they had done to their kings. Triumphal arches; flags flying in every town, village and hamlet; roads lined with *olla* fringes for miles together; monster audiences gathered together to hear and see us—these evidences of exuberant joy and warm affection astounded us. In India we had been so reviled by Christians, so frowned upon by the authorities with chilling disdain, and so given the cold shoulder by the Natives, to stay with whom and work for whose welfare we had come so far, that this greeting of the Sinhalese profoundly moved us to gratitude. We felt a sincere desire to do something, even if only a little, to show them that we were not insensible to such kindness. During our short stay of two months, eight Branches—seven Buddhistic and one scientific—were organised by us. But when the popular enthusiasm had had time to cool, and our members forced the practical difficulties of carrying on so tremendous a reform as the one we had in view in Ceylon, they found they had not the needed experience, and begged me to return and help them. So I went there in April last, and stopped until mid-December. During those 212 days I gave sixty public addresses at temples, school houses, colleges, and in the open air; held two conventions, or councils, of Buddhist priests; travelled hundreds of miles within the

Western Province; largely increased the membership of our Society; wrote, published, and distributed 12,000 copies of a Buddhist catechism; had translated into the Sinhalese language several freethought tracts; and raised by national subscription the sum of about Rs. 17,000, as the nucleus of a National Buddhistic Fund for the promotion of the Buddhist religion and the establishment of schools. Here is the photograph of one of the schools we opened last year by private subscription, before there was any such thing as a National Fund thought of. You see here in this group about 250 boys, every one of whom was being educated under Christian influences before we took them in charge. The missionaries have, as appears from the latest Government Report, about 27,000 children of Buddhists in their schools. As a general rule, they do not convert them to Christianity, but make them lose all faith in, and respect for, their forefathers' religion. Of these, we have already recovered back about 1,000, and I can assure you that it is simply a question of time and money as to our getting the whole 27,000 children. Just here I wish to say one word in anticipation of the possible objection that it is a gross inconsistency that a society based upon the theory of absolute reciprocity in religious matters, should be thus helping to baffle missionary work in Asia. At a superficial glance this is a valid point, but that is all. Look twice at it, and you will see that we are working strictly within our stated boundaries. We demand reciprocity from the Christians for the Hindus, Parsis and Buddhists: it is refused; hence we take the side of the Asiatics, and treat the foes of their religions as our foes. Do they give reciprocity? Will they allow their childern to be taught by Heathen masters, out of Heathen school-books, to despise the creeds and philsophies of their forefathers? Will they let Asiatic missionaries invade *their* homes, coax away *their* wives and daughters, make *them* outcasts by breaking the long established social order of European and American communities? You know, and they best of all know, they would not do one of these things. Then why, I ask in the name of justice and fair play, should they expect the Indian, the Persian, the Sinhalese, or the Chinaman, to stand idly by while they are doing all they can to undermine the bulwarks of Asiatic social life? The cry of reciprocity is a very sweet sound to hear, when *both* parties utter it in unison. That is the attitude of the Theosophical Society; and *from the day when the Christians will act up to their so-called Golden Rule*—which they borrowed from India and China, where sages taught it before there was any Palestine, or any Jew, in existence—*you will never hear a word spoken or see a line written by us against the missionaries or their religion.* For, if Christianity is no better, it is certainly no worse than some other popular faiths, and its morality is as sublime as that of other faiths, though *not* more sublime. We should and do respect the feelings of all who sincerely believe it, *and practise its precepts.* And this, by the way, reminds me of a proposal that appeared in the *Bombay Gazette* of the 10th inst. that my countryman, the Rev. Joseph Cook, now in this city, and I should get up a religious controversy. I disapprove of controversies as a rule; they are not apt to be convincing, and often excite angry feelings. It is the better way for each side to expound their views, supported by authorities, and leave an impartial public to decide. As regards Christianity, it, like all other religions, is now being melted in the crucibles of science and logic to separate its gold from its dross. That it is in mighty throes of pain; that scepticism is flowing across Christendom with the rush of the swollen Ganges; that free-thought books and newspapers are multiplying every day, that the Church has had to revise the Bible to suit a more enlightened and critical public; that the late census returns and special canvasses of the sects of Protestantism show a marked falling-off in the ratio of conversions, and attendance at churches—these all are so true that not even my gifted countryman, Mr. Cook, can deny it. That is the naked fact, and it cannot be covered up by all the flowers of rhetoric he can shower upon it. You have heard him discourse upon the support that science gives to Christianity, but if I may judge from what Natives have told me, their acute logical intellects—and nowhere will he find minds more acute than here—reject his inferences while admitting his scientific facts. He is new to Bombay, and does not even seem to suspect that if he should succeed in uprooting those germs of infidelity Western culture has planted in the Asiatic mind, the young men will *not run out into Christianity* but *run back into the religions of their fathers*; becoming orthodox and continuing so. For Christianity is totally repugnant to the Hindu mind. I heard his lecture in this Hall on Tuesday evening, and enjoyed it as an oratorical treat. But I could see—as I thought, though I speak under correction—that whatever fruit he might shake from the tree of Materialism would drop into the baskets of the Parsi Mobeds and the Hindu Sastrees. I shall not even touch upon his arguments, for I have not time; but perhaps your friend—also a countryman of Mr. Cook and myself—Mr. D. M. Bennett, Editor and Proprietor of the *Truth-seeker*, one of the greatest organs of the Western Freethought movement, who fortunately is here present, and, like Mr. Cook, is on a voyage around the world, may have a few words to say upon the subject.

But, to return from our digression: It was not enough to raise a fund in Ceylon; I had also to provide every possible guarantee that it would not be dishonestly appropriated, either while I myself was alive, or after my death. Taking advice, therefore, from counsel learned in the law, and the specially devoted and energetic members of our Colombo Branch, I drafted memoranda for two separate deeds, of which one created a Board of five Trustees, to receive, invest, and keep invested the proceeds of subscriptions, donations, legacies, and profits on sales of publications; and the other a Board of Managers to select the objects upon which money should be expended, and draw the cash as required, by drafts upon the Trustees to the order of the payees. As principal creator of the fund I was given a general supervisory power over the whole business, but without salary or remuneration of any kind. A commission was offered me, but at once declined; for, until now neither Madame Blavatsky nor I have been paid one penny for our services to the Society, nor do I expect that we ever will. If any friend of this our movement should henceforth hear us called unscrupulous adventurers, who are using Theosophy as a means to make money by, I ask you only to repeat what the Treasurer's Report, just read, shows, *viz.*, that Theosophy has cost us thousands instead of paying us a farthing. And you may add, if you choose, that to us two it is "a pearl without price," for which we would give not money alone, but even life.

Now why may we not do something for India of a similar character to that which we are doing for Ceylon. I could not undertake to give my whole time to the raising of an Indian National Fund just at present; but still I could do *something*, and after all the *first* step is the hardest of all to take in every serious business. After short visits to Poona, Calcutta, and Madras, I will return to Ceylon, where I am under engagement with our Galle Branch to deliver more than seventy lectures within the Southern Province on behalf of the Fund. This wlll occupy a few months, after which I hope I may be free to work in India. My only difficulty is to know for what the Indian Fund should be raised. I am most anxious to have sound advice upon the subject from our best Natives throughout the country. I should stipulate that whatever the Fund might be called, a portion of its annual income must be spent in promoting Sanskrit literature and the study of Aryan philosophy, arts and sciences. I mean to help to strengthen the Indian national aspirations for a revival of Aryan glories, not to stifle or weaken them. I would make *any* sacrifice to cause the Hindus to have a proper respect for the old Rishis, or for the Parsis to understand and imitate the learning and virtue of the ancient Magusthi: but I would not sacrifice the value of a *chopatty* or a *hoppa* to see created a whole generation of such intellectual and moral hybrids as are many of those who have been baked dry in the scholastic ovens of Elphinstone College, and turned adrift, with the imprint "B. A.," that was stamped into them when they were but on soft dough in the hands of a Materialistic or a Christian Professor. My dream for India is of a day when the Pandit will come up to the old standard of moral, intellectual, excellence as described in the *Bharat*;

when he will be the true guide and , exemplar of the people, and not a mere walking dictionary of Sanskrit *Slokas*, whose private character is oftentimes no better than that of the unlearned masses. Of a day when funished with all the helps that Western scholarship can give him to compare his ancestral ideas with the progress of science, he will, as in the olden time, be revered as a philosopher and a *guru*; and when the students of Europe will gather about his feet, as once gathered the students of Greece and Egypt about the feet of the Yogis and Sastrees of North India. Of a day when it will not be thought clever for beardless lads from college to smirk and sneer at those who affirm that Patanjali taught nothing but exact truth about Yoga Vidya.

Some wonder that I can so warmly and impartially labor with Hindu and Parsi, with esoteric Christian and esoteric Mussalman, to promote the best interests of their so contradictory faiths, when I am with all my heart and strength working with the Buddhists for the restoration and reform of their religion. That I, in short though a philosophical Buddhist, am yet endeavoring to equal the votaries of all these other creeds in zeal for their welfare. But man never yet made a creed that could bind me, as with an iron chain, when my brother man needed my help. My religion is the Welfare of Humanity my help is pledged to every one who, like myself, is trying to discover religious truth. I would spurn and stamp upon any creed or bible that bade me love only my fellow religionists, and hate all others; or that would forbid my allowing to my fellow truth seeker of any race, or color or creed, the same right of private judgment that I claim for myself. I recognize the Vedas as the earliest of extant religious writings, the repository of the highest thought of archaic man, the spring source of all subsequent philosophies. And I believe that if modern India could be brought to study and understand the true meaning of the Vedas, they would find in them so much that is noble, so much to satisfy the strongest spiritual yearnings of the national Indian heart, that not one young man, whether college-bred or not, would be tempted either to lapse into infidelity or fly off at a tangent into Christianity. Esoteric Buddhism satisfies my ideal of a philosophy, but though it is almost identical with esoteric Hinduism and esoteric Zoroastrianism, I no more expect my Hindu and Parsi brothers to agree with my views upon that subject than with my likings or dislikes for certain foods and dresses. The world is wide enough for us all, if we will only bear with each other's prejudices; but, without charity, even the universe is too little for two litigious pandits or padris.

I should also stipulate, before attempting to raise our Indian National Fund, that it should be made clear to everybody, rich and poor, that neither I, nor my Society, nor any one connected with it, should receive any profit or commission for raising the money. I must be able to face India as I am facing Ceylon, without a blush of shame for unworthiness of motive. Then I should require that in each Presidency a Board of Trustees, comprising the most honored patriot names among Natives, should be formed, and that their agent should go about with me, to take account of the subscriptions and receive all the money on their behalf. I should, as in Ceylon, require that there should be a Deed of Trust under which the money should be invested on specified security, and the annual interest only be used on given objects, in definite proportions. All this is secured already in the Ceylon deeds. When these points are covered, then I will be ready to begin. I will go from town to town, and village to village, and, telling the people what Aryavarta once was, and what it may be made again by united effort, will ask them to give whatever they can spare, whether a rupee or a lakh. In Ceylon we made one rupee the theoretical unit of subscription. Those who are too poor to give a rupee at lump give it by instalments of four annas and we issue to such tickets representing values of four annas, eight annas, and one rupee. The names of subscribers of two rupees and over are printed in the vernacu-weekly owned and conducted by members of our Ceylon Branch, Practically, we find that the wish to see their names in print induces many to give at least two rupees who, otherwise, would have pleaded poverty. There is human nature as well as pearls in Ceylon!

The Ceylon Fund is to be invested at the uniform rate of 10 per cent. on primary mortgages, in sums of Rs. 3,000 or less; no more than three thousand to be loaned on any one piece of property. Of the net income one-half is to be expended on Education, one-fourth on Publications of sundry kinds, and one-fourth on Miscellaneous Worthy Objects promotive of Buddhism. And finally—not to take up your time with details that can be read in this month's THEOSOPHIST—both Deeds provide that any Trustee or Manager who may be detected in taking a percentage or other pecuniary advantage out of the fund, shall be expelled from the Society in disgrace, and his offence made known to all Ceylon.

Various schemes have been suggested to me by patriotic Hindu gentlemen as proper objects for the raising of such a fund. A Madras pensioned Deputy Collector, Mr. Jyaloo Naidoo, names the sending of clever but poor youth to Europe and America to learn trades and bring their technical skill to India. A Parsi gentleman thinks it would be well to grant a certain stipend to young men who would obligate themselves to attend one of the Government colleges of Agriculture and then to take up land and farm it. I have this note from him:—

MY DEAR COL. OLCOTT,

With reference to our conversation the other evening in regard to raising a national fund in India on the model of one you have raised in Ceylon, under the auspices of the Theosophical Society, and meant to be devoted to the material advancement of the masses, in proof of the practical interest the Society takes in the welfare of the people of this country, I would suggest the advisibility of devoting a portion of the fund, if raised, to the following two purposes :—

1 Young educated boys of poor parentage should be allowed a monthly stipend from the fund, provided they would join any of the agricultural classes opened by the Government of India and engage subsequently in agricultural pursuits. One of the great wants of the country is a refined system of agriculture, and since the Government has thought it right to devote its attention to this important subject by establishing an Agricultural Department, our young men would do well to acquire the art and thereby become the means of spreading a knowledge of the principles of the much needed refined system of agriculture throughout the land.

2. Similar allowance may be made from the fund to young educated men who may be desirous of following the profession of any handicraftsmen in preference to mere clerkships in offices. In connection with this subject, I would draw your attention to an article in *The Bombay Chronicle* of to-day, headed "Clerks vs. Handicraftsmen," which I enclose. I trust you will take up these suggestions and mention them in your public Address. We shall talk more about the subject when we meet.

Yours fraternally,

A Poona friend broached a scheme for the organisation of a model village, a sort of Aryan Arcadia, where every want of the intellectual, moral and physical man would be thought of, and, to a degree, provided for. Your and my eminent friend, Mr. R. Ragoonath Rao, late Dewan of Indore, writes as follows :—

DAER SIR,—I think yourself and your Society can render eminent and good service to India in various ways. You can rouse up people to establish schools, quite different from those now in use, which are absolutely necessary for the improvement of MIND and HEART. You can induce people to open new industries, such as paper manufacture, machine making, &c., &c., &c. You can make people attend to religion, to cultivate self-reliance, to become loyal and good citizens, to induce the English and Americans to take more brotherly interest in the welfare of the Indian Aryans. I have no doubt that the Society will use its influence in bringing about the well-being of us all.

I remain, Dear Sir,
Yours Obedient,

3rd December, 1881. R. RAGOONATH RAO.

This is highly complimentary, and I shall be glad if we may be found to deserve his good opinion. I have myself thought, among other things, of the endowment of a professorship of Aryan Technology at Benares College; the chair to be filled by the most competent man who can be found. The lectures to include everything about the ancient Aryan arts, trade rules, recipes, processes, &c., that can be extracted out of Sanskrit and Vernacular literature. In connection with this chair, a technological museum might be opened at Benares, the one city of all India to which people are constantly thronging at all seasons of the year. However, all this is premature. As I said before, I will not even ask for a single pice towards the proposed fund, until all the preliminaries before noted have been amply provided for. My object to-day is to merely throw out the idea, and ask all true Indian patriots to favour me with the names of the seven or seventeen best men in each of the Presidencies whom I ought to consult and co-operate with. The Theosophical Society is here *not* for the sake of notoriety or show, but to do good, in all practical ways, to the country of our adoption.

The past year of our Society was fruitful of sensations connected with phenomena of the kind which tradition always has taken to illustrate the intimate knowledge of natural law in the department of Force possessed by the Aryan sages and transmitted from generation to generation of their followers. Though some sceptics will deny it, yet a large majority,—perhaps, we may say most—intelligent Hindus regard this reaffirmation and substantiation of the truth of Aryan Occult Science as the most important fact in the history of the theosophical movement in India. Thousands who were pre-disposed to believe the Yoga Sastras true, had still lost heart, for Western Science had declared such phenomena impossible and the Indian writings but the wildest fiction. Even the most learned Pandits of Benares, as I was told by a very high Anglo-Indian official of the N.-W. Provinces, had admitted that if ever such phenomena had occurred, their day had passed by, and no one now living knew the Yoga Vidya practically. But when we came and said that the old record was true; that these wonder-working powers are inherent in man; that discipline, under proper conditions, would develop them to-day as they had in the day of Gautama and Sankaracharya; and that to believe in their existence did not oblige one to believe in the possibility of miracle, but, on the contrary, made one realise that miracle is *not* possible—these doubters were rid of their perplexity. The other evening, my countryman, Mr. Cook, held up a copy of the Bible and declared that he did not fear the power of the combined science of the world to overthrow it. In like manner I challenge the whole array of materialistic men of science, of decorated Hindu collegians, and of clergymen, padris, priests, bishops, cardinals, and *gnastikas*, to disprove the truth, taught by Patanjali and a score more of Indian sages, and confirmed by the phenomenal demonstrations given by thousands of initiates, in many lands and among many peoples—that the ancient progenitors of your race, and my race, knew the secret laws of Matter and of Force, which Western Science is groping after, but as yet without avail. And India, the unworthy but yet not quite effete successor of her Aryan Mother, is the dusky casket in which the splendid secret has been locked throughout all these unhappy ages. Search, search for the key, ye, men of Modern Science. Not in the ooze of ocean's flood, where your deep sea dredges bring up quaint specimens of the busy life of the abyssal fannæ; not in the dust of powdered aërolites; not in the sporules of infection; not in coloured cells of the vaunted protoplasm; nor, though you turn from the glass that magnifies the things of the little-thing world, to the Greenwhich refractor that brings the seas of Mars and the moons of Jupiter within the range of the eye's most wondrous sweep, will you find out the secret of your being. No, but if you drag the depths of the ocean of human nature, if you study the laws of your own self, if you turn the eye of intuition to those profounder depths of natural law, where the demiurgic Hindu Brahma manages the correlations of forces and the rhythmic measures of the atoms, and the eternal principle of motion, called by the Hindu Parabrahm, outbreathes and inhales universes, —*there* will the golden key of this Ineffable Knowledge be found.

AN ADDRESS TO LADY THEOSOPHISTS.

A good many motives may incline a lady to desire to join the Ladies' Theosophical Society. Amongst these may possibly be reckoned—

1. Curiosity as to what it is and means, and, perhaps, a hope of finding out, through it, all about the Parent Theosophical Society to which some of her male relatives may belong.

2. A love of novelty; a desire for some new plaything, in fact.

3. A desire to take part in something from which her fellows are excluded, and thus have something to talk of, or pride herself on, wherewith to excite their curiosity or envy.

4. A wish to be thought more learned or of more importance than her neighbours.

5. The hope of witnessing some of those marvels that the members of the *first* section of the Theosophical Society are thought to have the power of effecting, or possibly of acquiring for herself, some of these wonderful powers. Or lastly—

6. A sincere desire to raise and improve herself mentally and morally, and to learn how better to do her duty.

No one, not firmly actuated by this last desire, and not willing cheerfully to undergo the labour and make the sacrifices that all such upward progress entails, should think of joining the Society. No good can ever come of it. No entering or belonging to a society like this can ever profit any who have not in their own hearts the steadfast desire to grow wiser and better.

Look around at the Parent Thesophical Society, with its thousands of members. By what whit are nine-tenths of these in any way wiser or better for writing "F. T. S." after their names? And why? Because instead of putting their own shoulders to the wheel, struggling to conquer all bad habits, all evil passions, and live pure and beneficent lives, they drag on in their old, worldly ways, waiting forsooth for some adept to perform a miracle, and transform them, and purify their natures without trouble to themselves!

But no such miracle is ever wrought; each man and woman must transform *themselves*; it is in their own hearts that the battle of good and evil must be fought out, and if any of you join the Ladies' Society without an earnest heartfelt aspiration for a higher and purer life, you will no more profit by such joining than have the greater mass of our fellows, by joining the Parent Theosophical Society.

If you are to continue to cherish angry passions or ill will towards any one, friend or foe, high or low; if you are still to set your whole hearts upon fine clothes, jewels, money, position or the pleasures of the senses; if you are still to allow your idle thoughts to stray to unfitting subjects; if you are not ready to struggle steadfastly to lead an useful, rational, and pure life, to labour untiringly for the welfare of others, and find your chief happiness in doing good; then never think of joining the Society; it will do *you* no good, while the grievous worldly taints still clinging about *you*, may insensibly injure the purer and more sincere members of the Society.

There may be some, however, who feel within their hearts a pious longing for a higher, purer life, though they may not as yet have wholly made up their minds to face the sacrifices, that such lives involve. Like would-be bathers on the banks of some cold, holy stream, they stand hesitating. Their better impulses urge them, now at the propitious conjuncture, to bathe and issue thence purified, but their weak, earthly, comfort loving natures plead that round them on the bank the flowers are blooming sweetly and the sun is shining warmly, that the water is cold and dreary, that there is no knowing whether any good *will* come of the plunge, and that at any rate it were best to wait a little longer! "There is no hurry, a little later will surely do as well, and then the water *may* be warmer;" and so, too often, they wait and wait until the hour is past, and the opportunity lost for ever.

"But why should we make the plunge?" May some, who read this, say—"It is true that we have had glimpses of higher things, and that we know that we waste much time in nonsense, leave undone much that it were perhaps wiser to do, and do and say and think many things that were better left alone; but after all the nice clothes, and jewels and money, and all those other things you wish us to cease to care for are very pleasant: we get on very well, on the whole, as we are and why should we turn our backs on all enjoyment to become a set of Yogees, disguised in hideous saffron tinted robes?"

But this is all a mistake. As for saffron coloured dresses, it matters nothing, spiritually, what colours or what raiment you wear. It is not by the robe that covers this poor body, but by the spirit that fills the heart that the good and pure are to be known. Each must in all externals conform to what is suitable to her position, no one desires you to put away nice clothes or jewels; if you are married women, it is part of your duty to make your husbands' homes bright and cheerful, and yourselves pleasant and comely in their sight. But what *is* needful is that you should cease to long for, or love for themselves, these mere worldly vanities, cease to plan and scheme and crave for them so earnestly, and, recognising their true value, their intrinsic nothingness, set your hearts instead on leading good and useful lives, and on unselfishly ministering to the happiness of others.

In this beautiful, though delusive, world innumerable sources of innocent and lawful pleasure are opened to one or other of us. Let none give a thought to what is denied to them; let all take and soberly enjoy what life freely gives, but without setting any great store thereby. Be ever ready to dispense with them without regret; never grieve or think twice about what has been lost or missed. Accept gladly what comes; ignore what fails to come or departs. At the best, all such are but dreams, easily broken, soon passed away; things of the earth whose influence for good cannot overpass the limits of this little life, while their influence for evil, if misused and allowed to grow into the heart, may extend; alas! *who* can say how far? But the heart, fixed upon things spiritual, that craves for purity of deed, of word, of thought, that finds its happiness untainted by selfish cares in the welfare of those around, has compassed joys against which Time, and Fate, and Death are powerless—joys that will wreathe with flowers every step of the immeasurable future that lies before each of us, not wholly lost, beyond the verge of this brief present life.

To some these will seem but idle words. "What," they will say, "do we know of any future? A few short fleeting years—alas, how short—and why should we not enjoy them while we may? A few brief years, and then the curtain falls for all, and the gloomy earth or blazing pile closes the vista for ever!"

For ever, indeed, to the eyes of the blind mortals who remain behind, but not so to those departing. The traveller leaves your hospitable door; he passes into the wood. You see him, hear of him, perhaps, no more. But he ever travels on, though you know nought of it, well or ill, according to the foresight and wisdom with which he has equipped himself before starting. We all are wanderers and travellers, resting but for a brief period on earth, and when we start thence it fares well or ill with us according as we have used or misused the opportunities afforded here. Those who have clung persistently to material pleasures, whose hearts have become bound up in evil or earthly things, nrawn down by the bonds of a self-erected attraction for matter, pass to a lower, more material sphere, too seldom to rise again, too generally to sink after a period of suffering, the exact measure of their own transgressions, into annihilation.

These are the travellers—alas, too many—who perish by the wayside. Throughout the universe the inexorable law of the exact requital of good for good and evil for evil rules; and those who fail to fit themselves for the upward course, sink downwards and become extinct.

But they, on the other hand, the wise and prescient travellers, whose aspirations have been towards things spiritual, who, unblinded by the glamour of this world's empty shows, have fixed their soul's gaze over on the things beyond earth's prison walls, they, freed from the fetters of the flesh, pass on rejoicing into peace and immortality.

It is not, however, to be concluded that even the majority of mortals, either thus sink into hopeless misery and annihilation, or pass in triumph to happiness and union with the universal. Too generally, human life is such a tangled skein of good and evil that even the fabled angels and devils would fail to unravel the black and white inextricably inter-knotted threads. Only when the entire tendencies are evil or material, and further development towards purity and spirituality is impossible, does the conscious self sink sadly into nothingness; only where perfect purity envelopes it with spotless robe can the soul win upwards the eagle wing, released for ever from the whirring groaning wheel of transitory existence, to the unchanging bliss of the immutable. In all other cases *each has* to work its way upwards, step by step, life by life and word by word, through the whole circle of necessity, rapidly and comparatively happily, or slowly and painfully, according to its merits. Each good deed in life blooms a flower of rejoicing in the next; each evil one rankles a thorn of suffering sharper than a serpent's tooth. As we sow, so, for ever and for ever, shall we reap.

The first great truth, then, that each must take to heart is that this life here is but as one day's sail in the vast voyage that all must make, who escaping utter shipwreck and destruction, would fain safely cross the stormy seas of material existences to that tranquil haven where all is peace—their birth-place and their home.

The second and even more vital truth is, that throughout this entire pilgrimage, our fates are in our own hands. We shall perish miserably by the way; we shall win onwards, slow or fast, in storm or sunshine, just as during each fresh departure we act, speak or think. There is no stern deity punishing, no merciful one forgiving. Let no one dull the sense of your own individual responsibility by such doctrines, but your own deeds, words, and thoughts here are their own avengers, or rewarders in the next life, and so on ever throughout the mighty series of existences that culminate where Change and Death can never enter.

You say, well "a few brief years, and then the curtain falls!" Who then, so mad as to barter for the brightest gewgaws earth can boast, the endless happiness open to all beyond? Who so foolish as not during this brief period to prepare aright for that, if they so will it, endless future?

Once bring home to your hearts your real position here on earth, once realize the dread significance of all your actions, all you are in this life, and you will cease to wonder *why* you *should* make the plunge; *why* you should cease to covet and crave for the pleasures and glories of this world; and while thankfully enjoying these as does the wayfarer the beautiful scenery, the tuneful birds, the perfumed flowers that ever and anon gladden his pilgrimage, suffer none such to beguile you to the right or left, but keeping your eyes steadfastly fixed on the distant goal, march onwards to it straight, gathering only as you pass those jewels of a pure heart and all loving soul that will alone avail you there.

And, remember, it is not only your own eternal welfare that may hang upon the issue—there are the children whose very lives are yours —the husbands, mothers, fathers you so dearly love. More than we think do each and all of us possess the power of influencing for good or evil those near and dear to us. More often than we realize are the entire lives of children coloured by the precepts instilled by the examples set before their eyes, in earliest childhood by their mothers. If you cannot be brave and pure for your own sakes, shall your children have to curse you in dark under-worlds for your evil influence, or bless you in brighter spheres for that light, which your loving cares first kindled in their soul.

Dear sisters, it is an awful responsibility which rests on all of us, men and women—a responsibility, real and from which there is no escape. You may glide onwards, dragged and blinded by the delusive pleasures and attractions of the earthly life, dragging with you, perhaps, to the bottomless pit of destruction, those or some of them, to save whose earthly lives you would so gladly lay down your own; or you may be strong and wise in time, and bursting the gilded chains of material pleasures and desires, rise triumphant, spirit buoyed, over the abyss drawing after you by silken threads of love, and reverence all to whose hearts, in life, you have been the sunshine.

"It is so hard!" It does, indeed, *seem* so, but nothing worth the having, nothing even of earth's empty glories was ever won without toil and trouble.

"It is impossible for us to become perfectly pure and good?" It is so! So long as the spirit continues prisoned in this home of clay, some material taints will ever cling to it. Natures too differ, and purity and spiritual exaltation, comparatively easy to one who has learnt the solemn lesson of existence in early life, are to be attained by another, when evil habits and desires have long had sway, only after a bitter struggle and sore travail of mind. But one and all can be better than they *are*; one and all can hunger and thirst after righteousness; one and all can surely, even if slowly, trample out, one by one, the noxious weeds sown by material influences in the gardens of their souls; one and all can, step by step, scale the peaks of snowy purity, whence the spirit can soar to another and a brighter world. Yes; all can strive in earnest to rise, to grow purer, more unselfish, more beneficent, and no one, man or woman, ever thus tried, patiently and perseveringly, but soon or late, reaped a rich harvest of their toil. It is not *really* so hard! it only *seems* so. How hard it seemed to level the dull gross mound that once stood yonder, and rear instead the noble temple pointing to the skies, that now delights all eyes! Yet, if you watched the work, you saw how by slow degrees, before the patient workman, shovel by shovelful, and basket by basketful, the gloomy mass waned and how, too, stone by stone, in long years, the temple rose and waxed, until at last its golden pinnacle shot up, untarnishable into the smiling heavens.

Take courage! It is *not* so hard even to begin; you have but to will; to turn your heart to the task in sincerity and patience, and the worst is over. Day by day the voices of the world calling to its phantom feasts will grow fainter and fainter, and day by day the low whispers from heaven will wax clearer and sweeter, until, after a while when you look back, you will wonder how you ever even thought it hard.

"But what are we to do?" We truely believe that there is not one of you who reads this that does not for herself know this far better than we can hope to tell it. Deep in each heart is planted the knowledge of good and evil: you *may* need preachers to arouse you to the terrible consequences of a wrong choice, to warn you of the eternity that depends upon your clinging to the one and shaking off the other; but once you know and feel this, once you have chosen that better path, you can hardly need any teachers other than your own souls.

Do you not know! You know full well? Your own darling sin, be it sloth, extravagance, sensuality, greed, anger, pride, envy, or what not, you know it well. *That* sin you must beat down with steadfast purpose; on its neck you must set your heel—it or you must perish—the strife is one for your own existence, aye, and, more or less, for that of all who love you, all you love. Be strong and resolute, will that it *shall* die, and (for, in this universe, right will is omnipotent), slowly its snaky folds shall uncoil from round your heart, the hateful fetters crumble, and you shall once more be free and happy.

You are surrounded by people, some to whom you owe obedience, some subject to your authority. Need we tell you that you should serve the former in all sincerity and loyalty, not with lip service, but from your heart in truth, and love, as *you* would others should serve *you*? Or need we say that those others, high and low, good and bad, should find in you an ever gracious, forgiving and mother-like ruler? Some will lie, and some will steal or sin in other ways, and many will neglect their duties. Pity them, for they are weaving for themselves a retribution elsewhere which they can no more escape than *you* can escape the consequences of your own deeds. Pity them! for *them* the light that guides you has not yet shone. Endeavour by gentleness, by just constraint unmixed with anger, but above all by your own example, to teach them how good a thing it is to be honest, pure, and true, and to perform every duty of life thoroughly and cheerfully.

A hundred idle superstitious observances go on around you daily, but if any of those to whom you owe love and deference, reverence or cling to these, do not vex their minds by ridiculing or despising such. Remember that though in themselves of no avail, they have had in past days a value in reminding mortals (almost smothered in the cares and desires of this material life) of better and spiritual things, and that all of them (though the signification may long since have been forgotten,) typify by material, visible objects, things spiritual and unseen. Make for each seemingly futile form which you comply with, to save pain to others, a higher spiritual signification, and let the aspirations of your hearts glorify each empty rite. So let the grains of rice you scatter remind you of the good words and deeds that should fall softly from you all around; so let the flowers you place up on the shrine recall those holiest of offerings, those imperishable flowers, pure and loving hearts!

See, however, that your children are reared in the full comprehension of the frailty and nothingness, in *themselves*, of these and all mere outward observances, but above all things in the living, ever present consciousness, of the eternal verities they symbolize.

Ridicule, despise, no religious observance performed in simple faith and honesty of purpose. Many paths lead to the mountain top, and no soul, however ignorant and foolish, seeking in singleness of heart to find the way, ever failed sooner or later to reach that summit. Cherish your own better knowledge, labour silently, but untiringly, to spread it to all others capable of receiving it; but beware how you shock the feelings of weaker sisters, by condemning what they believe in, shaking perhaps their simple faith (foolish it may be, yet in so far as earnestly clung to, never without some saving power), and thus retard the upward progress of their timid souls. Strive gently, that the truth may, drop by drop, so distil into their hearts, that they may never risk the dangers of the sudden drowning out of old long cherished beliefs.

Intemperance and an addiction to spirituous liquors is one of the growing vices of the men of your race. There is no sensual indulgence which leads to more evil, none more destructive of the sinner's spiritual hopes, or more fatal to the peace, well being and happiness of families.

On purely selfish grounds, if for no higher motive, every woman should set her face against this pernicious practice. But you—you who have a higher goal than self in view—should struggle to put it far from you, and all you love, with all your strength and with all your hearts. No persuasions, no temptations should lead you ever henceforth to allow one drop to cross your own lips, and alike with husband, brother, son, you should strive, not by noisy reproaches or open preaching but with all the power of a good woman's silent, loving influence, to make, or keep, them equally temperate.

In this life we have the poor and suffering with us always. It is not by ostentatious subscriptions to public charities, it is not by formal alms to professional mendicants—whether these claim a religious character or no—that the best and highest work is to be done, but by the unblazoned relief of humble sufferers. Let your charity fall like heaven's dew, unheard of and unseen. There can scarcely be one amongst you who, through kinsmen or servants, does not hear from time to time of grinding poverty and bitter distress in human homes. Remember, as you mete unto others here, so shall it be meted unto you in the next life.

The waste of time for which many of you are responsible is grievous. Days, weeks, months, nay, almost the entire lives of not a few, pass in idleness or in occupations and amusements so useless and frivolous as to deserve no better name than idleness disguised. Let all realize how precious are the fleeting hours, how short the space within which we can work and fit ourselves for the coming journey and resolve—and *keep* that resolve—that thenceforth wasted and mis-spent time shall not be amongst their sins. How well might some of that time now wasted be devoted to thought and supervision that would make the home happier for all its members, to teaching and leading those amenable to our guidance into the path of truth, or to enquiring into and devising methods for alleviating some portion of the misery ever seething round us.

But why linger over details? To all in whom the spirit is truly awakened, a hundred paths of usefulness and beneficence are open, despite the apparent disadvantages of the positions in which many are placed. Be pure, be humble, and be loving to all earth's creatures, high and low, and not only will all love *you*, not only will you secure for yourselves, and help to secure for those dearest to you, imperishable joys in the unseen, but real and limitless universe that lies beyond and all around this little visible earth-clod of delusions, but even in this transitory life, where, at first, the waters of repentance seem so dark and dreary, you shall find a peace, a joy, a blessedness, far beyond aught that selfish earthly striving can ever yield, and unlike their fruits (which, at best, cloy, and too often turn to ashes on the lips), proof against sorrow and suffering, against time, and change and death.

THE SPIRIT OF THE ZOROASTRIAN RELIGION.

Delivered at the Town Hall, Bombay, on the 14th of February, 1882.

With great diffidence I have accepted your invitation to address the Parsis upon the theme of the present discourse. The subject is so noble, its literature so rich, its ramifications so numerous, that no living man could possibly do it full justice in a single lecture. Happy, indeed, I will be, if I succeed in communicating to one or two of the learned Parsi scholars, who honour me with their presence, some of the deep interest which I have had for years in the esoteric meaning of the Mazdiaznian faith. My hope is to attract your attention to the only line of research which can lead you towards the truth. That line was traced by Zoroaster and followed by the Magi, the Mobeds, and the Dasturs of old. Those great men have transmitted their thoughts to posterity under the safe cover of an external ritual. They have masked them under a symbolism and ceremonies, that guard their mighty secrets from the prying curiosity of the vulgar crowd, but hide nothing from those who deserve to know all. Do not misunderstand me. I am not pretending that *I* know all, or a fraction of all: at best I have had but a glimpse of the reality. But even that little is quite enough to convince me that, within the husk of your modern religion, there is the shining soul of the old faith that came to Zaratusht in his Persian name, and once illuminated the whole trans-Himalayan world. You—children of Iran, heirs of the Chaldean lore; you —who so loved your religion that neither the sword of Omar, nor the delights of home, nor the yearning of our common humanity to live among the memories of our ancestors, could make you deny that religion; you—who, for the sake of conscience, fled from your native land and erected an altar for the symbolical Sacred Fire in foreign countries, more hospitable than yours had become; you—men of intelligence, of an ancient character for probity, of enterprise in all good works—*you* are the only ones to lift the dark veil of this modern Parsiism, and let the "Hidden Splendour" again blaze forth. Mine is but the office of the friendly wayfarer who points you to the mouth of the private road that leads through your own domain. I am not, if you please—a man, but only a VOICE, I need not even appeal to you to strip away the foreign excrescences that, during twelve centuries of residence among strangers, have fastened themselves upon primitive Zoroastrianism, nor to recite to you its simple yet all sufficient code of morality, and ask you to live up to it more closely. This work has already been taken up by intelligent and public spirited members of your own community. But I am to show you that your religion is in agreement with the most recent discoveries of modern science, and that the freshest graduate from Elphinstone College has no cause to blush for the "ignorance" of Zaratusht! And I am to prove to you that your faith rests upon the rock of truth, the living rock of Occult Science upon which the initiated progenitors of mankind built every one of the religions that have since swayed the thoughts and stimulated the aspirations of a hundred generations of worshippers. Let others trace back the history of Zoroastrianism to and beyond the time of the Bactrian King Vistâsp; and reconcile the quarrels of Aristotle, Hermippers, Clement, Alexander, Polyhistor, and the other ancient as well as of modern critics, as to when Zaratusht lived and where was his birth-place: these are non-essentials. It is of far less moment to know where and of what parentage a religious reformer was born, than to be sure of what he taught and whether his teaching is calculated to bless mankind or not. Plotinus, the philosopher, so well knew this that he would not tell, even to Porphyry, his pupil and literary biographer, what was his native country, what his real name, or his parentage. As regards Zaratusht one thing is affirmed, viz., that about six centuries B.C. one man of that name lived—whether or not several others preceded him, as several highly respectable authorities affirm is the fact—and that the religion he preached, whether new or old, was of so noble a character that it indelibly stamped its impress upon the then chief school of Western philosophy, that of Greece.* It is also,

* In the oldest Iranian book called the "Desatir"—a collection of the teachings of the fourteen oldest Iranian prophets (to make the number fifteen and include, among them, Simkendesh, or "Secander," is a grave error, as may be proved on the authority of Zaratusht himself in that book)—Zartusht stands thirteenth in the list. The fact is significant. Respecting the period of Zoroaster the *First*, or his personality, there is no trustworthy information given by any of the Western scholars; their authorities conflicting in the most preplexing manner. Indeed among the many discordant notices, I find the earliest Greek classic writers who tell us that Zaratusht lived from 600 to 5,000 years before the Trojan war, or 6,000 years before Plato. Again it is declared by Berosus, the Chaldean priest, that Zoroaster was a founder of Indian dynasty in Babylon 2200 B.C.; while the later native traditions inform us that he was the son of Purushaspa, and a contemporary of Gustaspa, the father of Darius, which would bring him within 600 B. C. Lastly, it is mentioned by Bunsen that he was born at Bactria before the emigration of the Bactrians to the Indus, which took place, as the learned Egyptologist shows us, 3784 B.C. Among this host of contradictions, what conclusion can one come to? Evidently, there is but one hypothesis left: and that is that they are all wrong, the reason for it being the one I find in the secret traditions of the esoteric doctrine—namely, that there were several teachers of that name. Neither Plato nor Aristotle, so accurate in their statements, is likely to have transformed 200 years into 6,000. As to the generally accepted native tradition, which makes the great prophet a contemporary of Darius' father, it is absurd and wrong on the very face of it. Though the error is too palpable to need any elaborate

as I believe, certain that this man was an initiate in the sacred Mysteries, or, to put it differently—that he had, by a certain course of mystical study, penetrated all the hidden mystries of man's nature and of the world about him. Zoroaster is by the Greek writers often called the Assyrian "Nazaret." This term comes from the word *Nazar* or *Nazir*—set apart, separated. The Nazars were a sect of adepts, very ancient—existing ages before Christ. They are described as "physicians, healers of the sick by the imposition of the hands" and as initiated into the Mysteries (see

---

confutation, I may say in regard to it a few words. The latest researches show that the Persian inscriptions point out to Vistasp as the last of the line of Kaianìan princes who ruled in Bactria, while the Assyrian conquest of that country took place in 1200 B.C. Now this alone would prove that Zoroaster lived twelve or thirteen hundred years B.C., instead of the 600 assigned to him; and thus that he could not have been a contemporary of Darius Hystaspes, whose father was so carelessly and for such a length of time confounded in this connection with the Vistasp who flourished six centuries earlier. If we add to this the historical discrepancy between the statement of Ommianus Marcelinus—which makes Darius crush the Magi and introduce the worship of Ahurmazda—and the inscription on the tomb of that king which states that he was "teacher and hierophant of Magianism;" and that other no less significant and very important fact that the Zoroastrian *avesta* shows no signs of the knowledge of its writer or writers with either the Medes, the Persians, or the Assyrians, the ancient books of the Parsis remaining silent upon and showing no acquaintance with any of the nations that have been known to have dwelt in or near the Western parts of Iran,—the accepted figure 600 B.C. as the period in which the prophet is alleged to have flourished becomes absolutely improbable.

It is therefore safe to come to the following conclusions:—(1.) That there were several (in all *seven* say the Secret Records) *Ohuru-asters* or spiritual teachers of Ahurmazda, an office corrupted later into *Guru-asters* and *Zuru-asters* from "Zera-Ishtar," the title of the Chaldean or Magian priests; and (2) that the last of them was Zaratushta of the *Desatir*, the thirteenth of the prophets, and the seventh of that name. It was he who was the contemporary of Vistasp, the last of the Kaianian princes, and the compiler of Vendidad, the Commentaries upon which are lost, there remaining now but the dead letter. Some of the facts given in the Secret Records, though to the exact scholar merely traditional, are very interesting. They are to the effect that there exists a certain hollow rock full of tablets in a gigantic cave bearing the name of the Zaratushta under his Magian appellation, and that the tablets may yet be rescued some day. This cave with its rock and tablets and its many inscriptions on the walls is situated at the summit of one of the peaks of the Thian Shan mountains far beyond their junction with the Belor Tagh, somewhere along their Eastern Course. One of the half-pictorial and half-written prophecies and teachings attributed to *Zaratusht* himself, relates to that deluge which has transformed an inland sea into the dreary desert called Shamo or Gobi Desert. The esoteric key to the mysterious creeds flippantly called, at one time the Sabian or Planetarry Religion, at another, the Solar or Fire Worship, "hangs in that cave," says the legend. In it the great Prophet is represented with a golden star on his heart and as belonging to that race of Ante-deluvian giants mentioned both in the sacred books of the Chaldeans and the Jews. It matters little whether this information is accepted or rejected. Since the rejection of it would not make the other hypothesis more trustworthy, it may just as well be mentioned here.

treatise *Nazir* in the Talmud). The Jews returning from the Babylonian captivity were thoroughly imbued with Zoroastrian and Magian ideas; their forefathers had agreed with the Sabeans in the Bactric worship, the adoration of the Sun, Moon, and Five Planets, the SABAOTH and realms of light. In Babylon they had learned to worship the Seven Rayed God. And so we find running all throughout the Christian as well as the Jewish Scriptures, the septenary system, which culminates in the *Book of Revelation* (the final pamphlet of the Bible) in the Heptaktis, and a prophecy of the coming of the Persian Soorish under the figure of the Christian Messiah, riding, like the former, upon a white horse. By the Jewish sect of the Pharisees, whose great teacher was Hillel, the whole angelology and symbolism of the Zoroastrians were accepted, and infused into Jewish thought; and their Hebrew Kabala, or secret book of Occult Wisdom, was the offspring of the Chaldean Kabala. This deathless work is the receptacle of all the ancient lore of Chaldea, Persia, Media, Bactria, and the pre-Iranian period. The name by which its students in the secret lodges of the Jewish Pharisees (or Pharsis) were known was *Kabirim*—from Kabeiri, the Mystery Gods of Assyria. Zoroastrianism and Magianism proper were, then, the chief source of both esoteric Judaism and esoteric Christianity. But not only has this subtle spirit left the latter religion, under the pressure of worldliness and sceptical enquiry, it also long ago left Judaism. The modern Hebrews are not Kabalists but Talmudists, holding to the later interpretations of the Mosaic canon: only here and there can we now find a real Kabalist, who knows what is the true religion of his people and whence it was derived

The real history of Zoroaster and his religion has never been written. The Parsis have lost the key, as the Jews and Christians have lost that of their respective faiths, and as I find the Southern Buddhists have lost that of theirs. *Not* to the living pandits or priests of either of those religions can the laity look for light. They can only quote the opinions of ancient Greek and Roman, or modern German, French, or English writers. This very day nearly all that your most enlightened scholars know about your religion is what they have collated from European sources, and that is almost exclusively about its literature and external forms. And see what ridiculous mistakes some of those authorities make at times! The Rev. Dr. Prideaux, treating of the Sad-der, says that Zaratusht preached incest!—that "nothing of this nature is unlawful, a man *may not only* marry his *sister or his daughter, but even his mother!*" (*Ancient Universal History*, iv. 296). He quotes no Zend authority, nothing written by a Parsi, but only Jewish and Christian authorities, such as Philo, Tertullian, and Clement Alexandrinus. Eutychius, a priest and archimandrite at Constantinople, writes, in the 5th century, on Zoroastrianism as follows: "Nimrod beheld a fire rising out of the earth and he worshipped it, and from that time forth the Magi worshipped fire. And he appointed a man named Andeshan to be the priest and servant of the Fire. The Devil shortly after that spoke out of the midst of the fire (as did Jehovah to Moses ?) saying 'No man can serve the Fire or learn Truth in my Religion, unless first he shall commit incest with his mother, sister, and daughter! He *did as he was commanded*, and from that time the priests of Magians practised incest; but Andeshan was the first inventor of that doctrine." I quote this as a sample of the wretched stuff that has always been written against the Zoroastrian religion by its enemies. The above words are simply the dead letter mistranslation of the secret doctrine, of which portions are to be found in certain rare old MSS. possessed by the Armenians at Etchmiadzine, the oldest monastery in Russian Caucasus. They are known as the Mesrobian MSS. Should the Bombay Parsis show any real general interest in the rehabilitation of their religion, I think I may promise them the unpaid but, all the same, friendly assistance of Madame Blavatsky, whose friend of thirty-seven years standing, the Prince Dondoukoff Korsakoff, has just notified her of his appointment by His Majesty the Czar, as Viceroy of the Caucasus.

In one of such old MSS., then, it is said of the Initiate, or Magus, "He who would penetrate the secrets of (sacred) Fire, and unite with it [as the Yogi 'unites himself with the Universal Soul'] must first unite himself soul and body to the Earth, his *mother*, to Humanity, his *sister*, and Science, his *daughter*." Quite a different thing, you perceive, from the abhorrent precept ascribed to the Founder of your Mazdiasnian faith. And this example should serve as a warning to your so-called educated youth, against turning up his classical nose, at his ancestral religion as 'unscientific' and nonsensical.

A curious and sad thing, indeed, it is to see how completely the old life has gone out of Zoroastrianism. Originally a highly spiritual faith—I know of none more so—and represented by sages and adepts of the highest rank among initiates, it has shrunk into a purely exoteric creed; full of ritualistic practices not understood, taught by a numerous body of priests as a rule ignorant of the first elements of spiritual philosophy; represented in prayers of which not a word has a meaning to those who recite them daily: the shrivelled shell that once held a radiant soul. Yet all that Zoroastrianism ever was it might be made again. The light still shines, though in darkness, enclosed in the clay vessel of materialism. Whose shall be the holy hand to break the jar of clay and let the hidden glory be seen? Where is the Móbed who shall in our day and generation rise to the ancient dignity of his profession, and redeem it from degradation.* One so great as to oblige even a Parsi author (Mr. Dosabhoy Framjee, see his able work on *The Parsees*, &c., p. 277) say they "recite parrot-like all the chapters requiring to be repeated on occasions of religious ceremonies. . . . Ignorant and unlearned as these priests are, they do not and cannot command the respect of the laity." . . . "the position of the so-called spiritual guides has fallen into contempt;" and to add that some priests have "given up a profession which has ceased to be honourable and . . . become contractors for constructing railroads in the Bombay Presidency." Some of the present Dasturs "are intelligent and well informed men, possessing a considerable knowledge of their religion; but the mass of the priesthood are profoundly ignorant of its first principles." (*Ibid* 279.)

I ask you, men of practical sense, what is the certain fate of a religion that has descended so low that its priests are regarded by the Behedin as fit only to be employed in menial services, such as bringing things to you from the bazaar, and doing household jobs of work. What is it? I put it to you. Do you suppose that such a dried corpse will be left long above ground by the fresh and critical minds you are educating at College? Nay, do you not see how they are already treating it; how they abstain from visiting your temples; how sullenly they "make kusti," and go through their other daily ceremonies; how they avoid as much as possible every attention to the prescribed ordinances; how they are gathering in clubs to drink pegs and play cards; how they are defiling themselves by evil associations, smoking in secret, and some even openly, and prating glibly the most sceptical sophistries they have read in European books, written by deluded modern theorists? Yes,—the cloud gathers over the fire altar, the once fragrant wood of Truth is wet with the deadly dews of doubt, a pestilential vapour fills the Átash Behrám, and unless some Regenarator is raised up among you, the name of Zaratusht may, before many generations, be known only as that of the Founder of an extinct faith. . . . . .

In his Preface to the translation of the *Vendidad*, the learned Dr. Darmesteter (vol. iv. of *The Sacred Books of the East*, edited by Professor F. Max Müller) says, "The key to the *Avesta* is not the Pahlavi, but the Vedas. The Avesta and the Vedas are two echoes of one and the same voice, the reflex of one and the same thought: the Vedas,

* Not before he learns the true meaning of his own name, and strives once more to become worthy of it. How many among the modern priests know that their title of Mobed or "*Mog*bed comes from *Mag*, a word used by the prophet Zeremiah to designate a Babylonian Initiate, which, in its turn, is an abbreviation of Maginsiah—the great and wise? "Maghistom" was once the title of Zoroaster's highest disciples, and the synonym of wisdom. Speaking of them Cicero says: *Sapientium et doctorum genus magorum habebatur in Persis.*

therefore, are both the best lexicon and the best commentary to the Avesta" (p. xxvi,) This he defines as the extreme view of the Vedic scholars, and while personally he does not subscribe to them entirely, he yet holds that we cannot perfectly comprehend the Avesta without utilising the discoveries of the Vedic pandits. But neither Darmesteter, nor Anquetil Duperron, nor Haug, nor Spiegel, nor Sir William Jones, nor Rapp (whose work has been so perfectly translated into English by your eminent Parsi scholar, Mr. K. R. Cama), nor Koth nor any philological critic whose works I have read, has named the true key to Zaratushta's doctrine. For it, we must not search among the dry bones of words. No, it hangs within the door of the *Kabala*—the Chaldean secret volume, where under the mask of symbols and misleading phrases, it is kept for the use of the pure searcher after arcane knowledge. The entire system of ceremonial purifications, which in itself is so perfect that a modern Parsi—a friend of mine—has remarked that Zoroaster was the best of Health Officers—is, as it seems to me, typical of the moral purification required of him who would either, while living, attain the Magian's knowledge of hidden laws of nature and his power to wield them for good purposes, or, after a well-ordered life, to attain by degrees to the state of spiritual beatitude, called *Moksha* by the Hindus and *Nirvana* by the Buddhists. The defilements by touch of various objects that you are warned against, are not visible defilements, like that of the person by contact with filth, but psychic defilements, through the influence of their bad magnetic aura—a subtle influence proceeding from certain living organisms and inert substances,—which is antipathetic to development as an adept. If you will compare your books with the Yoga Sutras of the Hindus, and the Tripitikas of the Buddhists, you will see that each exact for the student and practitioner of Occult Science, a place, an atmosphere, and surroundings that are perfectly pure. Thus the Magus (or Yozdathraigur), the Yogi and the Arahat all retire, either to the innermost or topmost chambers of a temple, where no stranger is permitted to enter (bringing his impure magnetism with him), to the heart of a forest, a secluded cave, or a mountain height. In the tower of Belus at Babylon, virgin seeresses gazed into magical mirrors and aërolites, to see their prophetic visions; the Yogi retires to his subterranean *guha*, or to the jungle fastnesses; and the Chinese books tell us that the "Great Nachus" of the sacred doctrine dwell in the "Snowy Range of the Himavât." The books alleged to have been inspired by God, or by him or his angels delivered to man, have always, I believe, been delivered on mountains. Zaratusht got the Avesta on Ushidarinna, a mountain by the river Daraga (Vendidad xlix.); Moses received the tables of the Law on Mount Sinai (Exodus xxxiv.); Mahommed was given the Koran on Mount Hara (Am. Cyc. vol. xi, 612); and the

Hindu Rishis lived in the Himalayas. Sakya Muni left no inspired books but, although he received the illumination of the Buddhaship in the plains, under a Boa-tree, he had prepared himself by years of austerities in the mountains near Rajagrihá. The obstructive power of foul human, animal, vegetable, and even mineral auras, or magnetisms, has always been understood by occult students, from the remotest times. This is the true reason why none but initiated and consecrated priests have ever been allowed to step within the precincts of the holiest places. The custom is not at all the offspring of any feeling of selfish exclusiveness, but based upon known psycho-physiological laws. Even the modern spiritualists and mesmerists know this; and the latter, at least, carefully avoid "mixing magnetisms," which always hurts a sensitive subject. All nature is a compound of conflicting, hence counterbalancing and equilibrating forces. Without this there could be no such thing as stability. Is it not the contest of the centrifugal and the centripetal attractions that keeps our earth and every other orb of heaven revolving in its orbit? The law of the Universe is a distinct Dualism while the creative energy is at work, and of a compound Unism when at rest. And the personification of these opposing powers by Zaratusht was but the perfectly scientific and philosophical statement of a profound truth. The secret laws of this war of forces are taught in the Chaldean Kabala. Every neophyte who sets himself to study for initiation is taught these secrets, and he is made to prove them by his own experiments, step by step, as his powers and knowledge increase. Zoroastrianism has two sides—the open, or patent, and the concealed, or secret. Born out of the mind of a Bactrian seer, it partakes of the nature of the primitive Iranian national religion and of the near spirituality that was poured into it, from the source of all truth, through the superb lens of Zoroaster's mind.

The Parsis have been charged with being worshippers of the visible fire. This is wholly false. They face the fire, as also they do the sun and the sea, because in them they picture to themselves the Hidden Light of Lights, source of all Life, to which they give the name of Hormazd. How well and how beautifully is this expressed in the writings of Robert Fludd, the English mystic of the 17th century (see Hargreave Jennings' *The Rosicrucians*. p. 69 *et seq*) "Regard Fire, then, with other eyes than with those soulless, incurious ones with which thou hast looked upon it as the most ordinary thing. Thou hast forgotten what it is—or rather thou hast never known. Chemists are silent about it * * * Philosophers talk of it as anatomists discourse of the constitution (or the parts) of the human body * * *. It is made for man and this world, and it is greatly like him—that is, *mean*, they would add * * * But is this all? Is this the sum of that casketed lamp of the human body?—

thine own body, thou unthinking world's machine—thou man? Or, in the fabric of this clay lamp [what a beautiful simile!] burneth there not a Light? Describe that, ye Doctors of Physics! * * * Note the goings of the Fire * * * Think that this thing is bound up in matter chains. Think that He is outside of all things, and deep in the inside of all things; and that thou and thy world are only the *thing between*: and that outside and inside are both identical, couldst thou understand the supernatural truths! Reverence Fire (for its meaning) and tremble at it * * * Avert the face from it, as the Magi turned, dreading, and (as the Symbol) bowed askance * * * Wonder no longer then if, rejected so long as an idolatry, the ancient Persians, and their Masters, the Magi—concluding that they saw 'All' in this supernaturally magnificent element—fell down and worshipped it; making of it the visible representation of the very truest, but yet, in man's speculation, and in his philosophies—nay, in his commonest reason—impossible God."

And, mind you, this is the language, not of a Parsi or one of your faith, but of an English scholar who followed the shining path marked out by the Chaldean Magi, and obtained, like them, the true meaning of your Mysteries. *Occult Science is the Vindication of Zoroastrianism, and there is none other*. Modern physical Science is blind herself to spiritual laws and spiritual phenomena. She cannot guide, being herself in need of a helping hand—the hand of the Occultist and the Hierophant Chaldean sage.

Have you thought *why* the Fire is kept ever burning on your altars? Why is it? Why may not the priest suffer it to go out and re-kindle it again each morning Ah! there is a great secret hidden. And why must the flames of one thousand different fires be collected—from the smithy, the burning kiln, the funeral pyre, the gold-smith's furnace, and every other imaginable source. Why? because this spiritual element of Fire pervades all nature, is its life and soul, is the cause of the motion of its molecules which produces the phenomenon of physical heat. And the fires from all these thousand hearths are collected, like so many fragments of the universal life, into one sacrificial blaze which shall be as perfectly as possible the complete and collective type of the light of Hormazd. See the precautions taken to gather only the spirit or quintessence, as it were, of these separate flames. The priest takes not the crude coals from the various hearths and furnaces and pits; but at each flame he lights a bit of sulphur, a ball of cotton, or some other inflammable substance; from this secondary blaze he ignites a second quantity of fuel; from this a third; from the third a fourth, and so on: taking in some cases a ninth, in others a twentieth flame, until the first grossness of the defilement of the fire in the base use to which it was put has been purged, and only the purest essence remains. Then only is it fit to be placed upon the altar of Hormazd. And even then the flame is not ready to be the type of that Eternal Brightness: it is as yet but a body of earthly flame, a body which lacks its noblest soul. When your forefathers gathered at Sanján to light the fire for the Indian exiles, the only Dastur Darab, who had come with them from Persia, gathered his people and the strangers of the country about him in the jungle. Upon a stone block the dried sandlewood was laid. Four priests stood at the four cardinal points. The Gathas are intoned, the priests bow their faces in reverential awe. The Dastur raises his eyes to heaven, he recites the mystical words of power: lo! the fire from the upper world of space descends, and with its silvery tongues laps round the fragrant wood, which bursts into a blaze. This is the missing spirit evoked by the adept Prometheus. When *this* is added to the thousand other dancing flames the Symbol is perfected, and the face of Hormazd shines before his worshippers. Lighted thus at Sanján, that historic fire has been kept alive for more than seven hnndred years, and until another Darab appears among you to draw the flames of the ambient ether upon your altar, let it be fed continuously.

This ancient art of drawing fire from heaven was taught in the Samothracian and Kabiric mysteries. Numa who introduced the Vestal mysteries into Rome, thus kindled a fire which was under the care of consecrated Vestal Virgins, whose duty it was, under penalty of death for neglect, to constantly maintain it. It was, as Schweigger shows, the Hermes fire, the Elmes fire of the ancient Germans; the lightning of Cybele; the torch of Apollo; the fire of Pan's altar; the fire flame of Pluto's helm; the inextinguishable fire in the temple of the Grecian Athene, on the Acropolis of Athens; and the mystical fires of many different worships and symbols. The Occult Science, of which I spoke, was shared by the initiates of the Sacred Science all over the ancient world. The knowledge was first gained in Chaldea, and was thence spread through Greece to more Western and Northern countries. Even to-day the Fire-Cult survives among the rude Indian tribes of Arizona—a far Western portion of my native America. Major Calhoun, of the U. S. Army, who commanded a surveying party sent out by our Government, told me that in that remote corner of the world, and among those rude people, he found them keeping alight their Sacred Fire in their *teocalis*, or holy enclosures. Every morning their priests go out, dressed in the sacerdotal robes of their forefathers, to salute the rising sun, in the hopes that Montezuma, their promised Redeemer and Liberator, will appear. The time of his coming is not foretold, but from generation to generation they wait, and pray, and hope.

In her *Isis Unveiled,* Madam Blavatsky has shown us that this heavenly fire, however and whenever manifested, is a correlation of the Akasa, and that the art of the Magician and the Priest enables one to develop and attract it down. But to do this you must be absolutely pure—pure in body, in thought, in deed. And these are the three pillars upon which Zaratusht erected the stately edifice of his religion. I have always considered it as a great test of the merit of any religion that its essence can be compressed into a few words that a child can understand. Buddhism, with its noble comprehensiveness, was distilled by its Founder into seven words; Zoroastrianism is reduced to three—*Homutá, Aukhté, Vurushté.*

A Parsi gentleman, with whom I conversed the other day, explained the fact of your haviug no wonder working priests at present, by saying that none living was pure enough. He was right, and until you can find such a pure celebrant, your religion will never be again ensouled. An impure man who attempts the magical ceremonies is liable to be made mad or destroyed. This is a scientific necessity. The law of nature is, you know, that action and reaction are equal. If, therefore, the operator in the Mysteries propels from himself a current of will power directed against a certain object, and—either because of feebleness of will, or deviation caused by impure motives, he misses his mark, his current rebounds from the whole body of the Akasa (as the ball rebounds from the wall against which it is thrown to the thrower's hand) and reacts upon himself. We are told that they who did not know how to manage the miraculous fire in the Vestal and Kabiric mysteries "were destroyed by it, and were punished by the Gods" (Eunemoser. *Hist. of Magic,* II. 32). Pliny relates (*Histor. Nat.* xxviii., 2) that Tullus Hostilius had sought from the books of Numa "Jovem devocare a cœlo"; but as he did not correctly follow the rules of Numa, he was struck by the lightning This same rule applies equally to the attempt to use the black art unskilfully. The old English proverb says "Curses, like fowls, come home to roost," He who would use the powers of Sorcery, or Black Magic, is sure to be destroyed by them *first* or last. The old fables about sorcerers being carried off by the mocking "devils" whom, for a time, they had employed to gratify their unlawful desires, are all based upon fact. And, in Zoroastrianism, the Parsi is as carefully taught to eschew and fight against the powers of Ahriman, or the Evil Spirits of Darkness, as to cultivate intimacy with and win the protecting favour of the Ameshaspentas and Yazatas—the personified good principles of Nature. You will not find any of your European authorities speaking of these personifications with decent respect, any more than of the nature-gods of the Aryans. To their minds these are but the childish fancies of a florid

Persian or Aryan imagination, begotten in the infancy of our race. For a good reason too; not one of these spectacled pandits has the least practical reason to believe that there are such good and evil powers warring about us. But I am not afraid to say to them all in my individual, not official, capacity, that I *do* believe in them; nay, that I actually know they exist. And this is why you hear me, a Western man taught in a Western University and nursed on the traditions of modern civilization, say that Zaratushta knew more about nature than Tyndall does, more about the laws of Force than Balfour Stewart, more about the origin of species than Darwin or Haeckel, more about the human mind and its potentialities than Maudsley or Bain. And so did Buddha, and some other ancient proficients in Occult Science. Pshaw! Young man, of the Bombay University, when you have taken your degree, and learned all your professors can teach you, go to the hermit and the recluse of the jungle and ask *him* to prove to you where to begin your real study of the world into which you have been born! Your professors can make you learned but not wise, can teach you about the shell of Nature, but those silent and despised unravelers of the tangled web of existence, can evoke for you the soul that lurks within that husk. Three centuries before Christ the united kingdom of Persia and Media exercised a dominion extending over an area of three or four millions of square miles, and had a population of several hundred millions of people. And do you mean to tell me that the Zoroastrian religion could have dominated the minds of this enormous mass of people—nearly twice the present population of India—and could have also swayed the religious thought of the cultured Greeks and Romans, if it had not had a spiritual life in it that its poor remnant of to-day completely lacks? I tell you that if you could put that ancient life back into it, and if you had your Darabs and your Abads to show this ignorant age the proof of the reality of the old Chaldean wisdom, you would spread your religion all over the world. For the age is spiritually dying for want of a religion that can show just such signs, and for lack of them two crores of intelligent Western people have become Spiritualists and are following the lead of mediums. And not only your religion is soulless. Hinduism is so, Southern Buddhism is so, Judaism and Christianity are so likewise. We see following the Missionaries none of the "signs" that Jesus said should follow those who were really his disciples: they neither raise the dead, nor heal the sick, nor give sight to the blind, nor cast out devils, nor dare they drink any deadly thing in the faith that it will not harm them. There are a few true wonder-workers in our time, but they are among the Lamaists of Tibet, the Copts of Egypt, the Sufis and Dervishes of Arabia and other Mahomedan countries. The great body of the people, in all countries, are become so sensual, so avaricious, so materialistic and faithless, that their moral atmosphere is like a pestilential wind to the Yozdathraigur (those adepts whom we have made known to India under the name of BROTHERS.)

The meaning of your Haoma, you doubtless know. In the IXth Yagna of the Avesta, Haoma is spoken of both as a god—a Yazata—and the plant, or the juice of the plant, which is under his especial protection, and so is the *Soma* of the "Aitareya Brâmana."

"At the time of the morning-dawn came

1. Haoma to Zarathustra,
2. As he was purifying the fire and reciting the Gathas.
3. Zarathustra asked him : Who, O man, art thou ?
4. Thou, who appearest to me as the most beautiful in the whole corporeal world, endued with Thine own life, majestic and immortal ?
5. Then answered me Haoma, the pure, who is far from death.
6. Ask me, thou Pure one, make me ready for food."

Thus in the same line, is Haoma spoken of in his personified form and as a plant to be prepared for food.

Further on he is described as

52. "Victorious, golden, with moist stalks."

This is the sacred Soma of the Aryans—by them also elevated into a deity. This is that wondrous juice which lifted the mind of him who quaffed it to the splendours of the higher heavens, and made him commune with the gods. It was not stupifying like opium, not maddening like the Indian hemp, but exhilarating, illuminating, the begetter of divine visions. It was given to the candidate in the Mysteries, and drunk with solemn ceremony by the Hierophant. Its ancient use is still kept in your memories by the mobeds drinking, in the Yagna ceremony, a decoction of dried Haoma stalks, that have been pounded with bits of pomegranate root in a mortar and afterwards had water thrice poured over them.

The Baresma twigs—among you represented by a bunch of brass wires !—are a reminiscence of the divining-rods anciently used by all practitioners of ceremonial magic. The rod or staff was also given to the fabled gods of Mythology. In the fifth book of the Odyssey, Jupiter in the council of the gods, bids Hermes go upon a certain mission, and the verse says—

Forth sped he * * * * * *
Then taking his staff, with which he the eyelids of mortals
Closes at will, and the sleeper, at will, reawakens."

The rod of Hermes was a magic-staff ; so was that of Æsculapios, the healing wand that had power over disease. The Bible has many references to the magic-rod, notably, in the story of the contest of Moses with the Egyptian Magicians in the presence of Pharaoh, in that of the magical bidding of Aaron's rod, the laying of Elisha's staff on the face of the dead Shunamite boy, &c. The Hindu gossein of our day carries with him a bamboo rod having seven knots or joints, that has been given to him by his Guru and contains the concentrated magnetic will-power of the Guru. All magic-rods should be hollow, that the magnetic power may be stored in them. In the Yagna II., note that the Priest, holding the Baresma rods in his hand, repeats constantly the words "I wish"—properly, I will—so and so. By the ceremony of consecration of the sacred twigs a magical power had been imparted to them, and with the help of this to fortify his own will-force, the celebrant seeks the attainment of his several good desires, the heavenly Fire, the good spirits, all good influences throughout the several Kingdoms of Nature, and the law or WORD. In the middle ages of Europe, divining-rods were in general use, not only to discover subterranean waters and springs, and veins of metal, but also fugitive thieves and murderers. I could devote an entire lecture to this subject and prove to you that this phenomenon is a strictly scientific one In Baring-Gould's *Curious Myths of the Middle Ages* will be found highly interesting accounts of these trials of the mystical power of the rods which time forbids my quoting. At this day the rods are employed to discover springs, and the Cornish miners carry sprigs of hazel or other wood in their caps. The author of the work named, while ascribing the strange results he is obliged to record principally to the imagination, is yet constrained to add that "The powers of Nature are so mysterious and inscrutable that we must be cautious in limiting them, under abnormal conditions, to the ordinary laws of expereince." And in this he is backed up by the experience of many generations of witnesses, in many different countries.

We have mentioned the invocation of the divine WORD or Name in the Yagna. All the ancient authorities affirm that there is a certain Word of power by pronouncing which the adept subjugates all the forces of Nature to his will. It is mentioned by many authors. One of the latest is the author of a book called *Rabbi Jeshua*, who speaking of Jesus, says, "He had perhaps endeavoured to employ magic arts, and to bewitch the council by invocation of the Name through which all incantations were rendered effective" (p. 143.) Among the Aryans the Agnihotra priest used to prepare the sacrificial wood and, upon reciting the appropriate Mantra, the heavenly fire of Agni would descend and kindle it. In the Avesta, Zaratusht smites the fiends with the spiritual power of the word (Darmesteter, lxxvii.) It represents him as a saint-militant repelling force by force. In Fargard XI. Zarathushtra asks Ahurt

Mazda how he shall purge the house, the fire, the water, the earth, the cow, the tree, the faithful man and woman, the stars, the moon, the sun, the boundless light, and all good things. Ahura Mazda answers :—

> "Thus shalt chant the *cleansing words* and the house shall be clean, clean shall be the fire, &c. &c.
>
> "So thou shalt say these fiend-smiting and most-healing words thou shalt chant the Ahura Vairya five times &c."

Then are given various words to employ for different acts of cleaning. But *the* WORD, the one most potent—the name which, so says Proclus in his treatise upon the Chaldean Oracles—" rushes into the infinite worlds," is not written there.* Nor can it be written, nor is it ever pronounced above the breath, nor, indeed, is its nature known except to the highest initiates. The efficacy of all words used as charms and spells lies in what the Aryans call the Vach, a certain latent power resident in Akasa. Physically, we may describe it as the power to set up certain measured vibrations, not in the grosser atmospheric particles whose undulations beget light, sound, heat and electricity, but in the latent spiritual principle or Force—about the nature of which modern Science knows scarcely anything. No words whatever have the slightest efficacy unless uttered by one who is perfectly free from all weakening doubt or hesitancy, is for the moment wholly absorbed in the thought of uttering them, and has a cultivated power of will which makes him send out from himself a conquering impulse. Spoken prayer is, in fact, an incantation, and when spoken by the " heart," as well as by the lips, has a power to attract good and repel bad influences. But to patter off prayers so many times a day while your thoughts are roving over your landed estates, fumbling your money-bags, or straying away among any other wordly things, is but mere waste of breath. The Bible says, " the prayer of the righteous availeth much"; and so it does. There is the case of George Mueller, of Bath, England, who for thirty years has supported the entire expenses of his orphanage—now a very large institution of charity—by the voluntary gifts of unknown passers-by at the door who drop into his charity-boxes *the exact sum he prays for* to meet the day's necessities. History does not contain a more curious or striking example than this. This man prays with such faith and fervency, his motives are so pure, his labours so beneficient, that he attracts to him all the good influences of Nature, although he knows neither the " Ahura Vairya," nor the Aryan Mantras, nor the Buddhistic Pirit. Use what words you may, if the heart is clean, the thought intense, and

---

* Though properly the WORD or the NAME is neither a word nor a name in the sense we give it.

the will concentrated, the powers of Nature will come at your bidding and be your slaves. Says tho *Dabistan* (p. 2) :—

> " Having the heart in the body full of thy remembrance, the novice, as well as the adept, in *contemplation*
>
> " Becomes a supreme king of beatitude, and the throne of the kingdom of gladness.
>
> " Whatever road I took, it joined the street which leads to Thee ;
>
> " The desire to know thy being is also the life of the meditators ;
>
> " He who found that there is nothing but Thee, has found Thee, has found the *final* knowledge ;
>
> " The mobed is the teacher of thy truth, and the world a school."

But this mobed was not a mere errand-runner, or droner of Gathas perfunctorily without understanding a word he was saying, but a real mobed. So high an ideal of human perfectibility had he to live up to, Cambyses is said to have commanded the execution of a priest who had allowed himself to be bribed, and had his skin stretched over the chair in which his son and successor sat in his judicial capacity. *(Hist Magic.* 1., 2.) " Mobed" is derived from Mogbed—from the Persian *Mog*, and means a true priest. Ennemoser truly says that the renowned wisdom of the Magi in Persia, Media and the neighbouring countries, " contained also the secret teachings of philosophy and the sciences, which were only communicated to priests, who were regarded as mediators between God and Man, and as such, and *on account of their knowledge*, were highly respected." *(Ibid.)* The priests of a people are exactly what the people require them to be. Remember that, friends, and blame yourselves only for the state of religion among you. You have just what you are entitled to. If you yourselves were more pure, more spiritual-minded, more religious, your priesthood would be so. You are merchants, not idolaters, but—as Prof. Monier Williams pithily remarks in the *Nineteenth Century* (March 1881)—worshippers of the solid rupee. The genuine Parsi, he says, " turns with disgust from the hideous idolatry practised by his Hindu fellow-subjects. He offers no homage to blocks of wood and stone, to monstrous many-headed images, grotesque symbols of good luck, or four armed deities of fortune. But he bows down before the silver image which Victoria, the Empress of India, has set up in her Indian dominions "

And this, according to Zoroastrianism, is a crime as great. In his ecstatic vision of the symbolical scenes shown him by the angel Serosh-izad for the warning and encouragement of his people, Ardai Viraf, the purest of Magian priest at the court of Ardeshir Babagan, saw the pitiable state to which the soul of a covetous money hoarder is reduced after death. The poor wretch, penniless—since he could take not a *direin* with him—his heart buried with his savagely loved treasures, his once pure nature corrupted and deformed—moved the seer to profoundest pity. "I saw it," says he, "creep along in fear and trembling, and presently a wind came sweeping along, loaded with the most pestilential vapours even as it were from the boundaries of hell * * * In the midst of this wind appeared a form of the most demoniacal appearance * * *" The terrified soul attempts to escape but in vain; the awful vengeful shape by voice and power roots him to the spot. He enquires in trembling accents whom it may be, and is answered, "I am your genius [that is, his spiritual counterpart and now his mastering destiny] and have become thus deformed by your crimes (whilst you were innocent I was handsome) * * You have laid in no provisions for this long journey; you were rich, but you did no good with your riches * *; and not only did no good yourself, but prevented, by your evil example, those whose inclinations led them to do good; and you have often mentally said, 'When is the day of judgment? To me it will never arrive.'" (*Ardai Viraf Nameh*, by Capt. J. A. Pope, p. 56.) Say it is a vision, if you will, yet nevertheless it mirrors an awful truth. The worship of the silver image of Victoria on the rupee is even more degrading than the Hindu's worship of Ganesha or Hari; for he, at least, is animated by a pious thought, whereas the greedy money-getter is but defiling himself with the filth of selfishness.

The Parsi community is already half-way along the road to apostacy. Gone is the fiery enthusiasm that made your forefathers give up everything they prized rather than repudiate their faith; that supported them during a whole century in the sterile mountains of Khorasan or the outlying deserts; that comforted them in their exile at Sanjan, and gave them hope after the battle with their hereditary enemy Aluf Khan. Formerly, it was Religion first and Rupee last; now it is Rupee first and everything else after it. See, I, a stranger, point with one finger to your palatial bungalows, your gorgeous equipages, and your ostentatious annual squandering of twelve lakhs of money at festivals; with the other to the wretched subscriptions of Rs. 16,000 towards the support of the Rahanu Mai Mazdiasni Sabha—a good society for the promotion of your religion among your own children, and of Rs. 10,000 to the orthodox Parsi Society of Khetwady! The proverb says, "Figures cannot lie," and in this instance they do not. If I wanted the best test to apply to your real religious zeal, I should look at the sum of your expenditures for vain show and sensual enjoyment, as compared with what you do for the maintenance of your religion in its purity, and to the sort of conduct you tolerate in your priests. That is the mirror that impartial justice holds up before you; behold your own image, and converse with conscience in your private moments! What but conscience is personified in the "maid, of divine beauty or fiendish ugliness," according as the soul that approaches the Chinvad bridge was good or bad in life? (Yasht. XXII.)

> She, "the well-shapen, strong and tall-formed maid, with the dogs at her sides, one who *can distinguish* * * * and is of *high understanding*." (Avesta, Fargard XIX)?

You have asked me to tell you about the spirit of your religion. I have only the truth to tell—the exact truth, without fear or favour. And I repeat, you have already set money in the niche of faith; it only remains for you to throw the latter out of doors. For hypocrisy will not last for ever. Men weary of paying even lip-service to a religion they no longer respect. You may deceive yourselves, you cannot deceive that maiden at the bridge. Let three or four more generations of sceptics be passed through the educational mint of the College, ; and let the teaching of your religion be neglected as it now is; and the time will have come when it will be only the occasional brave heart that will dare call himself a Mazdiasnian. Let that stand as a prophecy if you choose: it *is* one, and it is based upon the experience of the human race. A black page will it be indeed, in the record of human events, when the last vestiges of the once splendid faith of Zarathushta shall be blotted from it, the last spark of the heavenly fire that shone from the Chaldean watch-towers of the sages be extinguished. And the more so, when that last extinction shall be caused, not by the sword of tyranny, nor by the crafty scheming of civil administrators, but by the beastly worldliness of its own hereditary custodians; those to whom the lighted torch had been handed down through the ages, and who dropped it into the quenching black waters of materialism.

Time fails me to enter into detailed explanation of the Zoroastrian symbols as perhaps I might—though I certainly am not able to do the subject full justice. The *sutra* and *kusti* with which you invest your children at the age of six years and three months have, of course, a magical significance. They pass through the hands of the Dastur, who, as we have seen, was formerly an initiate, and he imparted to them magnetic properties which converted them into talismans against evil influences. After that a set formula of prayers and incantations is regularly prescribed for the whole life. The wearer's thoughts are directed towards the talismanic objects constantly, and when faith is present, his or her will power, or magnetic aura, is at such times infused into them. This is the secret of all talismans; the object worn, whatever it may be, need have no innate protective property, for that can be given to any rag, or stone, or bit of paper, by an adept. Those of you who have read the Christian bible will remember that from the body of Paul, the Apostle, "were brought unto the sick handkerchiefs or aprons, and the diseases departed from them, and *the evil spirits went out of them.*" (Acts XIX., 12.) In the Ormazd-Yasht of the Khordah-Avesta (25), it is written "by day and night, standing or sitting, grit with the Aiwyâonhana (*kusti*) or drawing off the Aiwyâonhana.

> "Going forwards out of the house, going forwards out of the confideracy, going forwards out of the region, coming into a region,
>
> "Such a man the points of the Drukhs-souled, proceeding from Aêshma, will not injure in that day or that night, not the slings, not the arrows, not knives, not clubs; the missiles will not penetrate (and) he be injured" (Haug's *Avesta* p. 24, Khordah-Avesta, Eng. Ed. of 1864). Similar protective talismans are given by every adept to each new pupil.

The use of Nirang for libations and ablutions is a survival of very ancient—probably pre-Iranian—mythic conceptions. There is nothing in the fluid itself of a disinfectant or purificatory character, but a magical property is given to it by ceremonial magical formulas, as a glass of common water may be converted into a valuable medicine by a mesmerizer by his holding it in his left hand and making circular passes over it with his right. The subject is treated in Darwesteter's Introduction to the Vendidad (lxxxviii.) "The storm floods that cleanse the sky of the dark fiends in it were described in a class of myths as the urine of a gigantic animal in the heavens. As the floods from the bull above drive away the fiend from the god, so they do from man here below, they make him 'free from the death-demon' (frânasu), and the death fiend flees away hellwards, pursued by the fiend-smiting spell: 'Perish thou, O Drug . . . never more to give over to Death the living world of the good spirit!'" It may be that there is a more valid reason for the use of Nirang, but I have not yet discovered it. That an occult property *is* imparted to the fluid by the ceremonial is clear, since, if it be exposed to certain influences not in themselves putrefactive it will speedily become putrid; while, on the other hand, it may be kept for years in a fresh condition without the admixture of antiseptic substances, and notwithstanding its occasional exposure to the air, if certain ceremonial rules be followed (of course, I have this from Parsi friends and not from my own observation: I would not express an unqualified opinion before investigating the subject). I recommend some Parsi chemist to analyze specimens of different ages, especially to determine the relative quantities of nitrogenous constituents.

When Professor Monier Williams vents his Oxonian scorn upon the ceremonies of the Parsis, he thereby only provokes the pity of such as have looked deeper than he into the meaning of ancient symbolism. "Here and there," says he, "lofty conceptions of the Deity, deep philosophical thoughts, and a pure morality are discoverable in the Avesta like green spots in the desert; *but they are more than neutralised by the silly puerilities and degrading superstitious ideas* which crop up as plentifully in its pages as thorns and thistles in a wilderness of sand." (XIXth Century Mag. Jan. 1881, p. 176). Mr. Joseph Cook, the other day, in this Hall, said the same. The good portions of the Vedas were so few as compared with the trashy residuum, that he likened them to the fabled jewel in the head of a filthy toad! It is really very kind of these white pandits to admit that there is anything whatever except rottenness and puerility in the old religions. Give each a statue!

In what has been said I have, you must remember, been speaking from the standpoint of a Parsi. I have tried to sink my personality and my personal religious preferences for the moment, and put myself in your place. That is the cardinal policy of the Theosophical Society. It has itself no sectarian basis, but its motto is the Universal Brotherhood of man. It was organized to bring to light the long buried truths of not one, but all the world's Archaic religions. Its members are of all respectable castes, all faiths and races. It has many intelligent Parsis among them. For their sake and that of their co-religionists this lecture has been given. I have tried most earnestly to induce one of them or some other Parsi to come forward, and show you that no religion has profounder truths, deeper spiritual truths, concealed under its familiar mask, than yours. That I am the incompetent, though willing, spokesman for the ancient Yozdathraigurs is your fault, not mine. If I have spoken truth, if I have suggested new thoughts, if I have given any encouragement to the pious or pleasure to the learned, my reward is ample.

"Zathâ ahû Saîryô:—The riches of Vohumanô shall be given to him who works in this world for Mazda * * *" is the promise of the Avesta (Fargard XXI.) Bear it in mind, ye Mazdiasnians, and remember the maiden and her dogs by the Chinvat bridge. I say this especially to my Parsi brothers in our Society, for I have the right to speak to them as an elder to his junior. As Parsis they have a paramount duty to their co-religionists, who are retrograding morally for want of the pure light. As Theosophists their interest embraces all their fellow-men of whatever creed. For we read in one of the most valuable of all books for the thoughtful Parsi—the *Datrotan*, or *School of Manners*:

"The world is a book full of knowledge and of justice,
The binder of which book is destiny, and the binding the beginning and the end;
The future of it is the law, and the leaves are the religious persuasions. * *"

For three years we have been preaching this idea of mutual toleration and Universal Brotherhood here in Bombay. Some have listened but more have turned the deaf ear. Nay they have done worse—they have spread lies and calumnies about us, until we were made to appear to you in false light. But the tide is turning at last, and public sympathy is slowly setting in our favour. It has been a dark night for us; it is now sunrise If you can see a good motive behind us, and an honest purpose to do good by spreading truth, will you not join us as you have other societies, and help to make us strong? We can perhaps be of service in aiding you to learn something more than you know about the spirit of Zoroastrianism. As I said before there are many important secrets to be extracted from ancient MSS. in Armenia. Perhaps they may be got at if you will join together and send some thoroughly competent Parsi scholars to make the search, in co-operation with the Tiflis Archæological Society. See how the Christians have organised a Palestine Exploration Society to search for anything in the shape of proof that can be found to corroborate their Bible. For years they have kept engineers and archæologists at work. Is your religion less important to you? Or do you mean to sit on your guineas until the last old MS. has been burned to kindle Armenian fires, or torn to wrap medicines and sweets in, as I have seen bibles utilised in India and Ceylon by heathen *boras*? One of our members (see *Theosophist* for July 1881) went over the most important ground a few months ago. At the monastery of Soorb Ovanness in Armenia there were in 1877 three superannuated priests: now there remains but one. The "library of books and old manuscripts heaped up as waste paper in every corner of the pillar-cells, tempting no Kurd, are scattered over the rooms." And he says that "For the consideration of a dagger and a few silver *abazes* I got several precious manuscripts from him"—the old priest. Now does not this suggest to you that through the friendly intermediation of our Society, and the help of Madame Blavatsky, you may be able to secure exceptional advantages in the matter of archæological and philological research connected with Zoroastrianism? We do not ask you to join us for our benefit, but for your own. I have thrown out the idea; act upon it or not as you choose. Beaten with Parsi children's shoes ought the Parsi to be that next gives a gaudy nautch or wedding *tamasha* unless he has previously subscribed as liberally as his means allow towards a fund for the promotion of his religion.

At the fifth annual meeting (in September last of the Archæological Society of Tiflis, Caucasus) a very valuable report was made by Count Ouvarof, the Nestor of Russian Archæologists and Founder of the Society, upon the recent explorations and discoveries in the districts formerly inhabited by the Mazdiasnians. This Caucasian Viceroyalty was once the heart of ancient Parsiism. It includes Armenia, Derbent, Osetiya, and the land of the Khabardines, besides other countries that should be explored by your agents. Among other curious facts brought to light was that the old Mazdiasnians had two kinds of burial structures—one for use in the hot weather, the other for the winter season. They found proofs that your faith was not less than 11,000 years old: which bears rather hard upon those authors (among them your own Mr. Dosabhoy Framjee) who date its birth from the time of the appearance, in the 6th century B. C., of a certain Zarathushta at the court of Darius Hystaspes. The learned Count Ouvarof says that the Ossetines, a warlike mountain tribe of half Christianized Mahomedans, formerly Masdiasnians, to this day bring a dog to look at the corpse before sepulture. In Tibet, too, towards the Northern border, the corpse is exposed to the view of a dog and a *djak*—a bird of prey, perhaps of the vulture species. Throughout Tibet the corpses of all but Lamas of the higher grades are given to be eaten by a breed of sacred dogs bred for the purpose. The Lamas above referred to are either burned or embalmed and entombed in a sitting posture. I have been unable to learn from any Parsi, even the most intelligent whom I have consulted with, what is the explanation of this ancient custom of exposing the corpse to inspection by dogs. Upon enquiry in another direction, however, I am told that its original purpose was to show the dog that here was food for him, and that immediately after seeing it, the animal would rush off to its fellows and bring a whole pack to share in the repast. His instinct (or shall we not rather say his mesmeric sensitiveness) told him when life had actually quit the cadaver. This seems to me a very clear and sensible explanation of a long-veiled practice. Moreover, I read in Mr. K. R. Cama's translation of Prof. Duncker's *Geschichte des Altertums*, that in the time of Agathias, the Persians carried their dead outside the gates of a town and exposed them to be eaten by dogs and birds: regarding it as a most clear proof that the deceased had led an impure life if the corpse was not directly consumed. What more likely, then, than that the relatives showed the corpse to the one or two dogs at the house, so that by the time the procession should reach the place of exposure, the pack would be there ready to complete their work? As for the theory that the glance of a dog frightens away the Drukhs-Naçu, it appears to be a mere hypothesis. In the Secret Doctrine it is taught that the most fatal current in the ether of space (*Akasa*) sets in from the North. This is the current of terrestrial magnetism. Experience has also warned mesmeric practitioners to make their subject sit with his back to the North and feet towards the South. The Hindus lay their dead in the same direction. Baron Reichenbach also discovered that his odylic sensitives could not sleep East and West, but would instinctively turn North and South, even when their beds had been purposely placed in the transverse way. In Occult Science the North is the habitat of the worst "elemental spirits" (a very clumsy name for the occult forces of nature), and in Eliphas Levi's books (*Dogme et Ritnel de la Haute Magie*, and others) are given instructions to guard against their irruption. If a corpse be traversed by this boreal current, the latter takes up certain psychically bad influences, which, if absorbed by the living who are sensitive to them, have a very evil effect. The Drukhs-Naçu is this boreal current, and contains in itself a number of varieties of malignant influences. This, I am told, is the Secret Doctrine.

I told you in commencing that this subject of the spirit of Zoroastrianism is limitless. In consulting my authorities I have been perplexed to choose from the abundance of material, rather than troubled by any lack of it. There are a few more facts that I would like to mention before closing.

Abul Pharaj, in the *Book of Dynasties* (p. 54) states that Zarathusht taught the Persians the manifestation of the *Wisdom* (the Lord's Anointed Son, or Logos, the Persian "Honover"). This is the living manifested word of Deific Wisdom. He predicted that a Virgin should conceive immaculately, and that at the birth of that future messenger a six-pointed star would appear, and shine at noonday. In its centre would appear the figure of a Virgin. This six-pointed star you see engraved on the seal of the Theosophical Society. In the Kabalat the Virgin is the Astral Light or Akasa, and the six-pointed star the emblem of the Macrocosm. The Logos, or Sosiosh to be born, means the secret konwledge or science which reveals the "Wisdom of God." Into the hand of the Prophet Messenger Zarathusht were delivered many gifts. When filling the censer with *fire from the sacred altar*, as the mobed did in ancient days, the act was symbolical of *imparting to the worshippers*, the knowledge of divine truth. In the '*Gita*,' Krishna informs Arjun that God is in the fire of the altar. "I am the Fire ; I am the Victim." The Flamens, or Etruscan priests, were so called because they were supposed to be illuminated by the *tongues of Fire* (Holy Ghost) and the Christians took the hint—(*Acts* II). The scarlet robe of the Roman Catholic cardinal symbolizes the heavenly Fire. In an ancient Irish MS. Zarathusht is called *Airgiod-Lamh* or he of the Golden Hand—the hand which received and scattered celestical Fire (Ousley's *Oriental Collections* I., 303). He is also called Mogh Nuadhat, the Magus of the New Ordinance, or dispensation. Zarathusht was one of the first reformers who taught to the people a portion of that which he had learned at his initiation, viz., the six periods or *Gâhambârs* in the successive evolution of the world. The first is *Midyuzeram*, that in which the heavenly canopy was formed; the second *Mid-yirshân* in which the collected moisture formed the steamy clouds from which the waters were finally precipitated; the third, *Piti-shahim*, when the earths became consolidated out of primeval cosmic atoms; the fourth, *Iyaseram*, in which earth gave birth to vegetation; the fifth *Midiyarim*, when the latter slowly evoluted into animal life; the sixth, *Hamespita-midan*, when the lower animals culminated in man. The seventh period—to come at the end of a certain cycle—is prefigured in the promised coming of the Persian Messiah, seated on a horse; *i. e.* the sun of our solar system will be extinguished and the "Pralaya," will begin. In the Christian *Apocalypse* of St. John you will find the Persian symbolical prophecy closely copied; and the Aryan Hindu awaits the coming of his Kalanki Avatar when the celestial White Horse will come in the heavens, bestridden by Vishnu. The horses of the sun figure in all other religions.

There exists among the Persian Parsis a volume older than the present Zoroastrian writings. Its title is *Gjavidân Chrad*, or Eternal Wisdom. It is a work on the practical philosophy of Magic, with natural explanations. Hyde mentions it in his preface to the *Religo Veterum Persarum*. The four Zoroastrian *Ages* are the four races of men—the Black, the Russet, the Yellow, the White. The four castes of Manu are alleged to have typified this, and the Chinese show the same idea in their four orders of priests clothed in black, red, yellow, and white robes. St. John sees these same colours in the symbolic horses of his Revelation. Speaking of Zoroaster, whom he admits to have possessed all the sciences and philosophy then known in the world, the Rev. Oliver gives an account of the cave temple of which so much is said in Zoroastrian literature; "Zoroaster," he writes, "retired to a *circular* cave or grotto in the mountains of Bokhara, which he ornamented with a profusion of symbolical and astronomical decorations, consecrating it to Methr-Az. . . . Here the sun was represented by a splendid gem . . . in a conspicuous part of the roof . . . and the four ages of the world were represented by so many gloves of gold, silver, brass, and iron." (*History of Initiation*, p. 9.)

And now, gentlemen—orthodox and heterodox—leaders among the Parsi community—a word with you on practical matters before we part. In three days more I shall leave Bombay on a long journey and the accidents of travel, to which we are all liable, may prevent my ever addresing you again. I pray you, therefore, to listen to what a sincere friend has to say : a friend who is none the less one in that he never asked you for a pice of your money for himself and never will.

I have lived among you for three years. During this whole time I have been associating on terms of confidential intimacy with some of your most intelligent young men. I have admitted them, and in some cases their wives with them, into our Society. Thus I have perhaps had exceptional opportunities to learn the real state of your people and religion. I find both in sore need of an organized, unselfish and persistent effort among yourselves. Your people look up to you as their best advisers, the mobeds respect your influence and court your favour. You have it in your power to do a world of good. Will you do it? You now spend annually from twelve to fifteen lakhs of rupees upon stupid tamashas—that do not belong to your own religion at all; that give you no real pleasure; that crush many poorer than you to the very ground with debt; that defile your own natures with disgusting pride and conceit; that encourage intemperate habits in the young; and that weaken pious inclinations. The burden upon the community is so sore, and common sense of your best men so revolts at them, that years ago you would have returned to the simpler pleasures of your forefathers, but that you lacked the moral courage to combine. A reform like this is never to be effected alone; the leaders must combine. Take two of the fifteen lakhs you now worse than waste and put it aside as a fund for the promotion of the Mazdiasnian Religion, and see what you might do for your children and children's children. Do not tell me you cannot afford to create such a fund, when the whole world knows that you are ready to give thousands to every object suggested by a European for the benefit or flattery of some one of his race, and even to rear statues to those who are not the friends of your religion. "Charity begins at home;" give, then, first for your own people, and of your remaining surplus to outside objects.

There is a fatal inactivity growing apace among you. Not only are you not the religionists you once were, you are not the old time merchants. You are being elbowed out of commerce, and it is not very uncommon to see your sons going from door to door in search of employment at salaries of from fifty to seventy-five rupees per month, with their pockets full of Matriculation papers or F. A., and B. A. diplomas. And instead of your being as in the olden time the kings in Indian trade and commerce you are jostled by successful Bhattias, Borahs, Maimans and Khojohs who have accumulated fortunes. You are making no proper effort to impart a practical knowledge of your religious principles and tenets to the educated rising generation ; hence very naturally they are largely becoming sceptics and infidels. They do not as yet actually despise it *en masse* —the time for that has not quite arrived. But on account of your neglect to show them its sublimity and make them deeply respect it, they have reached the stage of indifference. One needed step would be to have your prayer books translated into the vernacular and English, with foot notes to explain the text, and especially, commentaries to show the reconciliation of Mazdiasnian philosophy with modern science. It is worse than useless—it is highly injurious to one's faith—to chatter off prayers in an unknown tongue, encouraging the hypocrisy of pretending to be pious while one has not the food at hand for a single pious thought. I have watched both priests and *behedin* at their prayers, morning and evening, and seen more that were not attending to the business in hand than that were.

If you wish to revive your religion, you should, besides organising the exploring expeditions and archæological surveys I previously spoke of, also rear a class of Parsi preachers who would be able to expound it thoroughly, and maintain it against all critics and enemies. These men should be highly educated, and versed in Sanscrit, Zend, Pehlve, Persian and English. Some should know German and French—like my honoured friend, Mr. Cama. With Western literature they should be familiar. Some should be taught oratory, so as to expound in a popular style the sacred theme. It might also be well to found travelling scholarships, as the Europeans have, to be given to especially meritorious students.

A stricter moral example should be set by you to your youth, who have, as I said above, fallen in too many cases into evil ways. They do not regard truth, nor show as much respect to elders as formerly.

As your understanding of the spirit of your religion has decreased, you have been growing more and more superstitious; essentials are neglected, and non-essentials given an exaggerated consequence.

Finally, and chiefly, the priestly class needs a thorough reformation. There are more than you need to perform the offices of religion, and the profession being over crowded, their influence is continually decreasing, and they have come, as a Parsi gentleman once remarked to me— to be looked upon as licensed beggars. A state of things which must certainly grieve your really learned Dasturs more than any one else.

The foregoing thoughts are submitted to you with great deference and in the hope that they will be pardoned in view of the kindly interest which prompts them. Before embodying them in this discourse I have taken the counsel of one of my most respected Parsi friends; so that you may regard them as in fact the views of one of your own community.

And now I ask you, as a final word, if the crisis has not arrived when every man of you is called upon, by all he holds sacred, to be up and doing. Shall the voice of Chaldean Fathers, which whispers to you across the ages be heard in vain? Shall the example of Zarathusht and Adam be forgotten? Must the memory of your hero forefathers be dishonoured? Shall there never more arise among you a Darab Dastur to draw down the celestial flame from the azure vault upon your temple altar? Is the favour of Ahura-Mazda no longer a boon precious enough to strive for and to deserve? The Hindu pilgrims to the temple-shrine of Jotir Math at Badrinath, affirm that some, more favoured than the rest, have sometimes seen far up amid the snow and ice of Mount Dhavalagiri— a Himalayan peak—the venerable figures of Mahatmas—perhaps of Rishis—who keep their watch and ward over the fallen Aryan faith, and wait the time for its resuscitation. So too—our travelling Brother in Armenia writes— there is a cave up near the crest of Allah-Dag, where at each setting of the sun, appears at the cave's mouth a stately figure holding a book of records in his hand. The people say that this is Mathan, last of the great Magian priests; whose body died some sixteen centuries ago. His anxious shade watches from thence the fate of Zoroaster's faith. And shall he stand in vain? Is he to see that faith die out for want of spiritual refreshment? Ye sons of Sohrab and of Rustam, rouse! Awaken' ere it is too late! The Hour is here; where are the MEN?

THEOSOPHY, THE SCIENTIFIC BASIS OF RELIGION.

Delivered at the Town Hall, Calcutta, on the 5th April 1882.

NOTWITHSTANDING the very complimentary terms kindly employed by my honored friend, the Chairman, in bespeaking your attention to the remarks I shall make, I feel most keenly my incapacity to deal with our subject as it deserves. When I face this vast audience, and recollect that it represents the highest culture of Bengal; when I think that we are met under the very shadow of the Calcutta University; when I reflect that these walls have resounded to the voices of Native orators, whose eloquence can hardly be surpassed by the most eminent senators in Western parliaments and congresses, and that, from the very spot where I stand, you have been addressed upon the most burning questions in religion and politics by Kally Churn Bannerji, Lalmohun Ghose Keshub Chunder Sen, Surendra Nath Bannerji, Kristo Das Pal, Sivanath, Sastri, and Protap Chunder Mozumdar—a sense of personal inferiority to those great masters of rhetoric and logic oppresses and warns me. But I have a message to deliver—a message of reproach in part, but also one of encouragement. I may not soothe your ears with the melody of your own gifted speakers; but I must deliver it, though all of them were here; and aye! though all the great dead of the past generations who gave renown to the name of Bengal were to cluster about this platform. I would they might do so; indeed, I should feel more sure of the moral regeneration of India, if those glorious ancestors of yours could but confront you for one short hour. If you could but hear what they would say of the ways in which you are maintaining their honor and sustaining their dignity, I think I would not need to utter a single word: one look at the expression of their faces, as their glance of mingled reproach and displeasure shot through to the very marrow of your being, would be quite enough. If you want to estimate Modern Bengal, with its foreign clothes and foreign vices, at its proper valuation, put it beside the Ancient Bengal. Call out your pertest Babu, who has suckled Spencer and Mill until he fancies himself able to build a new religion, or even a new planet; clothe him with all his academic honors; stuff his hands full of his diplomas; gather around him all the paraphernalia of Western culture, including the spirituous aids to reflection. If we were to ask this B. A. —this Bad Aryan—to give to this audience his candid opinion of himself, he would probably tell you that he was the type and the *beau ideal* of Hindu development,— a fair representative of what Young India might become under the fertilising sprinkles of the college watering-pot. But if we had the power to evoke the shades of the great Menu, of Kapila,

Goutama, Patanjali, Kanada, and Veda Vyasa, of Jaimini, Narada, Marichi, Vasishta, and other really great Hindus, and could place them before you on this platform, how would our trousered B. A. appear then? That is the gist of the whole question. A nation which has had representatives such as those I have named, need not go to any foreign teachers for an *imprimatur* of culture. When *they* can match the Aryan *Rishis*, then it will be time enough to look up to them as the gods of the academic *Brahmaloka*. And that is part of my message to Young Bengal.

I know, Mr. Chairman, that the first question that arises in the minds of my audience, is what motive I have in talking thus. You listen in surprise to hear a white man speak, as hitherto you have only heard your own orthodox Hindus speak. And as you have always observed that a motive underlies all human action, you must be asking yourselves what is my motive? I must preface my discourse with some personalities, therefore.

Elsewhere in India it is pretty well known how we Theosophists came here, and why. For three years, that is, since February 1879, we have been living under the public eye at Bombay, and every body knows what sort of people we are, how we live, and what we do. We have lived down serious suspicions and calumnies. I could not give you a better proof of this than to refer you to the action of the Hindu and Parsi educated public the other day when a ranting clergyman from my own country indulged in insulting and false remarks about us in one of his public lectures. The response the Natives made, showed most unmistakably that his slanders had increased rather than diminished their friendliness for their theosophist friends. It will be so here. Though this is my first visit to Calcutta, it will not be my last. I expect henceforth to spend at least two or three months of each year in Bengal, and you will thus have ample opportunity to become acquainted with me. We are not birds of passage; we have not come to India, as Sinbad did to the Valley of Diamonds, to pick up what we can, and after a time flit away. We have not the least intention of returning to our own countries to reside. India is our chosen home—the land of our adoption, and the Hindus are our dearest friends, if not our brothers. We were not driven out of our Western homes. If we had chosen to stop there, we should now be enjoying all comforts and pleasures. In my native land, where the highest offices of State are open to all aspirants, I might even now, if I should return, hold, as I have for many years before, posts of honor and importance. One of our most influential New York journals, a journal which circulates a lac and a quarter of copies every week day, and of its Sunday Edition, 167,000 copies, asked the other day, why I should expatriate myself, and why I did not return to my own people to teach them about Asiatic philosophy. Nor did I leave America to better my fortunes. A sorry way it should be to improve one's prospects to give up an income of thousands of rupees, and devote every moment of one's time to the interest of a philanthropic society, for whose support I must pay thousands annually out of my private means! There are the Treasurer's accounts, audited and certificated by the Council of the Society, which show that I am stating the bare fact. They show that since we began at New York our preparations to depart for India, Madame Blavatsky and I have given towards the expenses of our Society more than Rs. 25,000. And since we came we have not asked a Hindu, a Parsi, a Buddhist, or any one else to give us one solitary rupee for our private benefit. Well, admitting all this to be true, the question will all the more press home upon you--what is our motive, why should we take up this life of public drudgery, move over Asia like uneasy ghosts, expose ourselves to the darts of slander and the stings of suspicion? I shall tell you, the answer is simple enough. We follow an idea; and for it we face obstacles, discomfort, and danger, incur expense and trouble, resign as worthless what men usually prize, and, relinquishing family and home, country and friends,—make a new home in Asia, and seek friends and brethren among her ancient races. We are covetous; yes, but it is for knowledge. We are ambitious; yes, but only for a place among those who have loved humanity, irrespective of caste, race, and creed. We are conspirators; yes, but only with the good and true souls who have deep religious aspirations, and who, deploring the darkened spiritual state of mankind, would point back to the beacons of hope that the *Rishis* of old lit on the mountain peaks of Aryan philosophy. When you come to know us, you will recall my present words, and be ready to testify that I told you only the truth.

But how comes about this wonder that we foreigners should feel so deep a reverence for Hindu philosophy, and why even then should we have left our country to come here?

In the year 1874 Madame Blavatsky and I met. I had been a student of practical psychology for nearly a quarter century. From boyhood, no problem had interested me so much as the mystery of man; and I had been seeking for light upon it wherever it could be found. To understand the physical man, I had read something of Anatomy, Physiology and Chemistry. To get an insight into the nature of mind and thought, I had read the various authorities of orthodox science, and practically investigated the heterodox branches of Phrenology, Physiognomy, Mesmerism and Psychymetry. To understand Mesmerism, one must have read Von Reichenbach's "Researches on Magnetism, Electricity, &c, &c, in their Relations to the Vital Force," and I venture to say that no one can possibly comprehend the *rationale* of the astounding phenomena of modern spiritualism, who has not prepared himself by a look at all these subjects above enumerated. So, then, this had been my bent of mind since boyhood, and although I always took an active part in all that concerned my country and fellow countrymen, and an especially active one during our late Civil War, yet my heart was not set on worldly affairs. In the year above mentioned, I was investigating a most startling case of mediumship, that of William Eddy, an uneducated farmer in whose house were nightly appearing, and often talking, the *alleged* spirits of dead persons. I will not go into particulars just now, for I have other things to speak about; perhaps I may make it the subject of some future discourse. Suffice it that with my own eyes I saw within the space of about three months some 500 of these apparitions, under circumstances which, to my mind, exclude the possibility of trickery or fraud. My observations were communicated to a New York daily journal during the whole period, and the facts excited the greatest wonder. Madame Blavatsky and I met at this farm house, and the similarity of our tastes for mystical research led to an intimate acquaintance. She soon proved to me that, in comparison with even the *chela* of an Indian *Mahatma*, the authorities I had been accustomed to look up to, knew absolutely nothing. Little by little, she opened out to me as much of the truth as my experiences had fitted me to grasp. Step by step, I was forced to relinquish illusory beliefs that I had cherished for twenty years. And as the light gradually dawned in my mind, grew apace my reverence for the unseen teachers who had instructed her. At the same time, a deep and insatiable yearning, possessed me to seek their society, or, if I could not do that, at least to take up my residence in a land which their presence glorified, and incorporate myself with a people whom their greatness ennobled. The time came when I was blessed with a visit from one of these *Mahatmas* in my own room at New York—a visit from him, not in the physical body, but in the "double," or *Mayavi Rupa*. When I asked him to leave me some tangible evidence that I had not been the dupe of a vision, but that he had indeed been there, he removed from his head the *puggri* he wore, and giving it to me vanished from my sight. That cloth I have still and in one corner is marked in thread the cypher or signature he always attaches to the notes he writes to myself and others. This visit and his conversation sent my heart at one leap around the globe, across oceans and continents, over sea and land, to India, and from that moment I had a motive to live for, an end to strive after. That motive was to gain the Aryan wisdom; that end to work for its dissemination. Thenceforth I began to count the years, the months, the days as they passed, for they were bringing me ever nearer the time when I should drag my body after the eager thought that so long preceded it. In November 1875, we founded the Theosophical Society as a nucleus around which might gather all those of every race and land, who were in sympathy with our mode of research; and as no such body could have any permanence unless we should eliminate the ever obvious causes of disagreement among men—religious bigotry and social intolerance—we organised it on the basis of Universal Brotherhood. The idea was a good one, since it has succeeded. I doubt if any society of a cognate character has ever so rapidly increased as ours. We have already Branches in most parts of the world, and we are fast overspreading India with our organizations. The Branch I shall to-morrow form at Calcutta, will be the twenty-fifth in this country, established since February 1879, and by the time I reach Bombay there will be twenty-eight. But I am getting ahead of my subject: let me turn. Within the three years when I was waiting to come to India, I had other visits from the *Mahatmas*, and they were not all Hindus or Cashmeris. I know some fifteen in all, and among them Copts, Tibetans, Chinese, Japanese, Siamese, a Hungarian, and a Cypriote. But, whatever they are, however much they may differ externally as to races, religion, and caste, they are in perfect agreement as to the fundamentals of occult science, and as to the scientific basis of religion.

The long wished for time came at last; our private affairs were settled, the New York Society was placed in competent hands; and my colleague and I embarked. Many friends accompanied us to the vessel to say good-bye, and their waving handkerchiefs, which we watched as long as we could see them, were a testimony to the exiles that they left loving hearts behind. How thoroughly, however, I had transferred my love to my new country, you may imagine when I tell you that as our steamer passed out of the harbour to the ocean, I cast no "longing, lingering look behind." Though I was leaving the native land I had loved so dearly, and had even risked my life for, and though I never expected to behold it again, I did not even give it the tribute of a sigh; but, descending to my cabin, I opened the map of India, and sent my thought to my Land of promise. But when after buffeting the storms of various waters, we neared Bombay, then far into the night, alone I paced the forecastle to catch the first glimpse of the beacon light that waited to welcome me *home*. The passengers were fast asleep, and only the watch on deck and I were there to see the stars of the Indian sky, and the fire seething waves of the Indian sea. The midnight bells were struck, but still the lighthouse could not be made out. At last, at one in the morning, the officer on duty, who knew my anxiety, relieved it by pointing to a faintly luminous speak at the water's edge, and telling me that that was Bombay light. My heart gave a throb, as perhaps throbs the heart of an old Hindu who has been long away in foreign countries; and a feeling of joy and pleasure came across me to think that my journey was ended, and my real life about to begin. I had pictured to myself a Hindu nation homogeneous, at least, as regards spirituality and love of their ancestors,

—one great family, rejoicing in the Aryan name, and with a religious faith that was built upon the assurance, if not the knowledge of theosophical truth. Though I knew there were religious sects and cliques I thought that these barriers were not high enough to keep the Hindus apart. I had written to Keshub Babu to ask him to join in our work, and was ready to serve in any subordinate capacity, under and with anybody, no matter whom, in the interest of India and Indians. I only asked some little corner, however small, where I might incorporate myself with their national life and thought; and as I asked nothing but the privilege to learn and to work, I hoped to be taken at my word and viewed as a friend. But I was not: the back of the hand, not the palm, was offered me. Dogged by the Police of Government as suspects, my colleague and I were not happy enough to find a sure refuge in Indian hearts. One Hindu we had most trusted, secretly maligned us to the authorities, while professing to love us like a brother; another was coward enough to desert us at the mere casual expression of a wish by his official superior; our characters were traduced by the enemies of Indian religion without a protest from the followers of that religion; it seemed, in fact, as though we were doomed to see every hope crushed,—every one we had an affection for, turn his back upon us. Thus under a black sky of trouble, we went on for weary months together, keeping up our courage by remembering what goal we had in view, and by degrees learning to pluck success from the very thorn bush of disaster. We founded our Bombay Branch, then another and another; we established our magazine, the *Theosophist*, and made it a success; we went to Ceylon, and were greeted with enthusiasm, and though some who mistook us for sectarians have broken with us, the third year of our Indian work now opens up bright and full of promise. The worst, we think, is over; and every month as I remarked in a recent lecture, we are being drawn nearer and nearer to the Indian heart. I venture to take the size of the present audience as a proof of this fact, for I do not believe it is only an idle curiosity that has brought all of you together. Our appeals to you to remember the glories of Aryavarta and strive to revive them, have not fallen upon deaf ears; the dry bones are stirring with the flutter of a higher and nobler spiritual life; the echoes of sympathy are coming towards us from the North and the South, the East and the West. Bombay has spoken, the North-West has spoken. Madras has spoken, and there have even been whispers from Bengal, though we have never until now spoken to Bengali audiences. Away with despondency and dejection. The morn is breaking, and if we wait but a little longer, we may see the perfect day.

No one feels more sensibly than I the anomaly that a white man should be appealing to you to study your religion. This is work for your learned Pundits. But they are silent ; and what is to be done ? I met the greatest Pundits of India at Benares, and, after showing to them the effects of Western culture upon the religious thought of Young India, implored them to rise to the occasion, and do their duty. As though the voice of the *Rishis* were speaking by my lips, I arraigned them at the bar of their country, and said that history would not hold them guiltless, if the entire body of our youth should fall into materialistic scepticism. I begged that they would at least compile tracts and catechisms, which should embody the great principles of morality and religion, the broad outlines of philosophy and spiritual science that are laid down in the Sastras, so that it might be seen that a Hindu need look nowhere outside his own literature for inspiration to noble deeds and noble living. The Pundits listened, applauded, signed articles of union between their Sabha and our Society, and then—did nothing more. I am waiting on and hoping almost against hope that from among the greatest of your living scholars will differentiate himself a moral Regenerator to lead you back from your desultory wanderings to the solid ground of Hindu philosophy. Must India call in vain ? Must the empty voice give back the hollow echoes of her appeal ? Is there not, even in Bengal, one Aryan heart that can be touched with the fire from the sacred altars of religion ? Where is the Brahmin who is able, like his pure and holy forefather, to perform the *Agnihotra* in the true way, and draw from the ambient sky the fire of *Agni* upon his *kusa* grass ? Where is the Brahmin who has the fire of *Agni* in the hollow of his hand ? Alas ! there comes no answer. There are thousands of Brahmins, but no adept *Agnihotris*. Among these swarming millions, and amid this teeming life, the aspirant for spiritual instruction finds scarcely a single *Guru* who can practically teach the *Yoga* science. Hundreds of bright young men are suffering from spiritual starvation. Can we help them ? Is their no hope to offer the youths who have learnt to regard modern science as the sole authority in questions of a religious and scientific nature ? For that is the ordeal that the advocates of Aryan philosophy must pass. It is useless to try to cover it up, or evade the alternative : either we must prove Hinduism to stand upon the ground of science, or we must leave it to its fate. I think we can hold out this hope, and can give this assurance. I believe that modern research has arrived at certain facts which help us to understand our subject if we collate and adjust them to each other. And this brings us to consider the second part of our discourse—an explanation of the word Theosophy, and its application to the *Yoga Vidya*.

Properly speaking, Theosophy may be defined as the knowledge of "Divine" wisdom. If there were a Western science of Psychology, worthy of the name, this would be its crowning glory ; the seeker after knowledge of the " soul" would end by becoming a Theosophist

For one can gain what is called Divine wisdom only in one way—through the developement of the psychic powers. Religion is most strictly a personal affair: every man makes his own religion and his own God: that is to say, if he has any idea at all about religion or God, they must be his own ideas, not some body's else. Another man can no more think for you in these matters, so as to do you any good, than he can eat or sleep for you. You may think some man very great, and be ready to wash and garland and swing him like an idol, and eat the dust of his feet, and all that sort of thing; and you may fancy that his commonest utterances are divinely inspired. You may call yourself a *Tantrika*, a *Sivavite*, a *Vaishnava*, a Buddhist, or whatever you like. But, after all, when it comes to your actual religious experience, it will be *your* experience, measured and limited by *your* own personal, physical, and theosophical capacity. It is simply tyranny to try to force a particular religion upon any man. So, as I said before, religion is something personal; and it is also something sacred, something not to be rudely interfered with and pried into. The true moralist will exert his influence to make his fellowmen live up to the best features of their respective faiths; it is the most audacious of experiments to try to give together bits of a number of good religions into a new mosaic.

I shall not enter here into a discussion as to what is meant by the word "Soul." I have my ideas, and they may conflict with yours. Call it what you like, the only radical point to reach is the fact that in the nature of man there *is* this department which is called psychical, and which is not to be included in the most objective, or physical and mechanical part of the self. The orthodox psychologist will deny you this point. He will meet you at the very threshold of the enquiry, and affirm that there is no more of man than is embraced in the ingenious mechanism of his body. The English poet Pope coined an expression to signify his scorn of a man who was devoid of great qualities—one who was

> "Fixed, like a plant, to its peculiar spot,
> To draw nutrition, propogate and rot."

But if you add to this the intellectual capacity as the result of cerebral function, have we not here the type of the "man" of modern Psychology? What does that science make of the human being but a digesting, locomotive, procreating, and thinking mechanism? Can you find anything better than this in the concepts of Herbert Spencer and the entire *a posteriori* school? I will give you a year to pour over Mr. Spencer's *Principles of Psychology*, or over *The Emotions and the Will*, and *The Senses and the Intellect* of Professor Alexander Bain, whom some of the greatest critics of our day consider as the master Psychologist of the age—and then defy you to find the secret of true psychology; or, if you choose, you may con the works of James Mill, Cousin, Locke, Kant, Hobbess, Aurtley, Hegel, Fichte, Huxley, Hæckel, John Stuart Mill,

Comte, and all the learned writers of the kind. You will see a good deal of protoplasm, and protogen, and monads; but you will not discover the nature of "soul" in any of them. After wading through their heavy volumes, you will arrive at the conclusion that they are little better than obscurationists—intellectual clouds between you and the sun of spiritual truth. You will find some of them light, fleecy clouds, some so thin and vapoury as to let through a good deal of light; others black and murky clouds, bursting with suppressed lightnings. If you go on far enough, you will see that these heavier intellectual masses, like the prototypes in Nature with which we are comparing them, will discharge their thunders at each other as they come into opposition, and then there is a great noise and heavy discharge of critical artillery. But the net result, after all is over, and you digest your notes and collect your confused thoughts, will be what I said—you will have puzzled your brain with a multitude of words and got no clear idea of Psychology. For, you see, they confuse the intellectual experiences of the human brain with the other and totally different experiences of the real *Psyche!* And though they wrote ten times as many books, since they would all be written upon this false hypothesis, they would be no nearer the mark. These Western psychologists have, we may say, chopped man into minute shreds. There is not an atom of him, (and by him I mean their 'him,' not the complete man)' not a bone, a muscle, a nerve, a cell, a ganglion, that they have not dissected out, and fumbled over, and analyzed. He has not a feeling, an emotion, a cognition; not a single or a complex intellectual process that they have not pulled about, weighed in the scales of logic, tested with the resolvents of reason, ticketed, and laid away in the psychological herbaria. But I defy the whole of them, from Locke to Bastian, and their whole army of followers, to show you one single discovery that explains the psychic phenomena whose occurrence has been observed in India from the remotest ages, and the laws of whose causation are explained in the Aryan Sastras. The earnest searcher after Divine wisdom—the true Theosophist—will turn away from western 'authorities' with a sense of weariness and despair. To express it truthfully in one word, I must call the soul-science of the Aristotelians of the now dominant European school, subcuticular—skindeep—Psychology, the Psychology of what lies inside the human skin! *Their battles are all fought under the epidermis;* they understand the psychological effect of external objects and phenomena upon the human mind; but a transcuticular man is to them a scientific absurdity. Their man is acted upon centripetally by Nature, but does not react centrifugally upon it. Asiatic philosophers recognize man as comprising three groups or divisions of selfhood. There is, *first, Sthul Sharira*—the physical—the grosser, more material, objective and perceptible; *second, Mayavi Rupa*—the psychical, or less perceptible, though still material; *third,* the

Atma,—the *spiritual*, or imperceptible and transcendental. With a minuteness of analysis that matches that of the European psychologists, they have again sub-divided these three groups into sub-sections. But there is this inestimable advantage on their side, that they prove their propositions experimentally. When they talk of a "double," or *Mayavi Rupa* or *Sukshma Sharira*, they produce the thing itself: *they show themselves to you in their doubles.* They will leave their physical bodies (*Sthul Sharira*) in *samadhi*, a state of lethargy, at some distant place, force the "double" out through its pores, and to that transferring their conscionsness with all its train of intellectual and intuitional cognitions and feelings, visit and make themselves visible to you. Fancy Professor Bain, or Mr. Mill, or Mr. Spencer, undertaking to argue on Psychology with a man in the *Mayavi Rupa*! Where would be then all their "quips and quibilets," their hard Greek and Latin terms, their speculative hypotheses? Until that moment, they would have thought themselves authorities but now the spectres of their books would rise before them only in reproach. Their antecedent mental state, as contrasted with their present one might be likened to those of a phillosopher who had speculated upon the possibility of aerolites, but of a sudden had been hit hard by a fragment of one tumbling on him from the sky. Or we may take an example even more extreme. Let us suppose Mr. Spencer sitting in his arm-chair at dusk in his library. He has been writing the 17th. Chapter of the 2nd volume of his *Principles of Psychology*, and worked out the problem of the "Completed Differentiation of Subject and Object" to his perfect satisfaction. He has satisfied himself that the phase of emotion is stimulated by memories of past experiences; his hand has just traced these words:—"Such components of consciousness, pleasurable and painful, divisible into classes and sub-classes, differ greatly from the components thus far described; being extremely vague, being unlocalizable in space and being but indefinitely localisable in time" (op. cit. p. 467). He has described to us the effect produced upon his state of quiescence by hearing at his back a voice which he recognizes as the voice of a friend: and, as he tells us, "a wave of pleasurable feeling" upsets certain antecedent sets of "vivid states," known to him as the parts of his body, a feeling of muscular tension is excited, "the emotion felt goes on presently to initiate other muscular tensions, and after them special sounds"—he speaks. And now, his chapter finished and his pen thrown aside, he muses. A wonderful phenomenon occurs—one that has happened to other great scholars, and by them recorded. But out of the reasoning, analysing, digesting machine that the world, by visual, auditive, and tactual observations recognize as Mr. Spencer, oozes a whitish vapour which at first a cloud, condenses into a man. It is not only a man but that very man, Mr. Spencer—his actual counterpart or "double," his *Mayavi-rupa*. At last it is fully formed and in the same degree as the light of intelligence comes into its eyes, the same light diminishes in the eyes of the musing philosopher. The synthetic man, who but just now was building air-castles with walls and foundations of words, has divided into two parts, and the supreme intellectual activity, as well as the supreme consciousness of selfhood, is transferred to that part which is now outside the skin that was the philosopher's *ultima thule* but just now. Can we not imagine what this new born self would say to the heavier body before it? Let it speak—"Here I am, and there you are, O man! I am Ego—Self; you a machine. You are my prison and jailor; but see I have escaped. Henceforth I leave you, I enter you, at will. You cannot detain me, you cannot ignore me, you *shall not silence me.* I am the conscious entity, you a vegetating mechanism of bones, and flesh, and nerves. How now about your emotions and will, your grey-matter vesicles and your white-fibre telegraph lines? Come, Philosopher, rouse yourself and debate with me. I would have you teach me Psychology. You write learnedly about subject and object. You have cleverly told your readers that you cannot 'frame any psychological conception without looking at internal co-existences and sequences in their adjustments to external co-existences and sequences:" (op. cit. I. p. 133) "now here we are—you there with your thinking machinery inside, and I here, with my intellectual powers outside the physical Mr. Spencer. Come, since you are fond of sequences, *follow me,* if you can, to the high plateau of the Himavat. There we shall find men who *know* Psychology instead of dreaming about it; men who are the successors of a thousand generations of Aryan and Hindu sages, who, all this time, have known what man is, and what are his powers. Your school of Metaphysics, not yet a century old, is a thing of yesterday as compared with the hoary science of the *Rishis,* the *Arahats,* and the Medean Magi. In the pride of their recently enfranchised intellects, your Western biologists and psychologists are trying to climb the sky of occult science, wherein alone can be found the truth about man and nature. Dull clod of earth, component of ashes, and gases, and water, it was I who illumined and inspired you; I who gave you such intuitions of Divine wisdom as you had, despite the incubus of your vaunted reason. I am *the* Spencer, you but my covering. You are of the ground, I of the infinite and eternal essence of Nature!" What can you answer—M.A. of the University of Calcutta—though you glitter with medals, and are clothed in honors as with a garment? Theory is one thing, fact another. Do you cling to the theory of Germany and Edinburgh, when you can learn the fact at the *asramams* of the Neilgherries and the Himalayas?

Mr. John Stuart Mill (*Dissertations and Discussions, III,* 97) makes a bold assertion. He says:—"The sceptre of Psychology has decidedly returned to this Island" (Great Britain). Sceptre, indeed! He talks as though it were some royal bubble, like the Koh-i-noor, that could be looted and sent home by a P. and O. Steamer! The sceptre of Psychology is wielded on the Himavat, and no modern empiric can clutch that rod of power, that staff of authority. The mesmerist knows something about Psychology, the modern spiritualist knows something, and so does the student of Psychometry. Their knowledge is based upon experimental research. They may not be learned anatomists, morphologists, or biologists; but, perhaps, they have a better idea of the whole nature of man than any of them. They have seen one from whom the conscious Ego had stepped out, and left the body not a dead thing but living, the *Jiv-Atma*, or life-principle, being in it. The dull eye of the body, in which no intelligence shines; the listless apathy and muscular relaxation; the reduced temperature of flesh; the stopped or fluttering heart—all these have convinced them that it is not the bodily mechanism that is the real man; and this conviction is made a certainty when one has seen a body thus inert, and, at the same time, seen the double of the man moving about, with full consciousness, doing intelligently the acts of a responsible being, and in very way showing that the physical body is but a habitable mechanism, of itself unspiritual, if not altogether irresponsible. In the ordinary experiments of Mesmerism, when the patient is thrown into the state of ecstacies, one usually observes that the body has passed into a state whose physical appearances closely resemble death. I have stood by a person in this death-like lethargy, and found there was neither pulse, animal heat, nor breath, while, at the same time, the inner self of the ecstatic was apparently soaring in the supernal spheres, keenly alive to its rapturous experiences. In a book of mine (*People from the other World*) which records my researches on the Eddy mediumistic phenomena, I have described the case of a woman, named Mrs. Compton whom I saw in such a dead alive condition after one of the most marvellous *seances* on record. Well, this something that comes out of the human body is, in the judgment of occultists, the soul-principle—the responsible entity, the part of a man which, whether inside or outside the body, is that which acquires the certainty of Divine wisdom. It is this that becomes the true Theosophist. And as this is not restricted by the hard limits of creed, race prejudice, caste, and other external relations which hedge about the material, or physical man, you will observe that when this self is thoroughly freed from the restrictive environments of society, it must be free from our prejudices, hatreds, and antipathies of one sort or another. This is the part of a man that becomes an adept, and the very name of *Mahatma* (great soul) that you have called it by since countless generations, shows how well this has been understood in India. When the *Yogi* practises *dharana*, *dhyan*, and *samadhi*, it is for the purpose of getting himself—that is his real self—disentagled from the illusions of the bodily senses which continually cheat us as to what is real and what unreal. He strives to evolve this astral self, and to purify that to the nearest possible approximation of absolute spirit. There are four stages of *Yoga* : in the first, the *Yogi* begins to learn the first forms of *Yoga*, and to fight his battle with the animal nature. In the next, having learnt the forms, he advances, towards perfect knowledge. In the third, the advance continues, and he overcomes all the primary and subtle, that is to say, he vanquishes the nature spirits or elementals, resident in the four kingdoms of nature ; and neither fire can burn, water drown, earth crush, nor poisonous air suffocate his bodily frame. He is no longer dependent upon the limited powers of the five senses for knowledge of surrounding Nature : he has developed a spiritual hearing that makes the most distant and the most hidden sounds perceptible, a sight that sweeps the area of the whole solar system, and penetrates the most solid bodies along with the hypothetical ether of modern science ; he can make himself as buoyant as a thistle-down, or as heavy as the living rock ; he can subsist without food for inconceivably long periods, and, if he chooses, arrest the ordinary course of nature, and escape bodily death to an inconceivably venerable age. Having learnt the laws of natural forces, the causes of phenomena, and the sovereign capabilities of the human will, he may make "miracles" his playthings, and do wonders that knock the conceit out of even the modern philosopher. He can walk upon water without even wetting the soles of his feet, or, sitting in *dhyan*, can, by inward concentration, so change the magnetic polarity of his body that it will rise from the ground and be self-suspended in the air. Or, if he throws himself into that deepest state of abstraction—*Samadhi*, he will then have so withdrawn the life-principle from the outer to the inner surfaces of the body, that you may tie him in a sack and bury him under ground for weeks together, and when dug up and rubbed and handled in a certain way, he will revive to perfect consciousness. Your most distinguished and honored countryman, Dr. Rajendralala Mittra, tells me that when he was a boy, he saw the *Sadhu* whom some wood-choppers found in the Sunderbunds jungle, and brought up to Calcutta. He was found sitting like a stiffened corpse with his legs twisted through the roots of a tree. At Calcutta, he unhappily fell into the hands of two fools, whose tipsy folly—as I am told, though I speak under correction made them practically his murderers. Not able to arouse him by shouting, pushing, and beating, they put fire into his hand, and plunged him into deep water in the Ganges with a rope about his neck as though he were a ship's anchor, and twice kept him there over-night. They pried his tetanous jaws apart, and put beef into his mouth, and poured brandy down his throat. Finally, to prove their own shamelessness and make their memory hateful for ever, this Hindu Rajah and this English physician set upon this poor saint whose emaciated body had been left by him, as he thought, in the safe solitude of the jungle, where tigers and serpents would not harm him, while his soul went out in search of Divine truth, these cruel, impious beasts of men set upon him an abandoned creature of the other sex to pollute him with her unholy touch ! Oh shame upon such specimens of humanity, I say. By their cruel violence they finally awoke the *Sadhu* from his lethargy, and his first utterance was, not a curse upon his tormentors, not a burst of indignant invective, but a plaintive and reproachful cry "O why, Sirs, did you disturb me : I had done you no harm ?" Shortly after he died from the effects of the food-poison they had forced into him.

This happened some forty years ago: do you suppose Calcutta is any better now, any safer place for a real *Sadhu* to trust himself in ? I think not ; and in my opinion if any one of you should want to find any better type of *Yogi* than the painted humbugs who perambulate your streets, you will have to go far away from the city grates.

At Lahore I met the son of a Native, still residing in a neighbouring place, who was an eye-witness to a burial of a *Sadhu* in the presence of Maharajah Runjit Singh—a case which is historical. The particulars are given in the work of Sir Claude Wade, the Political Resident (*The Camp and Court of Runjit Singh*), and Dr. McGregor, then Residency Surgeon (*History of the Sikh War*). This *Sadhu* was buried alive for forty days, a perpetual guard being kept, night and day, over the spot. The English officials saw him buried and also exhumed, and Dr. McGregor gives a professional diagnosis of the case. When uncovered, the man's body was shrunken and dried like a stick of wood ; the tongue, which at the burial had been turned back into the throat, had become like a piece of horn ; and eyes, ears, and every other orifice of the body had been stopped with plugs of *ghee*. Upon returning to his external consciousness the *Sadhu* told them that he had been enjoying the blissful society of *Yogis* and saints, and that if the Maharajah wished it, he was quite ready to be buried over again.

There is—to say nothing of the Aryan and post-Aryan Sastras which is you know, are full of such things—a whole literature of Mysticism among the European nations, and the anals of the Christian Church teem with testimonies of ecstatics and visionaries who, escaping from the body while alive, have penetrated the inner world and seen divine things. No one can read the mystical literature of the Christian and other churches without being struck with the idea that the visions of an uninitiated seer are invariably mixed up with his own individuality. His subjective prejudices and preconceptions give objective color and shape to the objects he encounters in his supra-physical life. The Christian sees the Heaven of his Apocalypse, or his Milton ; the Parsi, the Chinvat Bridge of Souls guarded by the dread Maiden and her dogs ; the Mussulman, the Gardens of the Blessed with their houris and never-ending delights. Swedenborg the Swedish seer, who developed his clairvoyance when he was past the middle age, and after he had devoted many years to scientific pursuits and religious thought, saw a system of correspondences which explained and illuminated, as he imagined, the dead-letter of the Bible, of whose divine authority he was already convinced. The visions of my almost life-long friend, Andrew Jackson Davis, have a similarly subjective character.

In all these cases, the seer has not passed out of the circle of illusion, he has not yet come into the forth stage of *Yoga* as defined by Patanjali. In this fourth stage " the *Yogi* loses all personality and all consciousness of separate existence ; all the operations of intellect become extinct, and spirit alone remains." The *Moksha* of the Hindu is this pure transcendental state indefinitely prolonged—an existence in which all the causes of sorrow being absent, there can be no sorrow ; and the causes of illusions being left behind, there can be no illusion, but the absolute truth is known in its unveiled splendour. The Theosophist is a man, who, whatever be his race, creed, or condition, aspires to reach this height of wisdom and beatitude by self-development, and, therefore, you will see that in a Theosophical Society like that we have founded—and that we hope many of you will join—to have one creed for our members to subscribe to, or one form of prayer for them to adopt, or any rules that would interfere with their individual relations to caste, or any other social and external environment not actually antipathetic to Theosophical research, would be impossible. You will also infer that, despite the false statements or ignorant misconceptions of our many critics, we are *not* preaching a new religion, or founding a new sect, or a new school of philosophy or occult science. The Hindu Sastras, the Buddhist Gathas, and the Zoroastrian Desatir contain every essential idea that we have ever propounded, and our constant theme, these past seven years, has been that of my present discourse, to wit, that Theosophy is the scientific and the only firm basis of religion. We deny that there is the slightest conflict between true religion and true science. We deny that any religion *can* be true that does not rest upon scientific lines, and we affirm that the outcome of scientific research will be to set religion upon such an eternal foundation, by breaking down the thick mystery of matter and tracing force up into that everlasting and immutable principle, called Motion by some, Spirit by some, and *Parabrahma* by the Vedantists. Theosophical research, therefore, is the prop and stay of both religion and science ; and by ignoring all those causes which keep men apart, and arm brother against brother, it is promotive of peace and harmony among men—in short, of Universal Brotherhood.

A great noice has always been made about certain striking phenomena which have occurred, not only in the presence of the mystics and saints of different religious sects above mentioned, but also in connection with the Theosophical Society. Minds, empty of healthy philosophical thought, hanker after the marvellous. Many such have joined our Society in the hope of seeing wonders, and even of obtaining *siddhis* (powers) without the usual training. Such are always disappointed, and, of necessity, foredoomed to disappointment. There is no royal road to Geometry. The Occult Science may be learnt by different methods, and by any one who can find a teacher, *provided he has the necessary psycho-physiological qualifications in himself.* For this department of research does exact very peculiar aptitudes. Can you learn law, or medicine, or theology, or chemistry, or astronomy, or any other science embraced in the college *curriculum*, without the special mental capacities that each demands? You know well that it is impossible, and that even where the mental capacity is not wanting, it takes time, and patience, and close thought and application to master your subject. There is not a professor, however prominent, who does not continue a student of his specialty to the very day of his death. Come, then, foolish man, do you imagine that this Theosophy, this science of sciences, which unlocks for you the corridors of nature and ushers you into the blazing splendour of the absolute truth, is less difficult than any of these pettier branches of knowledge? Do you think that in a few weeks or months or years, you can pierce the veils of the mysteries, while you are keeping on in your round of worldly occupations, indulge your animal pleasures, cower before your social prejudices, and wrap your nobler self in the tainted body of ignoble desires? The mere seeing of phenomena does no good except to a mind which has already obtained a thorough understanding of philosophy. This the *Yogi* knows so well that he does not allow himself to be diverted by them, even when produced by himself, from his ultimate object of reaching the fourth stage of *Yoga*. Patanjali says that even in the third stage the *Yogi* is liable to be overcome and even in the last, which is sub-divided into seven stages, he is not wholly safe from the "local gods," nor will be so till he has advanced beyond the fifth of these seven. In the course of training, adopted among certain mystics of Tibet, there are seven stages of an ascending series, and each of these is sub-divided into nine sub-stages. But whatever the training, there is the same object—emancipation from illusion and attainment of Theosophical knowledge. The untrained seers and religious ecstatics we have noticed above as having visions of a partially subjective character, are all beneath the fourth stage of *Yoga*. Their delusions result from their lack of training They see a spiritual light, but through a smoky glass, Patanjali's methods having been unknown to them, they have not developed their psychic powers by *dharana* and *dhyan*, that is, by "restraint of the mind," and "spiritual meditation." Hence, their actual psychic perceptions are mixed up with their intellectual pre-conceptions, as the Bible puts it—they "see through a glass darkly."

So we arrive at this point at last. If Psychology is a science,—and Psychology includes the learning of divine wisdom,—then this search after religious truth is the scientific basis of religion. Theosophy, therefore, is the scientific basis of religion, for this research is Theosophy. I think this is plain enough, and I cannot see how any fair man of any creed or sect could put himself in antagonism to us. If his sect or his bigotry are more precious than the learning of the truth, of course we need not argue with him. He could not understand us, or, if he could, he would not admit it. Perhaps, in his petulant dissatisfaction, he might even accuse us of falsehood. One of these sect-leaders said, the other day, in a Calcutta paper, that the study of occultism and spiritualism only pandered to "vain curiosity;" that "men will not believe in God and immortality, but they will believe in any amount of spirit-rapping and occultism." I could not offer you a better example of the spirit just described—a spirit which would have us put aside science and investigation of natural law, and blindly take on faith what any would-be leader chooses to tell us. "The more"—says this gentleman, himself an avowed religious teacher—"a man is found to disbelieve in the natural and legitimate object of faith, the more inclined he is to put his trust in all manner of magic, witchcraft, and spiritualism." What's the use of arguing with a mind like that? The little world of illusion in which it lives is quite enough to satisfy its every desire; if it thinks it can find emancipation in it, let it try. Of one thing those people are most certainly ignorant, and that is of *the spirit of the 19th century*. The day of blind faith has gone by, never, I hope, to return. If we are to have any religion—and every man of moral feeling longs for some religious convictions—it must be one that is in reconciliation with science and natural law. We are not going any more to be catching up our religions as though they were made of glass, and running for shelter behind the rampart of "faith" every time Darwin or Spencer throws a stone at them These men who want to prohibit our looking into the mysterious operations of Nature, are the lineal descendants of the theological doctors of Galileo's time. Some of these professors of Pisa and Padua behaved so absurdly about this theory of the heliocentric system that he has held them up to an immortality of ridicule in a letter to Kepler. "Oh! my dear Kepler," he writes, "how I wish we could have a hearty laugh together. Here at Padua, is the principal professor of philosophy, whom I have repeatedly and urgently invited to look at the moon and planets through my glass which he pertinaciously refuses to do. Why are you not here? What shouts of laughter we should have at this glorious folly and to hear the philosopher at Pisa laboring before the Grand Duke with logical arguments as if, with magic incantations, to draw the new planets out of the sky!" Dr. James Esdaile, from the Preface to whose work on *Natural and Mesmeric Clairvoyance*, I take this quotation, is the

Residency Surgeon, who under the patronage of Lord Dalhousie, then Governor-General of India, established a Mesmeric Hospital here at Calcutta, in the year 1846, at which were performed painlessly some hundreds of surgical operations upon mesmerised patients. His noble devotion to truth and purely philanthropic labors provoked the nasty spite of his professional colleagues. They behaved towards him with the same vindictive malice as some editors, preachers, and laymen have shown for the Theosophical Society. But he kept on with his work, despite all obstacles, until the use of mesmeric anesthesia was superseded by the application of chloroform to surgery. Dr. Esdaile lived down opposition and so was enabled to say in 1852, as the result of personal experience, that "like the camomile plant Mesmerism only flourishes the more for being trodden upon." Theosophy seems to enjoy the same vital property, for we have just seen that the stamp from the boot-heel of a missionary shouter from my own country, instead of crushing it as his party hoped, has done it a world of good. A Christian himself, and without a trace of infidelity in his opinions, Dr. Esdaile scouts the idea of the study of Mesmerism promoting *theism*; and, though he gives no sign of knowing the connection of his idea with Vedantism or *Yoga*, he says that by this research the life of man "will probably be found to be only a modification of the vital agent which pervades the Universe." Thence, he says, we may "come to understand the astounding sympathies and affinities sometimes developed between the organic and inorganic world, and be led to suspect the possibility of the finite mind of man passing for a time into relation with the infinite, and thereby receiving impressions otherwise than by the senses which regulate and circumscribe our knowledge of surrounding nature in our normal state of existence." These are the wise words of a true philosopher, and I may add, a true Christian in the better sense of the word. Mesmerism—a modern European discovery of an old Asiatic science—*is the key to the mystical phenomena of the Hindu Sastras*. Young gentlemen of the University, remember this, and withhold your flippant scepticism about your ancestral faith until at least you have mastered this subject. Yes, in Mesmerism is balm for the heart of the searcher after the hidden truth of Aryan philosophy.

Look, if you please, at this engraving. It is from a little work published two years ago at Lahore by Sabhapathy Swami. It represents the system of psychic development by *Raj Yoga*. Here is traced a series of lines and circles upon the naked body of a man sitting in the posture of *Padmasan*, and practising *Yoga*. The triple line passes down the front of the head and body making the circles at certain points, *viz*., over the *Vomer*, or nasal cavity, the mouth, the root of the throat, the heart, the umbilicus &c. The artist, to bring the whole system into one view traces for us the parts of the line and circles that would be out of sight, such as that over the lower end of the spinal column, the line up the spine, and over the cerebellum and cerebrum, until it unites with the front line. This line is the line travelled by the will of the *Yogi* in his process of psychic development. He, as it were, visits each of the centres of vital force in turn and subjugates them to dependance upon the Will. The circles are the *chakras*, or centres of forces, and when he has traversed the entire circuit of his corporal kingdom, he will have perfectly evolved his inner self—disengaged it from its natural state of commixture with the outer shell, or physical self. His next step is to project this " double" outside the body, transferring to it his complete consciousness and then, having passed the threshold of his carnal prison-house, into the world of psychic freedom, his powers of sight, hearing, and the other senses are indefinitely increased, and his movements are no longer transmelled by the obstacles which impede those of the external man. Do not understand me as saying that this is the only method of psychic evolution ; there are others than Patanjali's, and some better ones. The highest form of *Yoga*—to employ that as a generic term—is one by which there is rather a moral than a physical or semiphysical training and evolution, and, as I conceive, by this process the ascetic sooner and more perfectly breaks through the wall of *maya* or illusion, than he can by Patanjali's methods.

Perhaps, some one of the physiologists in this audience may feel like denying that consciousness can be thus transferred from the sensorium in the brain to other parts of the body. Such if they are here I will ask to refer to the back numbers of the *Zoist*, to Professor Weinholt's *Lecture on Somnambulism*, to the *Breslau Medical Collections*, to Dr. Bertrand's Treatise on *Somnambulism*, to Dr. Pettin's *Electricite Animale*, to the Proceedings of the Philosophical Society of Lausanne, to the Report of Signori Corini, Visconti and Mazzacorati of a case in the Hospital Della Vita at Bologna, to Dr. Esdaile's and Professor William Gregory's works, and scores of others I might mention. They will there find that in certain morbid states of the nervous system especially catalepsy and hysteria, the senses of hearing, sight, taste and touch are localized at the pit of the stomach, the finger-tips, the soles of the feet and the back of the head. I do not claim any especial weight for my own testimony, but still, as one always likes to have oral evidence when possible, I may tell you that I have seen examples of some of those psycho-physiological phenomena. Not to dwell upon others, I will mention but a single case—that of an American girl of 10 years, daughter of a friend of mine. This charming little child would in her waking state read any book, point or writing I held against the back of her head. The faculty, which she accidentally discovered, left her after a couple of years without apparent cause. Now, if nature thus spontaneously offers us examples of the higher mesmeric and other psychic phenomena, their possibility *is by nature herself proven.* The only remaining question is whether the *Yogi* or other mystic can, by intense concentration of his will upon a certain centre of vital activity, voluntarily excite an identical condition. And that he can, I know to a certainty.

I have spoken of Baron Von Reichenbach's masterly work: here it is. I affirm that this record of five years' experiments of an Austrian chemist of the first eminence contains in itself a master-key to Aryan psychological phenomena. That Von Reichenbach probably never read a single *Sastra*, or gave himself one moment's concern about *Patanjali*, does not in the least detract from the value of his researches. You see the silvery nimbus or cloud about the head of the *Yogi* in Sabhaputhy Swami's book, and here I show you pictures of the Hindu Gods, Siva and Krishna, with their Parvatis, Radhas, and Gopis. Around the head of each is the same aureole. These are not sketched after the conceptions of some modern artist; they represent the popular idea of hundreds and thousands of years ago. And now I show you a similar picture by a Christian artist of a Christian saint—where the same glory and of a transcending brightness is depicted.

In Buddhist temples, the image of the recumbent Buddha laying in the divine ecstasies, has a flaming aureole of this kind about the head; the lines of color not standing out like spikes, but wavy, like the coruscating splendours of the auroras of the North and South poles. In the rock-cut image of Zoroaster which is assumed to give, perhaps, the nearest idea of a personal likeness of that splendid seer, the same idea of a glory about the head is carried out.

Now, whence did the Hindu, the Buddhist, the Parsi, and the Christian get this impression that the head of a spiritual leader must radiate lights? Shall I surprise you when I say that we may find the answer in this book of Reichenbach? Look at this illustration. This figure B represents the actual luminous appearance of the human head, as seen by one of a class of persons of acute nervous sensitiveness with whose help the author made his researches. Repeated experiments with over fifty such sensitives, demonstrated that the human system, in common with every animate and inanimate natural object, and with the whole starry heavens, is pervaded with a subtle aura, or, if you please, imponderable fluid, which resembles magnetism and electricity in certain respects, and yet is analogous with neither. He called it Od, or Odyle. This aura while radiating in a faint mist from all parts of our bodies, is peculiarly bright about the head. These two spots of light are the eyes, and this third one is the mouth. Now this picture represents the aura of a young married lady; and we have only to imagine to ourselves—as we may from all the analogies of nature—how this aura would be intensified by enormous concentration of the will, to comprehend readily the intuition which first suggested the artistic conception of the aureole. In fact, we see that

Reichenbach was anticipated by the Aryans in the knowledge of the Odic aura. But all the same, remember kindly that we might never have understood what the nimbus about Krishna means, but for this Vienna chemist.

I must not pass on towards my conclusion before showing you that we can get some instruction from Reichenbach upon certain Brahminical customs prescribed in the *Sastras*, but which I have not yet found even one Brahmin to explain. You have had two kinds of Brahminic custom handed down, one primitive and essential, the other secondary and non-essential customs and practices no doubt invented by cunning priests to save profitable vested rights, when the caste had begun to lose its original spirituality. When Brahmins sit to eat, every man is isolated from his neighbours at the feast; he sits in the centre of a square traced upon the floor, grandsire, father and son, brother and uncle, avoiding touching each other quite as scrupulously as though they were of different castes. If I should handle a Brahmin's brass platter, his *lotah* or other vessel for food or drink, neither he nor any of his caste would touch it, much less eat or drink from it until it had been passed through fire: if the utensil were of clay, it must be broken. Why all these? That no affront is meant by avoidance of contact is shown in the careful isolation of members of the same family from each other. The explanation, I submit, is that every brahmin was supposed to be an individual evolution of psychic force, apart from all consideration of family relationship: if one touched the other at this particular time when the vital force was actively centred upon the process of digestion, the psychic force was liable to be drawn off, as a leaden jar charged with electricity is discharged by touching it with your hand. The Brahmin of old was an initiate, and his evolved psychic power was employed in the *agnihotra* and other ceremonies. The case of the touching of the eating or drinking vessel, or the mat or clothing of a Brahmin by one of another caste, of inferior psychic development, or the stepping of such a person upon the ground, within a certain prescribed distance from the sacrificial spot, bear upon this question. In this same plate of Baron Reichenbach's, the figure F represents the aura streaming from the points of the human hand. Every human being has such an aura, and the aura is peculiar to himself or herself as to quality and volume. Now the aura of a Brahmin of the ancient times was purified and intensified by a peculiar course of religious training —let us say psychic training,—and if it should be mixed with the aura of a less pure, less spiritualized person, its strength would of necessity be lessened, its quality adulterated. Reichenbach tells us that the Odic emanation is conductible by metals, slower than electricity, but more rapidly than heat, and that pottery and other clay vessels absorb and retain it for a great while. Heat he found to enormously increase quantitively the flow of Odyle through a metal conductor. The Brahmin, then, in submitting his odylically-tainted metallic vessel to the fire, is but experimentally carrying out the theory of Von Reichenbach. I will not, however, enlarge upon a branch of my subject which might well be made the theme of a series of lectures. The gathering obscurity of the twilight warns me to be brief as the breadth of one theme and its novelty to you permit, as also does the fear that I may have already overtaxed your patience. I must use my few remaining minutes by saying something more specific about the Theosophical Society.

The Society has no endowment, its current expenses being met as far as practicable, out of an Initiation Fee of Rs. 10. The deficiency is made good by Madame Blavatsky and myself out of our private resources. Our printed rules define the objects of our organization to be:—

First.—To form the nucleus of a Universal Brotherhood of Humanity, without distinction of race, creed, or color.

Second.—To promote the study of Aryan and other Eastern literature, religions, and sciences, and vindicate their importance.

Third.—To investigate the hidden mysteries of nature and the psychical power in man.

I have touched upon these sufficiently, I hope, to make it clear that our Society has not one feature of sectarianism in it; that it regards religion as a personal matter; that its founders do not believe that any actual knowledge can be obtained of Divine things except through psychical development; that it has not a shadaw of political character; that it is neither a propaganda, nor a special antagonist of any particular faith; that its influence must be in the direction of piety, personal purification, unselfishness, and patriotism in the noblest sense of that most abused word. Finally, you must infer that instead of undervaluing Western culture and scientific research, we have a thorough appreciation of the importance of both.

The question between you and myself at this present moment is whether you will take an active, practical interest in our work, and help us to make Bengal what it ought to be in virtue of its traditions and its world-wide reputation for intellectual, metaphysical, and scientific capacity, the centre of a Theosophical revival that shall thrill all India with the promise of a new spiritual era. I am not asking you to draw the rusty sword of Luxman Sen from its scabbard and deluge your land in blood. It is not war that India wants, but peace—peace to develop her prostrate industries; peace to improve her agriculture, and to re-adjust her population to territory, drawing away the surplus where it is overcrowding the land, and settling it in districts where labour can find vacant land and employment; peace to remove all obstructive barriers, and knit the races of the Peninsula into a brotherly and reciprocolly profitable union; peace to foster the taste for art, which was once so high that the land is filled with monuments which excite the world's wonder; peace to found Sanskrit schools wherever they flourished in the old time, so that once more the contents of Indian literature may be known, and this present foul reproach of ignorance of our *Sastras* may be removed; and peace that there may be born a generation of unselfish patriots, in place of the present one, which I need not describe: a generation which will esteem it the highest happiness as well as the highest honor to forget self, and work for the public good. Aye, "Peace hath its victories, as well as war." I have not come here to ask you to give us money, or ask to erect great temples of Theosophy, to stand as laughing-stocks of human vanity for the warning of coming generations. I am not asking you to overturn the alerts of your faith to make room for hybrid erections of ignorant iconoclasts. I do not ask you to trample under the feet of pert criticism the sacred literature of your forefathers, and substitute for the majestic rhythm and profound thought of its *slokas*, the crude rhapsodies of modern ideologists. I am not asking the educated among you to put aside the science your masters of the College have taught you, nor to tear up the diplomas which are the certificates of your industry and your culture. I am not come to tear down the *purdah*s behind which the lustful violence of your conquerors obliged you to hide your beloved mothers and sisters, wives and daughters. I am quite content to leave to time its changes, and to the increasing good sense of the Hindus the cure of all evils, and the extirpation of all abuses.

But I stand here as the unworthy mouthpiece of Ancient India, to speak a word of appeal on her behalf into the ears of the present generation. Since science has proved that your race and mine boast a common parentage, and that the streams of Aryan and European civilization flowed from a single fount I speak by right of heritage for the claims of Aryan philosophy. If you will it, we may together work in fraternal concord, and together snatch from the oblivion of neglect the science of Divine Truth, the Wisdom—Religion of archaic times. We care not what may be the name of your Samaj; if you are working for India, we will work with you.

The *Mahimnastava*, a hymn to Siva, daily chanted by the Brahmins (for an English translation of which I am indebted to my venerable friend, Babu Rajnarain Bose) expresses a sentiment which I would like every modern Hindu to take to heart. It mirrors the spirit of our Society, and is as follows:—

"As the Ocean is the goal of all rivers, so Thou art the ultimate goal of different paths, straight or divious, which men follow, according to their different tastes and inclinations."

I am asked how we shall set about this task, how to learn Occultism without teachers, and without text-books that we can read. For just such emergencies as these men always arise: we must create the teachers and compile the books. Meanwhile, we must turn to a quarter where we need never seek in vain. There is a Teacher within us who waits for us to unlock his prison-doors and set him free. That Teacher is our veritable Ego, our Inner Self. We can reach him by holy lives, abstract meditations, and the evolution of the powers of will. More than one road will lead us to the *Adytum* wherein he dwells; for adeptship is of no one creed, and is the life of all faiths. Look at the prescribed methods of training under different systems, and you will find that while they differ as to formulas, they resemble in essentials. *First*, the man must be pure—in body, mind, and aspiration. *Second*, the place chosen must be pure—in atmosphere and surroundings. It must also be quiet and safe. *Third*, the diet must be simple, digestable, and taken in as moderate quantities as the preservation of bodily health admits. The would-be adept must have physical stamina, for concentration makes a great drain upon vital force. And the experience of mediums shows that mediumship except in the highest form of mental impressibility, is usually concomitant with a scrofulous or phthisical taint in the blood. *Fourth*, the motive must be a noble and unselfish desire for divine wisdom, and lastly, the practice must be gradual and cumulative. Given these, and one may be sure of attaining his end—that of developing into an adept Theosophist.

My task is finished, my word spoken. It remains with you to crown our effort with practical success, or to suffer my voice to pass profitlessly, in widening ripples of sound, out into the ocean of air; remember only that what may be done to-day may be impossible to-morrow. Neglect has brought Hinduism to its present pass. Neglect has reduced the Brahmin Pundits already to a condition little better than that of half-starvation or genteel beggary. If they would not expose themselves to the rude rebuffs of the bazaar, and jostle with a crowd of painted impostors who masquerade as *Sadhus* to cheat the charitable, and secretly give loose rein to their beastly natures—they must seek Government employ and convert themselves into clerical automata. Their once famous schools are now only a memory, and their once grand debates on philosophy at the courts of kings survive only in legendary story. A wave of practicalism is sweeping away the last vestiges of Hindu originality, engulfing the fairest relics of Aryan greatness, as the muddy overflow from the crater Kilauea swallows up the trees and villages upon its slopes. Neglect, and sottish laziness has done all this. A few years—or perhaps a few generations more, and the foreign boot will be on every Hindu foot, the foreign brandy bottle in every Hindu hand, and what is a thousand times worse— the foreign heart will be beating in every Hindu body, for love of country's religion will have all died out. Are you prepared to face this ultimate? Burns there in corner of your breast a spark of that noble pride and self-respect that made the Aryan man ennoble by his personal virtues the Aryan name? If you would arrest the tide of national demoralization that is rushing the brandy shop and the opium den, you must set up again the old moral standard, and teach your children to live up to them. You can save your nationality and regain your spiritual mindedness, or you can impiously see them swept by the torrent of pretended "Progress," into the *Kala Pani* of commercial expediency. Some of your best men thought India had already reached that stage, for they wrote me, two years ago, from Bengal, that we Theosophists had come too late. India was dead, and hope extinguished. But I said No, and I say so now: a nation is never dead while one single patriot son survives. For he alone, by an extraordinary moral grandeur and spiritual insight, may re-infuse the vanished life into the decrepit frame, and laying his holy hand upon his mother's heart, cause it to beat again. No, Aryavarta—Queen-mother of nations,—is not dead. Her altar-fires burn feebler every year, and the recollection of her spiritual triumphs is becoming a tradition of a by-gone time; yet it is not too late for her children to labor for her, and sacrifice themselves for her dear sake.

The sacrifice will not be profitless, the labor not be vain. Remember and take heart from what an English Lord wrote:

> "Dejected India lift thy downcast eyes,
> And mark the hour whose steadfast steps for thee
> From Time's pressed ranks brings on the Jubilee."

THE COMMON FOUNDATION OF ALL RELIGIONS.

Delivered at the Patchiappah's Hall, Madras,
on the 26th April 1882.

———o———

Before proceeding with my discourse I must first express the profound thanks of Madame Blavatsky—my learned colleague—and myself for the warm and distinguished welcome we have received, from your Committee on our landing, and this immense assemblage which embraces so large a number of the educated men of this Presidency. We have thus had one more proof of the fact that the progress of our work in India is being watched with affectionate interest by the intelligent classes of the Indian Peninsula. Once more, upon visiting for the first time a Presidency town, we find ourselves among friends the sincerity of whose welcome cannot be misunderstood, and which unmistakeably proves that we are not received as strangers but as brethern are who return from a distant land to their own people. Let us hope that the fraternal ties now created between us may never be broken, but grow stronger and stronger as time makes us all to see the necessity for united effort on behalf of the sacred cause of Indian interests. I trust that you will give patient attention to the thoughts that I shall now offer for your consideration.

Religion is—according to Mr. Herbert Spencer—"a great (I should say the greatest) reality and a great truth—nothing less than an essential and indestructible element of human nature." He holds that the religious institutions of the world represent a genuine and universal feeling in the race just as really as any other institution. The accessory superstitions which have overgrown and perverted the religious sentiment must not be confounded with the religious sentiment itself. That this is done is a mischievous mistake, alike of religionists and anti-religionists. Science in clearing away these excrescences brings us always nearer the underlying truth, and is therefore the handmaid and friend of true religion. The substratum of truth is the one broad plateau of rock upon which the world's theological superstructures are reared. It is—as the title of our lecture puts it—"the common foundation of all religions."

And now what is it? What is this rock? It is a conglomerate, having more than one element in its composition. In the first place, of necessity, is the idea of a part of man's nature which is non-physical; next, the idea of a post-mortem continuation of this non-physical part; third, the existence of an Infinite Principle underlying all phenomena; fourth, a certain relationship between this Infinite Principle and the non-physical part of man.

The evolution of the grander from the lower intellectual conception in this graded sequence is now conceded, alike by the scientist and the theologian. This evolution is accompanied by an elimination, for in religion as in all other departments of thought the light cannot be seen until the clouds are cleared away. Primitive truth is the light, theologies the clouds; and they are clouds still though they glitter with all the hues of the spectrum. Fetish worship, animal worship, hero worship, ancestor worship, nature worship, book worship; polytheism, monotheism, theism, deism, atheism, materialism (which includes positivism), agnosticism; the blind adoration of the idol, the blind adoration of the crucible—these are the Alpha and the Omega of human religious thought, the measure of relative spiritual blindness.

All these concepts pass through a single prism—the human mind. And that is why they are so imperfect, so incongruous, so human. A man can never see the whole light by looking from inside his body outwardly, any more than one can see the clear daylight through a dust-soiled window-glass, or the stars through a smeared reflecting lens. Why? Because the physical senses are adapted only to the things of a physical world, and religion is a transcendentalism. Religious truth is not a thing for physical observation, but one for psychical intuition. One who has not developed this psychical power can never *know* religion as a fact; he can only accept it as a creed, or paint it to himself as an emotional sentimentality. Bigotry is the brand to put upon one; Gush that for the other. Back of both, and equally threatening them, is Scepticism.

Like man his religion has its ages: *first*, proclamation, propagandism, martyrdom; *second*, conquest, faith; *third*, neglect, self-criticism; *fourth*, decadence, tenacious formalism; *fifth*, hypocrisy; *sixth*, compromise; *seventh*, decay and extinction. And, like the human race, no religion passes *as a whole* through these stages *seriatim*. At this very day, we see the Australian sunk in the depths of animalism, the American Red Indian, just emerging from the Stone Age, the European in the full flush of high material civilization. And so, a glance at religious history shows us the cropping up of highly heretical schools and sects in each great religion, of which each represents some special departure from primitive orthodoxy, some separate advance along the road towards the final goal that we have sketched out. And I also note, as the physician observes the symptoms of his patient, that history constantly shows in the bitter mutual hatreds of these cliques and sects for each other, the clearest proofs that our postulate is correct when we say—as just now—that Religion can never be really known by the physical brain of the physical man. All these hatreds, bitternesses and cruel reprisals of sect for sect, and world's faith for world's faith, show that men mistake the nonessentials for essentials, illusions for realities.

We can test this statement most easily. Look away from this war of theologians to the class of men who have developed their psychical powers and what do you see? In place of strife, peace, agreement, mutual tolerance, a brotherly concord as to the fundamentals of religion. Whatever their exoteric creed they are greater than and far above it, and their innate holiness and gentleness of nature give life and strength to the church they represent, they are the flowers of the human tree, the brothers of all mankind; for they know what is the light that shines behind the clouds; under the foundations of all the churches they see the same rock. I ask those of you who wish to be convinced of this fact to read the *Dabistan*, by Mohsan Fani, who records in it his observations of the sadhus of twelve different religions two centuries ago. "Granting all the premises,"—the modern sceptic will say—"can you prove to me that science has not swept away all your religious hypothesis along with the myths, legends, superstitions and other lumber? Well, I answer "Yes." It is exactly on that datum line that the Theosophical Society is building itself up. Some people think us opponents of Science, but on the contrary we are its warmest advocates—until it begins to dogmatize from incomplete known data upon new facts. When it reaches that point we challenge it and fight it with all our strength, such as it may be, just as we fight the dogmatism of theology. For to our mind, it does'nt matter whether you blindly worship a fetish, a man, a book, or a crucible—it's blind idolatry all the same; and Science can be, and has been, as cruel and remorseless in her way as the Church ever was in her's.

The first step is to have an agreement as to what the word 'Science' means. I take it to be the collection and arrangement of observed facts about Nature. If that is correct, then I protest against half-measures: I want those observations to be complete, to cover all of Nature, not the half of it. What sort of an Ontology would it be which, while pretending to investigate the laws of our being, took note only of our anatomy, physiology and whatever relates to the physical frame of man, leaving out all that concerns his mental function? Absurd! you would say; but I ask you whether it is any more absurd to study man in his body without the mind, than to study him in body and mind while ignoring the trans-corporeal manifestations of his middle-nature. You want me to define what I mean by this "middle nature" and by its trans-corporeal manifestations: I will do so. I start, then, with the proposition that there is more of a man than can be burnt with fire, eaten by tigers, drowned by water, chopped to pieces with knives, or rotten in the ground. The materialist will deny this, but it doesn't matter; the proposition can be proved as easily as that he is a man. They have in Europe a science which they call Psychology: it is a misnomer—it is another kind of Ology—but we won't quarrel about words. Well, when you come to analyze the Western idea that underlies this term of Psychology, you will discover that it relates only to the normal and abnormal intellectual manifestations of the brain. One class of scientists—especially among the alienists, or students of Insanity—maintain that mind is a function of the gray vesicles of the lobes of the brain; injure the brain by any one of a dozen accidents and sensation is cut off, thought ceases, mind is destroyed, the thinking, hence responsible, entity is extinguished. All that is left is carrion, and out of this carrion, before the accident, sprang by magneto-electric energy all that distinguishes man from the lowest animal, as the lotus springs from slimy mud. The opposed party affirm that the brain is the organ of the mind, the machine of its manifestation, and that the thinking something in man thinks still and still exists even though the brain be shattered, even though the man die. The one reflects the tone of materialistic science, the other the tone of the Christian Churches and of the two crores of so-called modern Spiritualists. The Materialists regard man as an Unity, a thinking machine the other regard him as a Duality, a compound of body and soul. There is no ground for a "middle-nature" in either of these schools. True, here and there, you will find some casual allusion to a third and higher principle—the 'spirit,' as, for instance, in the Christian New Testament (I Thessalonians, v., 23) where Paul says, "I pray God your whole spirit and soul and body be preserved blameless unto the coming of our Lord Jesus Christ"—an expression which, however sound as theology, is dreadfully loose and heterodox as science. But the whole drift of christian teaching and of mediumistic teaching favors the duality theory; the body dead, the second principle enters on a new career of its own until it attains to a postulated *summum bonum* or *summum malum* state. Now, experienced observers of the mediumistic phenomena have seen many animated figures or more or less substantial apparitions of deceased persons, and these they regard as the returning souls revisiting the land of the living. They have no idea of this middle-nature. But the Hindu Philosophers make a far deeper analysis of man. Instead of a single part, or a duality, they affirm that there are no fewer than seven distinct groups which go to make up a human being. These are:—

(1.) The Material body—*Stoolasarira* ;
(2.) The *Lingasarira* ;
(3.) The Life Principle—*Jiva* ;
(4.) The *Kamarupa*, resulting as *Mayavirupa* ;
(5.) The Physical Intelligence (or Animal soul) *Manas* ;
(6.) The Spiritual Intelligence—*Buddhi* ;
(7.) The *Atma*.

And, so minute is their analysis, each of these groups is subdivided into 7 sub-groups. Generally speaking, the 1st, 4th and 7th principles mark the boundaries of the tripartite or trinitarian man. And the 4th, which comes just midway between the gross body (*Stoolasarira*) and the *Atma*, or divine and eternal Principle, is this Middle Nature of which we have been in search. Now the next question to be asked us is whether this 4th Principle, or Mayavirupa or human 'Double,' is intelligent or non-intelligent, matter or spirit; and the next, whether its existence can be scientifically accounted for and proved. We will take them in order. In itself the Double is but a vapour, a mist, or a solid form according to its relative state of condensation. Given outside the body one set of atmospheric, electric, magnetic, telluric and other conditions, this form may be invisible yet capable of making sounds or giving other tests of its presence; given another set of conditions it may be visible, but as a misty vapour; given a third set, it may be condensed into perfect visibility and even tangibility. Volumes upon volumes might be filled with bare paragraph abstracts of recorded instances of these apparitional visits. Sometimes the form manifests intelligence, it speaks; sometimes it can only show itself—I am now speaking of the apparitions of dead persons. I have personally seen more than 500 such apparitions at a place in America where hundreds more saw them, and I put my experiences in the form of a book, which was praised by some of the eminent scientists of Europe as a careful record of scientifically accurate observations. I only mention this to satisfy you that here is no case of hallucination or unsupported statements. Well, then, we have here the middle nature of man acting outside of and after the death of the physical body; though for my part—being a believer in Asiatic

Psychology—I do not believe that these post-mortem apparitions are the very man himself—the thinking, responsible Ego. They are, I conceive but the vapoury image of the deceased—matter energized by a residuum of the vital-force which is still entangled in the lingering molecules. But to prove our proposition we must show that this middle principle, this *Mayavirupa* or double, can be separated from the living body at will, projected to a distance, and animated by the full consciousness of the man. We have two means of proving this—(1), in the concurrent testimony of eye-witnesses as recorded in the literature of different races; and (2), in the evidence of living witnesses. In the Hindu religious and philosophical works there are many such testimonies. Not to mention others we may cite the case of Sankaracharya, who entranced his body, left it in the custody of his disciples, entered the body of a Rajah just deceased, and lived in it for a number of weeks; and that of Agastiya who appeared in the heat of the battle between Rama and Ravana, while his body was entranced in the Neilgherries. This story is given in the *Ramayana*. In Patanjali's Yoga Sutras this phenomenon is affirmed to be within the power of every Siddha who perfects himself in Yoga As to living witneses I am one myself, for I have seen the Doubles of several men acting intelligently at great distances from their bodies, and in this pamphlet that I now show you,* will be found the certificates of no less than 9 reputable persons—5 Hindus and 4 Europeans—that they have seen such appearances on various occasions within the past two years. And then we have the scores of similar attestations from credible persons living in different parts of the world, which are to be read in many European books treating upon these subjects. I do not pretend to say that a sceptical public can be expected to take this mass of evidence, conclusive as it may be, without reserve; the alleged phenomenon so surpasses ordinary human experience that to believe its reality each one must see for himself. I however do affirm that we have here a case of probable verity made out; for, under the strictest canons of scientific orthodoxy, we cannot suspect a conspiracy to lie among so many individual witnesses, who never saw or heard of each other, who, in fact, did not even live in the same generation, but yet whose testimonies corroborate each other.

But if we have a case of probable truth, the man of science will ask us what we next demand of him. Do we allege a natural and scientific,

---

* *Hints on Esoteric Theosophy*. Published at Calcutta, 1882, by a Member for the benefit of the Theosophical Society, and to be had for Re. 1, post free, through the Manager of the *Theosophist*.

or a supernatural, hence unscientific, explanation for the projection of the double of the living, and the apparition of that of the deceased man? I answer, most assuredly, the former. I am devoted enough of Science to deny, with all the emphasis I can give to words, the fact that a miraculous phenomenon ever took place, in this age or any age. Whatever has ever occured must have done so within the operation of natural law. To suppose anything else would be equivalent to saying that there is no permanency in the laws of the universe, but that they can be set aside and played with at the caprice of an irresponsible and meddlesome Power. We should be in a universe going by jerks, started and stopped like a clock that a child is playing with. This supernaturalism is the curse of all creeds, it hangs like an incubus around the neck of the religious and hatches the satire of the sceptic: it is the dry-rot that eats out the heart of any faith that builds upon it. This, it is, which, carried in the body of a church, foredooms it to ultimate destruction as surely as the hidden cancer carried in the human system will one day kill it. And of all epochs this XIXth century is the worst in which to come before the public as the champions of supernatural religions. They are going down in every land, melting before the laboratory fires like waxen images. No, when I stand forth as the defender of Hinduism, Buddhism or Zoroastrianism, I wish it understood that I do not claim any respect or tolerance for them outside the limits of natural law. I believe—nay I *know*—that their foundation is a scientific one, and on those conditions they must stand or fall so far as I am concerned. I do not say they are in equally close reconciliation with science, but I do say that whatever foundation they have, whether broad or narrow, long or short, is and must be a scientific one. And so, too, when I ask you to cease from making yourselves ridiculous by denying the existence of this middle nature in man, it is because I am persuaded, as the result of much reading and a good deal of personal experience, that the double, or Mayavirupa, is a scientific fact.

Well, then, to return—is it matter or something else? I say matter *plus* something else. And here stop a moment to think what matter is. Loose thinkers—among whom we must class raw lads fresh from college though they be ever so much titled—are too apt to associate the idea of matter with the properties of density, visibility, and tangibility. But this is very inexcusable. The air we breathe is invisible, yet matter—its equivalents of Oxygen, Hydrogen, Nitrogen and Carbonic Acid are each atomic, ponderable, demonstrable by analysis. Electricity cannot, except under prepared conditions, be seen, yet it is matter. The

Universal Ether of science no one ever saw, yet it is matter in a state of extreme tenuity. Take the familiar example of forms of water, and see how they rapidly run up the scale of tenuity until they elude the clutch of science: stone-hard ice, melted ice, condensed steam, superheated and invisible steam, electricity, and—it is gone out of the world of effects into the world of causes!

Well, then, with this warning before you, my cerebrally superheated young friend of the Madras University, pray do not contradict me when I say that the Hindu philosophy of man fits in with the lines of modern science much more snugly than that of either the supernaturalistic Christian or the materialistic man of science. As we have seen the successive forms of water running up into the invisible world, so, here, Esoteric Hindu Philosophy gives us a graduated series of molecular arrangements in the human economy at one end of which is the concrete mass of the *Stoolasarira*, at the other the last sublimation called *Atmā*, or spirit. "But how can all these exist together in one combination; is a man like a nest of boxes or baskets fitted into each other, or do you mean to say the scientific absurdity that two things can simultaneously occupy the same space?" This is a side question provoked by the main one, but we must dispose of it first. I will say, then, that, as the thing has been explained to me, each of these several sets of atoms which compose the seven parts of man occupy the interstitial spaces between the next coarser set of atoms. They are focalized as to their several energies in what the Hindus call the Shadadharams, or centres of vital force, crowned by Sahasraram, in which Atma is located. This supreme point is in the crown of the head: the others are located at the base of the spine, the abdomen, the umbilicus, the heart, the root of the throat, and the centre of the frontal sinus. The atoms of the *Buddhi* would, then, pervade the interstices of the *Manās*; those of the Manas those of the *Kamarupa*; those of the latter those of the *Jiva*; and those of the Jiva those of the *Stoolasarira*. And, as each coarser contains the particles of all the finer principles, therefore the Stoolasarira is the gross casket within which the several parts of the composite man are contained. Pervading and energizing all is the Atma, or that incomprehensible final energy which cannot be comprehended by the physical senses, and which is described to himself by the Brahman in the *Mandukyo Upanishad* by saying: "Thou art not this, nor that, nor the third, nor anything which the mind can grasp with the help of the physical perceptions." Your popular Telugu poet beautifully and allegorically depicts this idea in his poem

Sitárámá anjaniyam (cosmic matter) where Sita—who is herself the personification of Prakriti—is asked by the daughters and wives of the Rishis to point out her husband, but, through modesty, refrains. The ladies then pointing successively to a number of different men ask each time "Is this thy husband?" She answers in the negative, but when they point to Rama she is silent, for she cannot even speak of her heart's lord before strangers. So, the Poet would have us understand, while we may freely say what Atma is *not*, when we are required to say what it *is* we must be silent, for words are powerless to express the sublime idea.

We have now prepared the ground to answer both of the questions put to us by our imaginary critic. The Kamarupa when intelligently projected beyond the physical body by the developed energy of an initiate of Occult Science, contains in it all his Manas and Buddhi (including the *Chittham* and *Akankaram*—sense of individuality)—his Intelligence and Spiritual Intelligence. The initiate quits his earthly casket—in which are left the Jiva and Lingasarira—and for the moment lives, thinks and acts in this Double of himself. Its atomic condition being less dense than that of the corporeal body, it has enhanced powers of locomotion and perception. Barriers that would stop the body—for example, the walls of a room—cannot stop it, for its particles may pass, through the interstices of the gross matter composing the wall. It is in the subjective world and may traverse its space like thought, which is itself a form of energy. Or, if he likes, the initiate may simply project a non-intelligent image of himself and make it appear at the spot at which he may have focalized his thought. It depends upon him whether the image shall be but an illusionary form, or his own self; it may be mere matter, or matter *plus* himself. As to our accounting for the middle nature of man scientifically, I have already shown that we may do this by the collection of testimonies, and by personal observation. We may add that further proof is obtainable by the best and surest of all methods—that of going oneself through the necessary course of self-training and projecting one's own Double. For this is no exclusive science reserved for a favoured few: it is a true science based upon natural law, and within the reach of every one who has the requisite qualifications. The humblest labourer may lift the veil of mystery as well as the proudest sovereign or the haughtiest priest.

But, it is constantly asked why are not these secrets thrown open to the world as freely as the details of chemistry or any other branch of knowledge? It is a natural question—for a superficial reasoner to put;

but it is not a sound one. The difference between Psychic and Physical sciences is that the former can only be learned by the self-evolution of psychical powers. No college professor can evolve them for you, nor any friend, fellow-student or relative : you must evolve them for yourself. Can another man learn Music, or Sanskrit, or the art of Painting or Sculpture for you ? Can another eat, sleep, feel warm or cold, digest or breathe for you ? Then why should you expect him to learn Psychology for you ? Anyhow he cannot do it, however much you may expect it, and that's the final answer to all such questioners. Nor is it absolutely *certain* that, even though you should try ever so much, you could evolve these powers in yourself. Has every man the capacity for Languages, or Music, or Poetry, or Science, or Philosophy ? You know that each of these require certain clear aptitudes, and if you have them not you can never become musician, poet, scientist or philosopher. The branches of physical science are difficult to master even when you have the natural capacity; but psychical science is more difficult than either of them—I might almost say than all combined. That is why the Mahatma has been described as "the rare efflorescence of a generation of enquirers" (Sinnett's *The Occult World*, p. 101,) and in all generations the true Sadhu has been reverenced as almost a superhuman being. The term applies to him only in the sense of his being above the weaknesses, the prejudice and the ignorance of his fellowmen. With the most absurd blindness to the experience of the race, we, Founders of the Theosophical Society, are constantly being asked to turn its members into adepts. We must show them the short cut to the Himavat, the private passages to the Asraonums in the Neilgherries ! They are not willing to work and suffer for the getting of knowledge, as all have who have got it heretofore, they must be put into a first-class carriage and taken straight behind the Veil of Isis ! They fancy our Society an improved sort of Miracle Club, or School of Magic wherein for 10 Rupees a man can become a Mahatma between the morning bath and the evening meal ! Such people entirely overlook the avowed two chief objects of the Society—the formation of a nucleus of an Universal Brotherhood for the research after truth and the promotion of kind feelings between man and man; and the promotion of the study of ancient religions, philosophies, and sciences. They do not appreciate this purely unselfish part of the Society's work, nor seem to think it a noble and most meritorious thing to labour for the enlightenment and happiness of mankind. They have an insatiable curiosity to behold wonders, seeing which they would not, in many instances, be stimulated to search after the hidden springs of wisdom, but only sit with open mouth and pendulous tongue, to wonder how the trick was done and what would be the next one! Such minds can get no profit by joining the Theosophical Society, and I advise them to stay outside. We want no such selfish triflers. Ours is a serious, hard-working, self-denying society, and we want only men worthy to be called men and worthy of our respect. We want men whose first question will not be "what good can I get by joining?" but "what good can I *do* by joining?" Our work requires the services of men who can be satisfied to labour for the next generation and the succeeding ones; men who, seeing the lamentable religious state of the world—seeing noble faiths debased, temples, churches, and holy shrines thronged by hypocrites and mockers—burn with a desire to rekindle the fires of spirituality and morality upon the polluted altars, and bring the knowledge of the Rishis within the reach of a sin-burdened world. We want Hindus who can love India with so pure an affection that they will count it a joy and an honour beyond price to work and to suffer, even, for her sake. Men, we want, who will be able to put aside for the moment their puerile hatreds of race, and creed, and caste, as they put away a soiled cloth or a worn-out garment; and with a loving heart and clean conscience be ready to join with every other man—be he black or white, red or yellow, bondsman or freeman—whose heart beats with love for India and her wide-scattered children of many races throughout the world. We welcome most those who are ready to trample under foot their selfishness when it comes in conflict with the general good. We welcome the intelligent student of Science, who has such broad conceptions of his subject that he considers it quite as important to solve the mystery of Force as to know the atomic combinations of Matter; and feeling so, is not afraid or ashamed to take for his teacher any one who is competent, whatever be the color of his skin.

Now to take our scientific argument one step further. Granted that the existence of the Double has been proven and also its projectibility, how is it projected? By an expenditure of energy, of course. That energy is the vital force set in motion by the will. The power of concentrating the will for this purpose is one that may be natural or acquired. There are some persons who have it naturally so strong in them that they often send their doubles to distant places and make them visible, though they may never have given a day's study to the science of Psychology: I have known both men and women of this sort. But it is an uncommon power, and can never be exercised at all times except by the true proficient in psychological science. The operations of the brain in mechanically evolving the current of will-force have been more or less carefully expounded by Bain and Maudeseley, while Professors Tait and Balfour Stewart have, in their *Unseen Universe*, traced for us the dynamic effect of thought-evolution into the Ether or, as Hindus have called it, these thousands of years, the *Akasa*. They go so far as to say that it is not an unthinkable proposition that the evolution of thought in a single human brain may dynamically affect a distant planet. In other words, when a thought is evolved a vibration of etheric particles is set up, and this motion must continue on indefinitely. Now the Yogi evolves such a current and turns it in upon himself as a concentrated force; continuing the process until the power is sufficient to force his Double out of its corporeal encasement, and to project it to whatsoever locality he desires. We have thus shown the fact of the Mayavirupa, its capability to exist outside the body, and the energy which causes its projection. I cannot go into details to elaborate the argument, for I can only detain you an hour in this tropical heat. But I have at least, I trust, shown you that I rely only upon scientific principles, and claim no indulgence from the advocates of supernaturalism.

And now is this Double—which is none other than what is commonly called the "Soul" immortal? No, it is not. So much of it as is matter in aggregation must ultimately obey the law of dispersion which in time breaks up and forces out of the objective universe whatever is material. It is equally the law of planetary as of lesser forms. As all that is material in a star was primarily condensed from the loose atoms in space, so all that is material in the human body, however course or however fine they may be, were primarily condensed from the chaotic atoms in the Akasa. And to that dispersed condition they must return whenever the centripetal force that attracted them into the human nucleus ceases to resist the centrifugal force or attractions of the atoms of space. This brings us right upon the problem of a continuity of existence beyond the physical death. Here is the dividing line between the world's religions. The dualists affirm that this soul goes to heavenly or infernal places to be for ever blest or punished according to the deeds done in the body. Though they do not use the very word, yet it is the doctrine of Merit they teach. For even those extremely unscientific theologians who affirm that a punishing and rewarding Deity has from all time pre-ordained some to be saved and some to be damned, tell us that the merit of faith in a certain system of morals and discipline and a share in the vicarious merit of another, are pre-requisites to future bliss. We may assume, therefore, that merit, or KARMA, is a cornerstone of Religion. This is both a logical and scientific proposition, for the thoughts, words and deeds of a man are so many causes which must work out corresponding effects; the good ones can only produce good effects, the bad ones only bad—unless they are antagonized and neutralized by stronger ones that are good. I need not go into the metaphysical analysis of what is bad and what good. We may pass it over with the simple postulate that whatever has either a debasing tendency upon the individual or promotes injustice, misery, suffering, ignorance and animalism in society is essentially bad, what tends to the contrary is good. I should call that a bad religion which taught that it is meritorious to do evil that good may come; for good can never come out of evil, the evil tree produces not good fruit. A religion that can only be propagated at the point of the sword; or upon the martyr's pile; or under instruments of torture; or by devastating countries and enslaving their populations; or by cunning strategems seducing ignorant children or adults away from their families, and castes, and ancestral creeds—is a vile and devilish religion, the enemy of truth, the destroyer of social happiness. If a religion is not based upon a lie, the fact can be proved and it can stand unshaken as the rocky mountain against all the assults of sceptics. A true religion is not one that runs to holes and corners, like a naked leper to hide his sores, when a bold critic casts his searching eye upon it and asks for its credentials. If I stand here to defend what is good in Hinduism, it is because of my full conviction that that good exists, and that however fantastic and even childish some many think its tangled overgrowth of customs, legends and superstitions, there is the rock of truth, of scientific truth, below them all. On that rock it is destined to stand through countless coming generations as it has already stood through the countless generations, which have professed that hoary Faith since the Rishis shot from their Himalayan heights the blazing light of spiritual truth over a dark and ignorant world.

It is most reasonable that you should ask me what those of you are to do who are not gifted with the power to get outside the illusion-breeding screen of the body and acquire an intimate actual perception of "Divine" truth through the developed psychical senses. As we have ourselves shown that all men cannot be adepts, what comfort do we hold out to the rest? This involves a momentary glance at the theory of re-births. If this little span of human life we are now enjoying be the entire sum of human existence; if you and I never lived before, and will never live again, then there would be no ray of hope to offer to any mind that was not capable of the intellectual suicide of blind faith. The doctrine of a vicarious atonement for sin is not merely unthinkable, it is positively repulsive to one who can take a larger and more scientific view of man's origin and destiny than that of the dualists. One whose religious perceptions rest upon the intuition that cause and effect are equal; that there is a perfect and correspondential reign of Law throughout the universe; that under any reasonable conception of eternity, there must always have been at work the same forces as are now active—must scout the assertion that this brief instant of sentient life is our only one. Science has traced us back through an inconceivably long sequence of existences—in the human, the animal, the vegetable, and the mineral kingdoms—to the cradle of future sentient life, the Ether of space. Would a man of science, then, make bold to affirm that you and I, who represent a relatively high stage of evolution, came to be what we are without previous development in other births, whether on this earth or other planets? And if he would not, he must, inconformity with his own canons of the conservation and correlation of energy, deduce from the whole analogy of nature that there is another life for us beyond this life. The force which evolved us cannot be expended, it must run on in its vibratory line until its limit is reached. And that limit the Hindu, and the Buddhist, the Jain and the Zoroastrian adept, all define as that abstract world which lies beyond the phenomenal one of illusions and pain. Whatever they may call it—whether Mukti, or Nirvana, or Light—it is all the same idea: it is the outcome of the eternal Principle of energy after passing around a cycle of correlations with matter. That final limit the Middle Nature as a whole never reaches, for it is material as to its from, size, colour and atomic relations: if we call it the 'Soul,' therefore, we may say that the 'soul' is not immortal; for that which is material tends always to resume its primitive atomic condition. And the Hindu Philosopher, arguing from this premises, teaches that what does escape out of the phenomenal world is *Atmá*, the SPIRIT. And thus, while from the Hindu standpoint it is correct to say the 'soul' is not immortal, it must also be added that the 'spirit,' is; for, unlike the Soul or Middle Nature, *Atmá* contains no mortal and perishable ingredients, but is of its essence unchangeable and eternal.

The confusion of the words "Soul" and "Spirit," so common now, is perplexing and mischievous to the last degree.

It is no argument to bring against the Asiatic theory of Palingenesis, that we have no remembrance of former existences. We have forgotten nineteen-twentieths of the incidents of our present life. Memory plays us the most prankish tricks. Every one of us can recollect some one trifling incident out of a whole day's, month's, year's, incidents of our earliest years, and one that was in no way important, nor apparently more calculated than the others to impress itself indelibly upon the memory. How is this? And if this utter forgetfulness of the majority of our life-incidents is no proof that we did not exist consciously at those times, then our oblivion of the entire experiences in previous births is no argument against the fact of such previous births. Nor, let me hasten to add, are the alleged remembrances of previous births, affirmed by the modern school of Reincarnationists, valid proofs of such births: they may be—I do not say they *are* mere tricks of the imagination, cerebral pictures suggested by chance external influences. The only question with us is whether in science and logic it is necessary for us to postulate for ourselves a series of births, somewhere, at various times. And this I think must be answered in the affirmative.

So, then, conceding the plurality of births and comming back to our argument, we see that even though any one of us may not have the capacity for acquiring adeptship in this birth, it is still a possibility to acquire it in a succeeding one. If we make the beginning we create a cause which will, in due time and in proportion to its original energy, sooner or later, give us adeptship, and with it the knowledge of the hidden laws of being, and of the way to break the shackles of matter and obtain Mukti—Emancipation. And the first step in this beginning is to cleanse ourself from vicious desires and habits, to do away with unreasoning prejudices, dogmatism, and intolerance, to try to discover what is essentially fundamental and what is nonessential in the religion one professes, and to live up to the highest ideal of goodness, intelligence, and spiritual-mindedness that one can extract from that religion and from the intuitions of one's own nature. I regard that man as a mad iconoclast who would strike down any religion—especially one of the world's ancient religions—without examining it and giving it credit for its intrinsic truth. I call him a vain enthusiast who would patch up a new faith out of the ancient faiths, merely to have his name in the mouths of men. I call him a foolish zealot who would expect to make all men see truth as he sees it, since no two men can even see alike a simple tree or shrub, let alone grasp metaphysical propositions with the same clearness. As for those who go about the world to propagate their peculiar religious belief, without the ability to show its superiority to other beliefs which they would supplant, or to answer without equivocation the fair questions of critics—they are either well-meaning visionaries or presumptuous fools. But mad, or vain, or stupid, as either of these may be, if they are sincere they are personally entitled to the respect that sincerity always commands. Unless the whole world is ready to accept one infallible chief and blindly adopt one creed the wisest, the only rule must ever be to tolerate in our fellow-man that infirmity of judgment which we are ourselves always liable to, and never wholly free from. And that is the declared policy and platform of the Theosophical Society—as you may see by reading this pamphlet containing its Rules and Bye-Laws. It is the broad platform of mutual tolerance and universal brotherhood.

There must be elementary stages leading up towards adeptship, you will say: there are, and modern science has laid out some of them. I told you that Psychology is the most difficult of sciences to get to the bottom of, but still Western research has cleared many obstacles from the path. Mesmerism is by far the most necessary branch of study to take up first. It gives you (1). proof of the separability of mind from conscious physical existence; a mesmerized subject may show an active intellectual consciousness and discrimination while his body is not only asleep but buried in so profound a trance as to more resemble a livid corpse than a living man: (2), it gives you proof of the actual transmissibility of thought from one mind to another; the mesmeric operator can, without uttering a word or giving a perceptible signal, transmit to his subject the thought in his own mind: (3), it easily proves the reality of a power to hear sounds and see things occurring at great distances, to communicate with the thought of distant persons, to look through walls, down into the bowels of the earth, into the depths of the ocean and through all other obstructions to corporeal vision: (4), of a power to ook into the human body, detect the seat and causes of disease and prescribe suitable remedies, as also a power to impart health and restore physical and mental vigour by the laying on of the mesmerist's hands, or by his imparting his robust vital force to a glass of water for the patient to drink, or, to a cloth for him to wear: (5), of a power to see the past and even prognosticate the future. These and many more things Mesmeric Science enables a person, not an adept of the higher Asiatic Psychology, to prove completely to himself and others. I say this on the authority of a Committee of the Academy of France. And then, besides Mesmerism, there are the highly important branches of Psychometry, Odyle, Mediumism and others that to barely mention would be beyond the scope of my present lecture. Each and all help the inquirer towards the acquisition of 'Divine' wisdom, towards an intelligent and scientific conception of the laws of that 'Eternal Something,' as Herbert Spencer calls it, which you may call God or by any other name you like. Whatever name you may choose for it, the knowledge of it is the highest goal for human thought, and to be in a state of harmony with it the noblest, first and most necessary aspiration of intelligent man. The pursuit of this knowledge is, in one word, THEOSOPHY, and the proper methods of research constitute Theosophical Science.

And thus in a single sentence I have answered a thousand questions as to what Theosophy is, and what the object of theosophical research. Most of you, like the great mass of Hindus, have, until this moment, been imagining to yourselves that we were come to preach some new religion, to propagate some new conceit, to set up some "New Dispensation." You see now how far you have been from the mark, and what popular injustice has been done to us. Instead of preaching a new religion we are preaching the superior claims of the oldest religions in the world to the confidence of the present generation. It is not our poor ignorant selves that we offer to you as guides and gurus, but the venerable Rishis of the archaic ages. It is not an American or a Russian, but a hoary Hindu philosophy that we claim your allegiance for. We come not to pull down and destroy but to rebuild the strong fabric of Asiatic religion. We ask you to help us to set it up again, not on the shifting and treacherous sands of blind faith, but upon the rocky base of truth, and to cement its separate stones together with the strong cement of Modern Science. Hinduism proper *has nothiug whatever to fear from the researches of Science*. Whatever of falsehood may have come down to you from previous generations we may well dispense with, and when the time comes for us to see through our present *maya* (illusions) we will cheerfully do so. "The world was not made in a day" and we are not such ignorant enthusiasts as to dream that in a day, or a year, or a generation, long established errors can be detected and done away with. Let us but always desire to know the truth, and hold ourselves ready to speak for it, act for it, die for it, if necessary, when we may discover it. People ask us what is our religion, and how it is possible for us to be on equal terms of friendliness with people of such antagonistic faiths. I answer that what may be our personal preferences among the world's religions has nothing to do with the general question of Theosophy. We are advocating Theosophy, as the only method by which one may discover that Eternal Something, not asking people of another creed than ours to take our creed and throw aside their own. We two Founders profess a religion of tolerance, charity, kindness, altruism, or love of one's fellows; a religion that does not try to discover all that is bad in our neighbour's creed, but all that is good, and to make him live up to the best code of morals and piety he can find in it. We profess, in a word, the religion that is embodied in the golden Rule of Confucius, of Goutama, and of the founders of nearly all the great religions, and that is preserved for the admiration and reverence of posterity in the Edicts of the good King Asoka on the monoliths and rocks of Hindustan. Following this simple creed, we find no difficulty whatever in living upon terms of perfect peace with the adherent of any creed who will meet us in a reciprocal spirit. If we have been at war with the pretended Christians it is because they have belied the teachings of him whom they pretend to call Master, and by every vile and unworthy subterfuge have tried to oppose the growth of our influence. It is they who war upon us, for defending Hinduism and the other Asiatic religions, not we who war upon them. If they would practice their own precepts we would never use voice or pen against them; for then they would respect the religious feelings of the Hindu, the Parsi, the Jain, the Jew, the Buddhist and the Mussalman, and deserve our respect in return. But they began with calumny instead of argument, and calumny I fear will be their favourite weapon to the bitter end. In comparison with the unmanly conduct of my brawling countryman who lectured here the other day, denouncing the Vedas as filthy abomination and the Theosophists as disreputable adventurers, how sweet and noble was the behaviour of that Mahommedan Lawyer who defended Raymond Lully when a Mussalman tribunal was disposed to punish him for trying to propagate his religion in their city. "If you think it a meritorious act, O Moslems! for a Mussalman to try to preach Islam among the heretics, why should we be uncharitable to this Christian whose motive is identical?" I cannot remember the exact words, but that is the sense. The tender voice of Charity spoke by that Lawyer's lips, and his words were the echo of the Spirit of truth.

Come then, ye old men and young men of Madras, if ye call yourselves lovers of India, and would make yourself worthy of the blessings of the Rishis, join hands and hearts with us to carry on this great work. We ask you for no honours, no worldly benefits or rewards for ourselves. We do not seek you for followers; choose your proper leaders from among your wisest and purest men, and we will follow them. We do not offer ourselves as your teachers, for all we can teach is what we have learnt from this Asia; the Gospel we circulate is derived from the recluses of the Indian mountains, not from the professors of the West. It is for India we plead, for the restoration of her ancient religion, the vindication of her ancient glory, the maintenance of her greatness in science, the arts and philosophy. If any selfish consideration of sect or caste, or local prejudice bars the way, put aside at least until you have done something for the land of your birth, the renown of your noble race. In this great crowd I see painted upon your foreheads the vertical sect-marks of the Dwaitas and the Visishtadvaitis, and the horizontal stripes of the Sivas. These are the surface indications of religious differences that have often burst out in bitter words and bitter deeds. But with another sense than the eye of the body I see another set of sect-marks indicative of far greater peril to Indian nationality and Indian spirituality than those. These marks are branded deep upon the brains and hearts of some—though, happily, not all—of your most promising young men, the choicest children of the sorrowing Mother India, and they are eating away the sense of pride that they belong to this race and have inherited this noble religion. These are the B. A., B. L., and M. A., brands that the University over yonder has marked you with. After three years of intercouse with the Hindu nation and of identification with its thought, I almost feel a shudder when some noble-browed youth is presented to me as a titled graduate. Not that I undervalue the importance of college culture, nor the honourable distinction one earns by acquiring University degrees ; but I say that, *if such distinctions can only be had at the cost of one's national honour and one's spiritual intuitions*, they are a curse to the graduate and a calamity to his country. I would rather see a dirty *Bairagee* who has his ancestors' intuitive belief in man's spiritual capabilities, than the most brilliant graduate ever turned out of the University, who has lost that belief. Let me companion with the naked hermit of the jungle rather than with a graduate who, though loaded with degrees, has by a course of false history, and false science, been made to loose all faith in anything greater in the universe than a Hækel or a Comte, or in any powers in himself higher than those of procreation, thought or digestion. Call me a Conservative, if you will ; I am conservative to this extent that, until our modern professors can show me a Philosophy that is unassailable ; a science that is self-demonstrative, that is, axiomatic ; a Psychology that takes in all psychic phenomena ; a new religion that is all truth and without a flaw I shall proclaim that which I feel, I know to be the fact, viz., that the Rishis knew the secrets of Nature and of Man, that there is but one common platform of all religions, and that upon it ever stood and now stand in fraternal concord and amity the hierophants and esoteric initiates of the world's great faiths. That platform is THEOSOPHY. May the blessing of its ancient Masters be upon our poor stricken India !

An Address to Indian Graduates.

Delivered at the Patcheppa's Hall, Madras, on the 7th day of June 1882.

The hour of parting has come, and mine is the unwelcome duty of bidding you farewell. Were I not sure of seeing you again after the lapse of some months, and of renewing the friendships that we have formed with you, the task would be a hard one indeed. For we have learnt by experience what a Madras welcome means, and how much generous cordiality is included in the Madrassee's notion of hospitality to the stranger. I make no invidious comparisons when I say that we two, whom you have entertained like blood relations rather than like guests, will remember your attentions and your politeness as among the brightest features of not only our Indian but even of our whole experiences. In my last discourse in this Hall, I sketched for you the evolution of Aryan morals and greatness, and outlined the causes of their decline, together with the means necessary for their resuscitation. It is for others to busy themselves with the politico-economical aspect of the question. Our society and its officers have neither the taste nor the disposition to trench upon that ground. Our study is the moral and spiritual state of India and the world ; our task, the searching back through the dusky corridors of time for the spring sources of that secret science which unlocks for us the mystery of human misery and human happiness. As you already know, the Theosophical Society was founded nearly seven years ago, by persons who believed that, if our age could but get a full knowledge of Aryan science, philosophy and religion, it would be enriched and ennobled to a degree unattainable in any other way. Those founders were persuaded that the Wisdom-Religion, so called, of the archaic ages, was a system of spirituality and science wedded together. That this system, if you looked at it from one point of view showed the entire ground of scientific research completely covered, all mysteries laid bare, all doubts dispelled, Nature uncovered, like the Egyptian Isis or the Grecian Venus, so as to expose her every charm—and the last lurking place of vulgar superstition lighted up by the blazing torch of Science ; while if you viewed it from the other side, you would find religion presented to you in such an aspect as to win love rather than excite fear, invite confidence instead of arousing scepticism, and cause one's whole consciousness to be filled with a reverential feeling for the potential holiness of human nature. In short—as all educated India has by this time heard—our Society sprang into the lists of modern research, like some young Knight of the olden time, to do battle against pure materialism, with Aryan science as its weapons to strike with, and Aryan philosophy as a strong buckler to parry the blows of modern sceptics. I need not turn aside to say whether we have held our ground and made ourselves felt; the intellectual agitation that has spread throughout this country, and the existence of our many Branch Societies are patent facts. No amount of argument or denial can blow them away. The chief matter for you and I, gentlemen graduates, to consult about is whether it is practicable to effect such a revival of Sanscrit literature, and arouse so general an interest in Aryan achievements in the departments of religion and morals, as to restore the ancient Aryan wisdom, virtue, and spirituality. Shall I waste time in showing you the need of such a revival? Are any of you bold enough to challenge me to the proof? Do you want me to hold up in one hand a picture of what your ancestors once were, and, in the other, another picture, made up from official statistics and Census reports, to show you what the Hindu of the present age is like? Or, shall I invoke the mystical powers of Nature to bring out the galleries of Eternity—where in fadeless colours the reflected images of all human events are for ever kept as leaves of History—and unroll before you a panorama of the dark thoughts, dark words, and dark deeds which have by slow degrees brought your race to the miry depths in which it is gasping and struggling? I could do it, but so can you, and I leave the labour in your hands; only asking and imploring you to study your national record in a spirit of fearless inquiry, and with the determination to profit by the facts you may learn.

There are no longer among Western scholars two opinions as to the importance of Sanscrit literature as a factor for shaping modern thought. Said Sir William Jones. "The Sanscrit language, * * * is more perfect than the Greek, more copious than the Latin, and more excellently refined than either." Says Mr. Talboys, in his preface to his translation of Adelung's Historical *Sketch of Sanscrit Literature*," Some * * * predict that it would exercise the same influence upon the learning and general tone of European society, as the introduction of Greek did in the fifteenth century." And he further remarks that "its great antiquity and its presumed connection with the religion, the arts, and the sciences, of Greece and Rome, are well calculated to excite a fond and anxious research into its literary remains—remains equally wonderful for their extent and the harmonious language in which they are composed, and containing treatises written * * * on philosophy, metaphysics, grammar, theology, astronomy, mathematics, jurisprudence, ethics, poetry rhetoric, music, and other sciences cultivated among the Hindus, at a time when Europe lay buried in the deepest shades of ignorance." Now this panegyric upon Sanscrit literature and Hindu learning was published at Oxford in June 1832, exactly fifty years ago. Look at the changes already wrought upon Western opinion since that time, and say whether the prophetic forecast there given was not a correct one. Until Sir William Jones brought Sanscrit to the notice of Europe, all Western writers were accustomed to estimate antiquity by the dates of Roman and Grecian history. A grudging half glance had been given to Egypt as the possible precursor of the two Mediterranean States, which later became her conquerors. The chronologies and histories of the Chinese were set down as exaggerations of barbarian liars. All writers, whether theologian or not, seem to have been in a tacit conspiracy to squeeze human events within the actual limit of 6,000 years, admitted by the Biblical chronologers. The very names still given to the several races, Semetic, Hamitic, Japhetic—show the absurd disposition to ascribe the great divisions of the world's population to the parentage of Shem, Ham and Japheth, the mythical sons of the imaginary Noah! But when the ancient historical mines of the Egyptian heiroglyphs, the Sanscrit sastras, and the Assyrian records were once opened, "antiquity" was pushed back countless centuries, and the Biblical Chronology fell to pieces. Then came all manner of compromises and subterfuges to save the shadow of Ecclesiastical authority, whose substance had departed for ever. Christian philologists tried to show Sanscrit a derivation from the Hebrew, and Father Roberto de Nobili, a Jesuit Priest, produced a forged edition of the Yajur Veda. The creative Days of Genesis were sketched into geological periods; and the unmistakably anterior religious symbols and myths, identical with the Christian, which were discovered in India, China, Tibet, Egypt, Babylonia and other lands, were boldly declared to have been prefigurations of the coming of Christ! A most amusing example of this spirit is given in Hac and Gabet's *Trăvels in Tibet, Tartary and China*, where those pious missionaries, having to their unspeakable dismay found every one of the fasts, feasts, ceremonies, and rituals of their church observed by the poor heathen Lamaists, without a chance of their having been learnt from the padris, exclaim that the

Devil had set up this Worship as a mockery of God's Holy Church! The intellectual agitation thus set astir as above desiribed has gone on so rapidly and so powerfully that not only is "Infidelity rampant," as that great American journal, the New York *Sun*, expressed it recently, but the thirst for information about the old Asiatic religion is growing deeper every day. It was on the crest of this wave that the Theosophical Society has been borne along, bringing me in the course of time to Madras and to your presence.

And now, what have you Hindus, you educated men of the University of Madras, done on your part? The University Calendar for 1882-83 tells me that 1,250 men have graduated from that *Alma Mater* since 1858, in Arts, Laws, Medicine and Surgery, and Civil Engineering. Of living graduates, according to Dr. Cornish, about 54 per cent. are Brahmins and 46 per cent. of other castes. Out of this whole number how many can you show me who have been "true to their colors"—have been loyal to their ancestral traditions by contributing to the glory of Sanscrit Literature? How many of them, O! B. A's and M. A's, B. L's and M. D's, L. M. S's and L. C. E's, have helped the West to discover the beauties, the superlative excellences of your national religion, and philosophies, your ancient sciences and laws? Answer me, for I bring you now to the bar of a more solemn tribunal than the Court of Queen's Bench—the bar of Indian History; and the Jury before whom I arraign you is the Indian people. Look around, you gifted and favored sons of Aryavarta, and see the condition of religion and morals among your countrymen. See how your Priests are mumbling slokas they cannot translate, to a public even more ignorant than themselves of the meaning of those religious symbols which for your ancestors embodied sublime conceptions. Heaven knows I have no personal prejudice against College bred men, for I am a University man myself, and like yourselves have worne the academical gown. But if Sanscrit had been the American classic tongue and I had seen in America my class mates and the graduates of other Universities and Colleges giving no thought after graduation to Sanscrit and the thoughts that are embalmed in it; if I had found them contributing nothing or next to nothing to our country's literature and giving no thought to its religion, I would, if I had had in America the very same feeling I now have in India, have upbraided, nay, implored them, as I do yourselves. Some of you have told me that it is unjust to charge the Madras graduates especially with materialism. But I do not. I am not aware that you are worse than the graduates of other Indian Universities. Nor am I aware that you are any better. If you are, prove it, and wherever I go I will publicly proclaim your merit. I will say that at Madras I found that eighth world's wonder, a body of graduates, out of whom not even lack of early religious instruction, nor ignorance of Sanscrit, nor much reading of misleading Western books, nor a long course of perversive training under Padris, and agnostical Professors, could shake their Hinduism ! None ever heard me speak ill of your B. A. title as a mark of College culture ; it was only when its obvious meaning, as applied to some native graduate, was Bad Aryan, that I felt called upon to deplore its importation. Look, then, around you, gentlemen, and see what a field there is in which to apply your education and talents. If you are G. A's (Good Aryans) and not those bad B. A's, you will be ready to prove it by devoting a part of your time, your thought, and your income unselfishly to the interests of Hindu Philosophy and Science. There is so much for you to do that I hardly know where to begin. But perhaps, as all the actions of a man spring from the man himself, we had better consider him first. Let us see :—The first duty of an educated Hindu is, I take it, to have a correct knowledge of the history of his country, the evolutions and progress of his ancestors, their achievements in science, philosophy and the arts, to know as clearly and minutely as possible, all about the principles of Hindu religion and philosophy. No sensible Hindu will contradict me I am sure. Substitute the name of any other nationality for that of Hindu, and my remarks will be equally applicable. How can you get this knowledge ? You have perhaps not learned Sanscrit, and so cannot get it first hand. This is a great detriment indeed ; for the most necessary thing for a Hindu is to know the language in which all his old national literature is written. But still, there are many valuable translations of portions into English and the Indian vernaculars, and many valuable treatises, criticisms and reviews, by both Natives and Europeans. All that I know myself has been derived from these sources, and though that is little, still it is something. And then there are many *Pandits* whom you can employ to translate for you, and whom you ought to help and support. They may not understand the spirit of the Vedic and Puranic writings, but you can train your intuitions so as to catch that. The spirit of Hinduism, subtle as it may be, difficult to get at without a master key or clue, can be grasped surely and certainly with that clue in your possession. And that clue is found in the Wisdom-Religion or Esoteric Doctrine of the initiated sages of antiquity ; which also, as I remarked before, gives the clue to all the ancient faiths of mankind.

Every religion the world ever saw has had its outer shell for the masses, and its inner soul a mystery for the initiates. Originally, or rather let us say, when they had evolved to the stage, when they had a philosophy and science—there were but two great classes among the Aryans —the Initiates and the non-Initiates. The divisions into Brahmins, Kshatriyas, Vaishyas and Sudras came later. There was no such thing as a born Brahmin. There is in reality no such thing now. For even now, as you know, the children of Brahmin parents are counted as Sudras, and are Sudras until, at the age of seven, they receive the sacred thread and become *Dvija*, or get their second birth. To show that they are really born again, they are now given a new name—a mystery or Brahminic name—and by this they henceforth designate themselves when coming into the presence of their religious superiors. This thread ceremony now made so meaningless and such a farcial travesty upon what was it meant to be, was originally a solemn and most potent mystery. The child was taken under special, painful, physical influences; the thread given him was imbued with mystical powers by the initiated Guru and made a talisman to protect against evil magnetisms. This power was imparted to the raw cotton, spun yarn, and the twisted thread with *mantrams*, and the mesmeric aura of the maker and finally of the officiating Priest. Priests were real Priests in those days. Tell me what they are now, when a temple Priest will sell admission to the holiest precincts of his Pagoda for Rupees—as one offered to do with me the other day—and when the three-fold cord is often made of twine from Manchester, that was twisted by greasy machinery? Some of my friends have thought that I was a little too severe upon the Brahmin graduates, but I shall show you before I close an authoritative description of the true Brahmin, that is far more severe upon them than I have been.

Well, then, having through translations of all sorts and the help of pandits, supplemented by your cultivated intuitions, acquired a knowledge of Sanscrit literature, the second step must be taken. Your Sanscrit works teem with allusions to wondrous physical powers enjoyed by initiated Brahmins, and to startling phenomena exhibited by them, often before multitudes of witnesses. I have scarcely found one translator or commentator, whether an educated European or educated Hindu, who does not slur these over with a sneer as idle tales of superstitious credulity. Ever since I lectured here, the other day, upon Theosophy, some of your class—who imagine themselves preternaturally clever, but are only preternaturally conceited—have been addressing me, in and out of the public prints, in a tone of lofty pity and benevolent contempt for affirming the existence of the *Kama Rupa.* These, I take it, are mainly beardless youths, whose opinion of themselves is at cent-per-cent premium, and who are totally unqualified to express any opinion about the subject, having neither read nor seen anything. Let them pass; when they are older and have had experience, we may talk with them. What I have said about these things is based upon thirty years of personal observation and reading, and yet I do not ask you to believe my words, but to study and experiment for yourselves. You can thus gain absolute knowledge about Asiatic Psychology, and you will come to know that, after allowing for all exaggerations and poetical colourings, there is a broad basis of fact of experimentally demonstrable acts under these Puranic stories, these mantrams, hymns, and dialogues. The key to Puranic phenomenalism is our western science of mesmerism—which has been aptly called experimental Psychology. I tell you, gentlemen, that one practical experiment with a mesmeric subject made clairvoyant under your own hands, and by the outflow of your own will-power, will give you more real knowledge of the subject of Psychology than the reading of all the books of all the learned speculators and word-jugglers of Europe combined, and it will give you also such a flash of light upon the mystical portions of Sanscrit literature, that the sneer will die upon your lip, and the scornful glance fade out of your eye, as you suddenly discover how foolish your ignorant raillery must have made you appear to those who had had similar experiences before you. There is not a devil-dance in your village, nor a case of *pisacha*-obsession, not one of healing a sick person by amulets, not one of snake-charming, snake-taming, or the prevention of snakes from entering a house by drawing around it a magic circle, not one of the subjugation of a tiger or other wild beast by a *bairagee*, not one of prophetic premonition of events or the discovery of thieves, or of lost property of persons by a *mantrika*, nor one of the bringing of fruit, sweet flowers or other objects from distances, by occult means, not one of the sudden disappearance of a *Sadhu* from one place, and his simultaneous appearance at another, miles away—not one of these but can be more or less comprehended by a practical study of Mesmerism in its various branches. Three-fourths of so called "vulgar superstition" is in my opinion mesmerism misunderstood. So I say to you, gentlemen, if you wish to understand Hinduism, learn the moden art that was introduced to the notice of polite Paris at the close of the last century by Anthony Mesmer.

And now having gained knowledge yourselves—not by hearsay, not by my telling you, nor any other man's telling you, but by personal research—you will be prepared to help others. You will now find that Hinduism is at its present low water mark (1st) because the Brahmin Priests do not understand it; (2nd) because the Brahmin graduates understand it still less; (3rd) because the non-Brahmin graduates are no better informed; (4th) because the masses of the people, who do know something of it practically, are left to their ignorant misconceptions, and mix nine parts of falsehood with each one part of truth. The first class for you to take in hand are the Priests. You must teach them what you have learned. They must be made to know the true meaning of the symbols, ceremonies, rites, prayers, charms, fables, legends, &c, that they have from boyhood been familiar with without understanding. This is a good work for you. They must be encouraged to live up to a higher standard, and make their caste once more respected as it used to be. Tell them that story from the *Bharat,* which *Rishi Markandeya* related to *Yudisthara* (See Aranyaparva Chapter 206, *Slokas* 24 to 47.) Do you all remember it? If not, I will give it you in a translation kindly made for me by an eminent friend of mine of Madras. I read an epitome of it long ago, and it recurred to my mind when I was thinking what ideal I could hold up to you. Here it is. A Brahmin once, who had practised *Tapas* and acquired some occult powers, was passing in a jungle when a bird by chance defiled his head. The incensed Brahmin cast it so angry a glance that it fell dead at his feet. He went on his way, and coming to the house of a *Pativratha* woman, asked for food. She told him to wait, and attended first to her husband's food. Then she brought some to the Brahmin. But he angrily asked her how she dared to make him wait. She answered that her first duty was to her husband. "What," he said, "and neglect Brahmins? Do you not know that Brahmins, if they choose, can burn up the globe?" She retorted (though she had not seen him in the jungle) "*I am not that bird*: give up your anger. What can you do to me with your cruel eye? I know what a Brahmin is. . . . . You killed that bird by anger, but him only who gives up anger the *Devas* call a Brahmin. He who speaks truth in this world, pleases his *Gurus*; though injured, does not retaliate—him the *Devas* know to be a *Brahmin.* He who has conquered his passions; who is religious; who continually studies [understandingly] the *Vedas,* who is clean [meaning in mind and body]; who holds desires and anger under control—him the *Devas* call a Brahmin. He who treats the world as [he does] himself and who knows *Dharma* [religion] and *who acts up to Dharma*—him call the Devas a Brahmin. He who teaches [what he has learned of] *Vedas,* and who continues learning; he who sacrifices and causes others to sacrifice; who gives charity according to his means—him call the *Devas* a Brahmin..............I see you do not understand *Dharma*. Go to a butcher's shop and take him for your Guru!" I fear that but a small proportion of the officiating Priests of either Indian sect—or, for that matter, of any other sect of Christendom—come up to this standard. And I wish I could say anything different for the great body of University graduates. I do hope and expect that a day will come when I might. For the regeneration of Hinduism must largely depend upon the intelligent and zealous co-operation together of your class. Modern scientific methods must be applied to it, and you are the only men who have learnt them. You are sceptics now, as a body, because of your ignorance of mesmerism and of Sanscrit literature, and its bearing upon Western culture, quite as much as because of the wrong notions put into your heads by your misguided teachers, and the equally misinformed authors of your psychological and biological text books. You have as much to unlearn as to learn, before you can get back to the starting point whence every Brahmin or Kshatriya lad, in the ancient times, went on to discover the true meaning of life and of nature.

The other day at Nellore and Guntoor respectively, I met two Brahmins who had become perverts to Christianity. The excuse of each was that he could not find any one of his caste to show him the superior merits of Hinduism, or refute the claims of the missionaries in favor of their religion. Now I ask you if that is not a shame to every Brahmin, especially to every officiating priest in the Nellore and Kistna Districts? But are you any better equipped, for all your University training? Supposing that these wavering young minds, ablaze with the excitement of doubt, and disturbed by the cunning sophistries of foreign propogandists had come to you—how many of you would have been ready to answer their questions, satisfy their reasonable doubts,and put before them fairly and succinctly the salient points of Hinduism and Christianity? Upon your answer I may gauge the urgency of the present Indian crisis. Upon it I may base my appeal to the B. A's and M. A's to form a national Union for the propagation and defence of the Hindu nationality, if not Faith. You are the flower of modern Indian youth by reason of your intellectual status, yet you are sadly ignorant of what is most essential for an Indian scholar to know. You blush for the unscientific absurdities that they tell you are to be found in Hinduism? You do not examine into the matter yourselves, but take for granted;

what interested critics tell you—and blush. But there are quite as many and as gross absurdities in Christianity, and science has pointed them out with as fine a scorn. Yet, all said, that does not prevent men of the highest families, after passing through the University, to enter Holy Orders; and if they and other men of culture turn sceptics, it is at least after they have studied Christianity through and through, and discovered the narrow base upon which it stands. Do as much by Hinduism, study it to the bottom, and then if you choose to turn perverts we will at all events know that you take the step with a full acquaintance with all the facts. "Knowledge is power," says the pervert, yet you are wasting your power in driblets for lack of a mutual understanding of an instinct of union. Your talents are given either to Government, in which case you have converted yourselves into clerical machines, running with groans and much friction—or to the sole pursuit of wealth, in which case you debase yourselves into mere plutomaniacs. And, I am told, that too often, the graduates of the latter class devote their first accumulations to gross pleasures, and stupid displays of vanity, in imitation of what they consider respectable European vices. If, now, you could but organize into one grand union throughout the three Presidencies, first for self culture, and then for the improvement of Hindu morals and spirituality, and the revival of Aryan science and literature; if you would encourage the foundation of Sanscrit schools, and create by popular subscription a national fund, for the support of Pundits; if you would print vernacular translations of the best parts of your old Sastras, and write and circulate able tracts, essays, and catechisms upon Hindu religious doctrines; if you would set your countrymen the example of virtue, and discountenance foreign vice in every form—then might we bless those who had founded these institutions of learning, and created for India a new caste to lead her back to prosperity, peace and happiness. It is a golden chance, my friends. Few have had such an opportunity to regenerate a fallen people, and make their names the subject of blessings in every village and hamlet throughout the boundaries of a mighty nation. Seize it—I beseech you by the memory of the great dead, the monuments of whose intellectual power in the Sanscrit language and what it contains, even now provoke the wonder of an astonished world. The hopes of humanity centre in this revival of the learning of the Aryan sages. The Western world is struggling through dark clouds for a glimpse of the light; and that light you can snatch for them, and for yourselves, out of the crypts of your ancestral past, where it was placed by your glorious forefathers.

When India asks your help, your ears are dull to the cry. Eyes have you, but you see not, tongues but you speak not. Split up into little cliques, blinded by flatterers, intoxicated by self adulation, you do not realize your power, your weakness, or your duty. A lowering standard of morality, an increased disposition to obey expediency at all costs, a hankering after paltry wealth and empty honors, a growing contempt for what is national—these are some of the dangers that beset and threaten you. There is safety only in union and reform. Choose in each Presidency the wisest and best man of your class, and make him your leader in this needed crusade against the evil tendencies of the times. Let him be your class-father and guide. Listen to his sage counsels, support him in all proper measures, and calling to your aid all good Hindus of whatsoever caste or sect, set to rolling over India a wave of reform, that shall sweep before it the last vestige of the abuses that now pollute your temples and the very springs of public virtue. The task is difficult, but yet feasible.

The secret is for you to learn discipline. You have only to look at any well organized Army to understand what I mean. Here is the British Army in India. You can see noblemen and the sons of noblemen and in subordinate rank to commoners. The former perhaps Captains or Lieutenants, the latter Majors, Colonels or Generals. Outside the Corps their superior social rank is recognized, but inside they are—whatever their birth—but integers in a vast whole which is guided and ruled according to a system of strict discipline and personal accountability. The same remark holds with respect to the Civil Service, and you who accept civil appointments quietly submit to departmental rules and do the special duty assigned to you. Something of this feeling must be fostered among you if you would make your class a moral power for good. It will require of you a certain measure of self-abnegation, but this concession is no more than every member of any social community makes for the sake of the public good. Even the Princes of the Blood pass through the usual subordinate grades of the Army and the Navy.

It is no Utopian scheme, no enthusiasts' vision. Such great things have been accomplished before. In our own days the devoted efforts of a single man weilded the several Provinces af Italy into a United Kingdom, and Garibaldi still lives in his highland home to see what a mighty work he accomplished. In the middle ages, a single Monk by his frantic appeals, caused a religious league to be formed by all Europe for the rescue of the Sepulchre at Jerusalem, and another Monk called Martin Luther preached for reform so effectively as to shake the Romish Church to its very foundations. The curse of African slavery was removed from England and America by the exertions of a few devoted men; and mighty achievements of this kind are frequent in History. This is no political cabal that I propose to you, but a sacred union in the interests of Religion, of Science and of good morals. Every good Hindu will approve of it in his heart, and it will be hailed as a work of true beneficence by every philanthropist in Great Britain and America. Come, then, men of the Colleges, show yourselves worthy of your titles and distinctions. Here lies the path, let him tread it who can say he loves his country and is ready to sacrifice something for its sake. There are many subjects that a graduates' union might take up. Among them I will only mention (a) the preparation and circulation of English and vernacular works, large and small, upon the philosophy of India, (b) the condition of temple property and the moral and intellectual condition of the temple priests; (c) a scheme for the religious education of Native children, and the gradual removal of all such from under proselytising influences; (d) the re-marriage and early marriage questions—they either are or are not prescribed by the highest—and by that I mean the oldest—Aryan authorities; your duty is to discover the facts, and having discovered, act up to them—; (e) the higher standard of moral accountability, not only among your corps, but also among the professional and mercantile classes in general; by the establishment of medical schools of a high grade where Native Physicians might be trained to administer native Medicines in an intelligent manner, to make fair diagnoses of diseases, and to perform the simple surgical operations. The works of *Sushruta*, son of *Viswamitra*, of *Charaka*, and other native authorities should be text books in such schools, and in my judgment this movement alone would be productive of incalculable benefit throughout India. The Managers of such Institutions should carefully enquire into all alleged methods of cure by mesmeric processes, such as monotonous chanting or dancing, stroking the patient with feathers or otherwise, the use of talismans, signs and charms—in vogue among the common people. If any of them should be found efficacious, *they should be explained scientifically to the students and recommended.* For in a native school of this sort at least, let us hope, there would be none of the stupid and bigoted prejudice which in our Western Medical schools prevents the Faculty from ever enquiring about remedies and remedial processes outside their imperfect text books. These subjects are of the highest importance and should be neglected no longer. But I shall not detain you with any longer enumeration of the branches of enquiry which a union such as I propose to you, should give its attention to. If a man like Rajah Sir T. Madhava Row, or Maharajah Sir Jotendro Mohun Tagore, or others, whose names will occur to you, would take the management of such an association, and loyally give to it his whole time and abilities; and if in each Presidency there should be chosen a man of commanding ability and high moral character as the local leader; and if the graduates were to come together and put themselves under a strict code of discipline, and work for the object with as much zeal as they now work for their worldly interests —this generation would not pass away before you would see a most wonderful improvement in the tone of native society. And, believe me (who know by life long experience the character of the Anglo-Saxon race) a union like this firmly, honestly and courageously managed would go far towards working a change in European feeling towards yourselves. If the paramount class do not respect you; if the picture of Anglo-Indian feeling drawn by the illustrious Mr. Justice Shore, afterwards Lord Teignmouth, Governor-General, be a faithful one—which I think it is—it is because you do not properly respect yourselves. And it seems you cannot afford to respect yourselves because there is on union, no *esprit de corps* no discipline among you. You have no moral power because you have no organization. If you cannot realize this you must be blind indeed. As the Brahmin's boy has a second and spiritual birth, to commemorate which he receives a mystery name, so you graduates have had a second or intellectual birth, and received from your Alma Mater a new name—the title of your degree. How shall you celebrate this palingenesis? Shall it be in labours for the enlightenment of your minds, the purification of your hearts, and the spiritual development of your natures; shall it be in the regeneration of your countrymen; shall it be by restoring to this generation that reverence for the *Vedas* which once prevailed throughout the whole of Aryavarta, and that dignity of character based upon a prevailing high standard of virtue, which made a Hindu's word a sacred and inviolable covenant? Or shall this title of honor, this badge of Academical distinction, this certificate of intellectual prowess and studious perseverance, be allowed to become less and less a restraint upon wordly desires and evil propensities, until things come to so bad a pass, that your class, instead of being viewed as the natural leaders of the people, their exemplars, best counsellors and friends, shall be regarded as unworthy of respect or confidence.? These, gentlemen, are the issues that you must consider: their decision is in the womb of the future, and who will bring us the answer after its revolution and changes have been accomplished?

"But a few brief years we labour,
Soon our earthly day is o'er,
Other builders take our places
And "our *place* knows us no more."

"But the work that we have builded,
Oft with bleeding hands and tears,
And in error and in anguish,
Will not perish with our years."

"It will be at last made perfect
In the Universal plan,
It will help to crown the labours
Of the toiling hosts of man."

[Felix Adeler]

And now, friends of Madras, farewell. May happier days dawn upon you, and may the golden light of the Aryan Wisdom shine thoughout India and the world.

ERRATA.

—:o:—

Page.	Line.	For.	Read.
4	16	stron hold,	stronghold
9	11	A. G. Davis,	A. J. Davis
18	20	Gnyana	Gayan
20	last but 8.	earn	learn
22	20	hand device	hand-vice
23	9	Elephanto	Elephanta
29	12	that we found that	then we found that our
29	13	must recast	that we must re-cast
29	18	the ancient Greeks	with the ancient Greeks
30	6	so much of	so much
30	29	Irdhi	Iddhi
30	last word	tendencies	tendency
32	6	ever	even
32	8	attrocious	atrocious
32	25	re now	are now
35	1	said	sad
35	16	Galee	Galle
39	10	trial	trait
39	18	enhemerization	euhemerization
40	21	Heracha	Heraclia
42	foot note	principal	principle
44	13	free, free.	free. Free ?
45	20	describes	descries
47	16	visitation	violation
61	18	stroke	struck
62	28	occurred	occurring
65	17	Dumaven	Dunraven
66	2	what	that
66	23	Chittender	Chittenden
68	17	his former	this farmer
69	11	went	wrote
69	16	shoud	should
73	20	order	orders
99	23	evey	every
115	39	belighted	benighted
117	23	blasted what	blasted,
117	25	became	become
125	4	funished	furnished
128	last but two	fannæ	faunæ
132	last but four	nrawn	drawn
145	3	Boa tree	Bo-tree
148	10	Homutá	Homuté
148	26	Eunemoser	Ennemoser
150	28	Yagna	Yaçna
151	last but 12	Do	Do
153	last but two	priest	priests
153	last	direin	direm

Page.	Line.	For.	Read.
184	last but 3	in corner	in no corner
184	last	rushing the	rushing through the
185	1	standard	standards
206	22	bring out the	bring out from the
210	1	a	or
210	14	was it meant	it was meant
210	15	painful, physical	psychophysical
210	32	physical	psychical
210	37	ever since	even since
211	11	acts	facts
213	29	propogandists,	propagandists
214	10	pervert	proverb
215	19	noblemen and	noblemen
215	last but 5.	weilded	welded
216	20	(e) the	(e) a
216	25	simple	simpler
217	20	on union	no union